The Dallas Cowboys Wives'

FAMILY COOKBOOK
and
PHOTO ALBUM

* SOUTHWESTERN EDITION *

(Compiled by the Dallas Cowboys' Wives)

Happy Hill Farm Academy/Home
Star Route, Box 56
Granbury, Texas 76048

DALLAS ★ COWBOYS
Super Bowl XXVIII Champions

HAPPY HILL FARM ACADEMY/HOME
Star Route, Box 56
Granbury, Texas 76048

DALLAS COWBOYS WIVES' FAMILY COOKBOOK
and PHOTO ALBUM
(SOUTHWESTERN EDITION)

First Printing: 25,000 copies, October, 1994

Other Dallas Cowboys Wives' Books:

DALLAS COWBOYS WIVES' COOKBOOK
(FIRST EDITION) 1991
First Printing: 10,000 copies, November, 1991

DALLAS COWBOYS WIVES' COOKBOOK
(SECOND EDITION) 1992
First Printing: 10,000 copies, October, 1992
Second Printing: 4,000 copies, January, 1993

DALLAS COWBOYS WIVES' FAMILY COOKBOOK
and PHOTO ALBUM
(SUPER BOWL EDITION) 1993
First Printing: 20,000 copies, October, 1993

Printed in the United States of America
Printed by
BRANCH-SMITH
Fort Worth, Texas

All of the proceeds from the sale of this cookbook go directly to the Scholarship Fund at Happy Hill Farm Academy/Home, supporting deserving boys and girls (ages 5-18), who live, work, and study on the 500-acre working-farm campus located just outside the Dallas-Fort Worth Metroplex. The Farm is licensed by the Texas Department of Human Services and accredited by the Southern Association of Colleges and Schools. Happy Hill Farm does not receive any State or Federal funding.

Jay and Yvette Novacek present Jerry Jones with "custom" Dallas
Cowboys' boots, used on the cover of this year's cookbook.

DALLAS ★ COWBOYS
Super Bowl XXVIII Champions

TABLE OF CONTENTS

Page

DALLAS ★ COWBOYS
Super Bowl XXVIII Champions

Page

JIM & TAMMY JEFFCOAT 93
Jim Jeffcoat's Fancy Tostadas 95
Tammy's Hot Cheesy Seafood Dip 95

JOHN & JACQUE JETT 97
John Jett's Chili Spaghetti 99
Jacque's Southwestern Shrimp 99

DARYL JOHNSTON 101
Daryl Johnston's Stuffed Mushrooms 103
Janice's Eclair Cake 103

ROBERT & MANEESHA JONES 105
Robert Jones' Chili Beans & Mac Casserole 107
Maneesha's Noodle-Crab Casserole 107

DEREK & DENISE KENNARD 109
Derek Kennard's Menudo 111
Denise's Shrimp Salad 111

DERRICK LASSIC 113
Derrick Lassic's Moist Supper Cake 115
Lassic's Sombrero Spread 115

LEON LETT 117
Leon Lett's Texas Fudge 119
Leon's Mexican Cornbread 119

BROCK MARION 121
Brock Marion's Blue Corn Bread 123
Keri's Chili-Corn Souffle 123

RUSSELL MARYLAND 125
Russell Maryland's Spanish Rice 127
Russell's Texas Ranger Cookies 127

GODFREY MYLES 129
Godfrey Myles' Western Baked Beans 131
Godfrey's Peanut Butter Meringue Pie 131

NATE & DOROTHY NEWTON 133
Nate Newton's Chicken Enchilada Woolum 135
Dorothy's Mexican Dip Woolum 135
Newton's Mexican Casserole Woolum 135

JAY & YVETTE NOVACEK 137
Jay Novacek's BBQ Spice Rub 139
Yvette's Indoor S'Mores 139

RODNEY PEETE 141
Rodney's Tucson Lemon Cake 143
Holly's Special Grilled Corn with Chile-Lime Spread 143

JIM & BRENDA SCHWANTZ 145
Jim Schwantz's Chicken Enchilada Supreme 147
Brenda's Cauliflower Salad with Guacamole Dressing 147

DALLAS ⭐ COWBOYS
Super Bowl XXVIII Champions

Page

ROOKIES

COACHING STAFF

DALLAS ⭐ COWBOYS
Super Bowl XXVIII Champions

Page

Jerry Jones, and Yvette and Jay Novacek, looking at the "new cover" for this year's cookbook.

Jerry Jones with Tom Landry, who was inducted into the "Ring of Honor" in 1993.

The Barry Switzer Family visiting with Jerry Jones at Cowboy Ranch.

DALLAS ✦ **COWBOYS**
Super Bowl XXVIII Champions

Super Bowl XXVIII -- "Back-to Back" Trophies.

DALLAS ★ COWBOYS
Super Bowl XXVIII Champions

FOREWORD

Our sincere thanks to the wonderful wives (and mothers!) of the Dallas Cowboys . . . players, coaches, and administration. Without their enthusiastic support, there could be no "Dallas Cowboys Wives' Cookbook". This year's Cookbook with an emphasis on "Southwestern Recipes" is all brand-new. This is "volunteerism" at its very best . . . and to Happy Hill Farm, volunteers are especially important. HAPPY HILL FARM ACADEMY/HOME, beginning its twentieth year of existence, has neither sought nor received any Federal or State aid. All of its support comes from individuals, foundations, corporations, and churches. All of the proceeds from the sale of this book go directly to the Scholarship Fund to underwrite the care of indigent children who live, work, and study at HAPPY HILL FARM ACADEMY/HOME. Neither the Cowboys' Wives, nor anyone in the Dallas Cowboys organization, receive any funds from this effort.

HAPPY HILL FARM ACADEMY/HOME is located just outside the Dallas-Fort Worth Metroplex. On its 500-acre working-farm campus live boys and girls whose personal problems have made it impossible for them to live in traditional home or school settings. The Farm is licensed as a basic child-care facility by the Texas Department of Human Services. Inter-denominational in nature, strong moral and spiritual teachings undergird the work. In its own fully-accredited (Southern Association of Colleges and Schools) private school (K-12 grades), the Farm's children are taught the merits of the free-enterprise system and the importance of hard work. A Board of Directors includes Bob Breunig, former Dallas Cowboys middle linebacker, and former Coach Tom Landry.

MANY CARING, SHARING SUPPORTERS MAKE THE MINISTRY OF HAPPY HILL FARM POSSIBLE. IF YOU WOULD LIKE TO KNOW MORE ABOUT HOW YOU CAN BECOME INVOLVED IN THE LIVES OF TROUBLED, NEEDY BOYS AND GIRLS, PLEASE WRITE OR CALL FOR INFORMATION.

HAPPY HILL FARM ACADEMY/HOME
Star Route, Box 56
Granbury, Texas 76048

Phone: (817) 897-4822

ACKNOWLEDGEMENTS

Enthusiasm for the "two-times-in-a-row" Super Bowl Champion Dallas Cowboys continues unabated! Cowboys' fans are found in every city, town, and village across America. Parades and parties accompanied the Super Bowl victory. The fans grabbed up everything that they could get their hands on to celebrate their team's triumphant 1993 season. This included the "Dallas Cowboys Wives' Family Cookbook and Photo Album (Super Bowl Edition)". Sales reached an all-time high.

This year, the players' and coaches' wives have teamed up to produce an even bigger and better, all-new "Dallas Cowboys Wives' Family Cookbook and Photo Album" -- *featuring "Southwestern Cuisine"*.

The new Cookbook contains all-new recipes, plus hundreds of photos of the players, coaches, wives, and families . . . including shots from Super Bowl XXVIII. The biographical section has been expanded to contain information, until now unpublished, about the Dallas Cowboys and their families.

The Cookbook Committee was directed by Yvette Novacek, and included the following: Tammy Hennings, Brooke Hellestrae, Tasha Tolbert, Secola Edwards, Ann O'Neill, and Maneesha Jones . . . but all of the wives, players, and coaches had a part in the production of the book. Again, our special thanks to Charlotte (Jones) Anderson, and her efficient assistant Doreen Bice, in the Special Events Office.

The cover photography, along with other photos used in marketing and promotion, were taken by Dave Edmunson of Edmunson and Father -- Dallas, Texas.

Design concepts and art for the Cookbook were produced by The Ad Place in Dallas. Special thanks to Earl Calhoun, Tracy Watson, and their very creative and dedicated staff.

xvi

ACKNOWLEDGEMENTS (continued)

My sincere gratitude and appreciation to Gloria, my wife, and Todd Shipman, our son, who set type, read proof, and did all the many things necessary for production.

Russ Russell, Jim Browder, and Bobbye Collier -- of the "Dallas Cowboys Weekly" -- have been especially helpful in allowing us to use "Weekly" pictures, as necessary, to supplement those provided by the players' families.

The members of the Jones' family and the Dallas Cowboys organization have graciously cooperated by supplying us with information and allowing us the use of the Cowboys' logo. To the many friends we have made throughout the front office, we are grateful. Your assistance and encouragement were invaluable. Special thanks to Marilyn Love.

A sincere word of appreciation to Jay and Yvette Novacek, who spearheaded this Cookbook project for the second year in a row. They encouraged others to help, wrote letters, made telephone calls, made personal appearances, and much more. To you both, our grateful appreciation.

To everyone who has had a part in the "Dallas Cowboys Wives' Family Cookbook and Photo Album (Southwestern Edition)" -- God bless you!

C. Edward Shipman
Executive Director
HAPPY HILL FARM ACADEMY/HOME

DALLAS ★ COWBOYS
Super Bowl XXVIII Champions

Super Bowl XXVIII -- Jerry Jones and Jimmy Johnson, Coach of the
Two-Times-in-a-Row Super Bowl Champs.

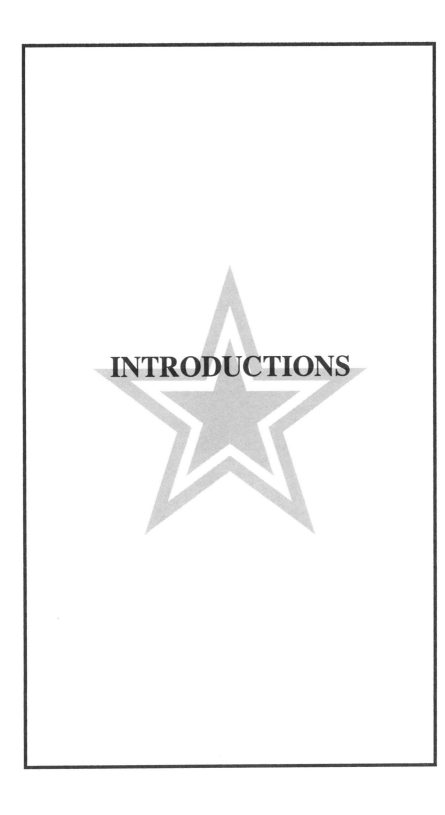

INTRODUCTIONS

Since moving to Texas seven months ago, I've enjoyed the friendliness of the people and the tastiness of the food. So many great eats; so little time.

Once again this year, the Cowboys' wives have managed to put some of the best recipes together in the "Dallas Cowboys Wives' Family Cookbook and Photo Album". This great effort benefits the kids at Happy Hill Farm Academy/Home.

Thanks, Cowboys' wives, from all of us at Channel 4.

Best of luck.

Mike Doocy
Channel 4 Sports
KDFW-TV

DALLAS ★ COWBOYS
Super Bowl XXVIII Champions

As the Dallas Cowboys began the 1993-'94 season, everyone wondered if they could repeat their championship play of the previous year. The answer came through loud and clear as the Cowboys won their second consecutive Super Bowl, beating the Buffalo Bills convincingly.

As Sports Director for Channel 8, I've been watching and working with the Dallas Cowboys for many years now. I've had the privilege of covering some of the great Cowboys stars. I've watched those stars move into the Ring of Honor and the Hall of Fame. Now, it's the "new" Cowboys turn to be great . . . and they certainly are just that. Who knows if the Cowboys can make it "three" Super Bowls in a row. It's never been done before, but if there is a team in the NFL that can rise to that challenge, it is this Dallas Cowboys team.

Those of us in the business, who have the opportunity of getting to know the players off the field, are pleased to join with them in this effort in behalf of troubled, needy boys and girls. Thank you, Dallas Cowboys and wives, who help support the kids at Happy Hill Farm Academy/Home through the sale of the "Dallas Cowboys Wives' Cookbook".

Dale Hansen
Sports Director
Channel 8 - WFAA-TV

xxi

Covering sports is what I do for a living . . . but it's not always as much fun as most people seem to think. Few teams win championships . . . which means that a lot of the time they're losing. Coaches and players don't particularly like to lose and they especially hate having reporters ask them to recount the loss.

That's one of the reasons that made the 1993 Cowboys Season so special. They were winning almost every week . . . and the players were always willing to talk about how they were kicking the rest of the League around. They were as accommodating as any athletes I've been around.

Covering a championship team is the best. It makes everyone's job easier. It was as much fun being around the Cowboys in '93 as anything I've done. Even though I had nothing to do with the team's success . . . I felt privileged to be involved in some small way. This year's team has a great chance of going to their third consecutive Super Bowl, but if it doesn't happen, that's okay . . . because at least it happened twice.

Timm Matthews
Channel 11 Sports
KTVT-TV

DALLAS ★ COWBOYS
Super Bowl XXVIII Champions

The Dallas Cowboys and Happy Hill Farm are similar in many ways. They both deal with discipline, they both are very dedicated, they both have great determination and they both have the desire to be the best. As a result of their great success, the Cowboys have fulfilled many of their dreams, and with the continued support of the "Dallas Cowboys Wives' Family Cookbook and Photo Album", Happy Hill Farm is able to help fulfill the dreams of hundreds of deserving children.

Thank you for your caring support!

Scott Murray
Sports/Director
KXAS-TV - Channel 5

DALLAS ★ COWBOYS
Super Bowl XXVIII Champions

Dear Cowboy Fans,

I'm delighted to have a chance to introduce you, through this book, to the Dallas Cowboys and their families.

First, it gives us all a chance to remember another run to the Super Bowl. More important, it serves as a reminder that a group of football players and coaches who win a championship have to be more than just a roomful of big strong guys. They have to be a family. And because the sport is so demanding, they need families who support and love them.

I've had the indescribable privilege of broadcasting Dallas Cowboys' games on the radio for 19 seasons now.

And the best part of what I get to do is getting to know, and hopefully help YOU get to know, the Cowboys as real people, not just names and numbers. That's the very best part of this book.

Happy reading, joyous holidays, and bon appetit!

Brad Sham
Sports
KVIL

DALLAS COWBOYS
1994

PRESIDENT - GENERAL MANAGER'S (WIFE)

Mrs. Jerry Jones (Gene)

VICE PRESIDENT'S (WIFE)

Mrs. Stephen Jones (Karen)

MARKETING and SPECIAL EVENTS COORDINATOR

Mrs. D. Shy Anderson (Charlotte Jones)

HEAD COACH

Barry Switzer

PLAYERS' WIVES

Mrs. Tommy Agee (Anchylus)
Mrs. Bill Bates (Denise)
Mrs. Larry Brown (Cheryl)
Mrs. Dixon Edwards (Secola)
Mrs. Kenneth Gant (Aris)
Mrs. Jason Garrett (Brill)
Mrs. Charles Haley (Karen)
Mrs. Alvin Harper (Jamise)
Mrs. Dale Hellestrae (Brooke)
Mrs. Chad Hennings (Tammy)
Mrs. Clayton Holmes (Lisa)
Mrs. Michael Irvin (Sandy)
Mrs. Jim Jeffcoat (Tammy)
Mrs. John Jett (Jacque)
Mrs. Robert Jones (Maneesha)
Mrs. Derek Kennard (Denise)
Mrs. Nate Newton (Dorothy)
Mrs. Jay Novacek (Yvette)

DALLAS COWBOYS

1994

PLAYERS' WIVES (continued)

Mrs. Jim Schwantz (Brenda)
Mrs. Tony Tolbert (Tasha)
Mrs. Mark Tuinei (Pono)
Mrs. James Washington (Dana)

SINGLE PLAYERS

Troy Aikman
Lincoln Coleman
Joe Fishback
Scott Galbraith
Daryl Johnston
Derrick Lassic
Leon Lett
Brock Marion
Russell Maryland
Godfrey Myles
Rodney Peete
Darrin Smith
Emmitt Smith
Kevin Smith
Mark Stepnoski
Ron Stone
Dave Thomas
Matt Vanderbeek
Erik Williams
Kevin Williams
Darren Woodson

ROOKIES' WIVES

Mrs. Larry Allen (Janelle)
Mrs. Cory Fleming (Tracey)

DALLAS COWBOYS

1994

SINGLE ROOKIES

Chris Boniol
Shante Carver
George Hegamin
Willie Jackson
Hurvin McCormack
Toddrick McIntosh

COACHING STAFF'S WIVES

Mrs. Hubbard Alexander (Gloria)
Mrs. Neill Armstrong (Jane)
Mrs. Joe Avezzano (Diann)
Mrs. Robert Blackwell (Diana)
Mrs. John Blake (Freda)
Mrs. Joe Brodsky (Joyce)
Mrs. Bucky Buchanan (Amy)
Mrs. Dave Campo (Kay)
Mrs. Don Cochren (Jan)
Mrs. Butch Davis (Tammy)
Mrs. Robert Ford (Janice)
Mrs. Steve Hoffman (Raffy)
Mrs. Hudson Houck (Elsie)
Mrs. Jim Maurer (Rosanne)
Mrs. Bruce Mays (Kathy)
Mrs. Mike McCord (Jan)
Mrs. Kevin O'Neill (Anne)
Mrs. Ernie Zampese (Joyce)
Mrs. Mike Zimmer (Vikki)

SINGLE COACHES

Jim Eddy
Mike Woicik

ADMINISTRATION

DALLAS ★ COWBOYS
Super Bowl XXVIII Champions

Jerry and Gene Jones at Texas Stadium with their team of grandchildren: Jessica Jones, Haley Anderson, and Jordan Jones.

DALLAS COWBOYS
Super Bowl XXVIII Champions

GENE & JERRAL (JERRY) WAYNE JONES
President and General Manager
Dallas Cowboys Football Club

BIRTH DATES: *Jerry* -- 10-13-42 (Los Angeles, California); *Gene* -- 2-14-42 (Little Rock, Arkansas)

COLLEGES: *Jerry* -- University of Arkansas (Masters -- Business Administration); *Gene* -- University of Arkansas (Liberal Arts)

GREATEST MOMENT AT SUPER BOWL XXVIII: Making a Great Comeback . . . and Winning!

HONORS OR AWARDS: *Jerry* -- Starred in Football as a Running Back at North Little Rock High School, Receiving Scholarship to Play at the University of Arkansas; Starting Guard and Co-Captain of 1964 National Championship Razorback Football Team (11-0); Boys Club Award; Awarded Best Sports Franchise Owner in the Metroplex, in 1991; Edelstein Pro Football Letter NFL Owner of the Year, in 1991; in 1992 -- "Big D Award" by the Dallas All Sports Association - ESPY Award for NFL Team of the Year - Golden Plate Award from the American Achievement Academy - Field Scovell Award - Business Leader of the Year - Waterford Crystal Trophy for Super Bowl Championship; in 1993 -- Entrepreneur of the Year, Presented by Ernst and Young and Inc. Magazine - Member of NFL's Broadcast Committee; in 1994 -- Financial World Magazine Recognized Jones as the Owner of the Most Valuable Sports Team in All of Professional Athletics - Only Owner (out of 11 Who Have Entered NFL in the Past 15 Years) to Guide His Franchise to a Super Bowl Championship (or Two!); Board Member for Dallas-Based Childworks International; *Gene* -- 1992 Arkansas Woman of Distinction; TACA Executive Board; Board Member of Children's Medical Center of Dallas; Mental Health Center; Willis M. Tate Distinguished Lecture Series; Easter Seals; Member of Symphony and Dallas Museum of Art

HOBBIES & INTERESTS: *Jerry* -- Tennis, Water Skiing, Snow Skiing, Hunting, and Playing with Grandchildren; *Gene* -- Being with Family, Snow Skiing, Walking the Beach, and Charity Involvement

FAVORITE AUTHOR: *Jerry* -- Tom Clancy; *Gene* -- John Grisham

FAVORITE TYPE OF MUSIC: *Jerry* -- Country Western; *Gene* -- Broadway Scores

FAVORITE SPORTS HERO: *Jerry* -- Vince Lombardi; *Gene* -- Husband Jerry

FAVORITE FOOD: *Jerry* -- Popcorn; *Gene* -- Cookies

CHILDREN & AGES: Stephen - 30 yrs.; Charlotte Jones Anderson - 28 yrs.; and Jerry, Jr. - 25 yrs.

GRANDCHILDREN & AGES: Jessica Jones - 2 yrs.; Jordan Jones - 1 yr.; and Haley Anderson - 15 months

3

Charlotte Jones Anderson, Jerry Jones, Stephen Jones, and Jerry Jones, Jr.

Karen Jones, Gene Jones, and Charlotte Jones Anderson at Super Bowl XXVIII.

DALLAS ⭐ COWBOYS
Super Bowl XXVIII Champions

Gene and Jerry Jones in the Georgia Dome at Super Bowl XXVIII.

* DEAN FEARING'S LOBSTER TACOS

4 - 1 lb. lobsters
6 - 7" *fresh* tortillas (*you may purchase*)
3 - T. corn oil
1 c. *grated* Jalapeno Jack cheese
1 c. *shredded* spinach leaves
"Yellow Tomato Salsa" - (*see following recipe*)
"Jicama Salad" - (*see following recipe*)

Preheat oven to 300 degrees. Fill a large stock pot with *lightly-salted* water; bring *to a boil* over *high* heat. Add lobsters; cook for about 8 minutes, or *until just done*. Drain; let lobsters cool *slightly*. Wrap tortillas *in foil*; place in preheated oven for about 15 minutes, or *until heated through*. Keep warm until ready to use. Remove meat from lobster tails *being careful not to tear apart*. Cut meat into *thin medallions* (or *medium-size* dice, if meat breaks apart). Heat oil in a medium saucepan over *medium* heat; saute lobster medallions *until just heated through*. Spoon *equal portions* of warm lobster medallions into the center of each *warm* tortilla. Sprinkle with *equal portions* of grated cheese and shredded spinach. Roll tortillas into a cylinder shape; place each one on a *warm* serving plate with the edge *facing the bottom*. Surround the taco with "Yellow Tomato Salsa"; garnish each side with a small mound of "Jicama Salad".

Yellow Tomato Salsa:

2 pts. yellow cherry tomatoes, or 1 lb. yellow tomatoes
1 *large* shallot, *very finely-minced*
2 T. *finely-minced, fresh* cilantro
1 T. champagne vinegar, or white wine vinegar
salt, *to taste*
2 serrano chilies, *seeded and minced*
2 t. lime juice
1 T. maple syrup (*use only if tomatoes are not sweet enough*)

In a food processor, *using the steel blade*, process tomatoes *until well-chopped*. Do not puree. Combine tomatoes *and their juices* with shallot, garlic, cilantro, vinegar, chilies, lime juice, and salt; *mix well*. Add maple syrup, *if needed to balance flavor and sweeten slightly*. *Cover*; refrigerate for at least 2 hours or *until very cold*. Note: *For a crunchier, more typical salsa, put tomatoes through fine die of a food grinder*.
* Executive Chef at The Mansion on Turtle Creek

Jicama Salad:

1/2 *small* jicama, *peeled and cut into fine julienne strips*
1/2 *small* red bell pepper, *seeds and membranes removed, cut into fine julienne strips*
1/2 *small* yellow bell pepper, *seeds and membrances removed, cut into fine julienne strips*
1/2 *small* zucchini (*only part that has green skin attached*), *cut into fine julienne strips*
1/2 *small* carrot, *peeled, and cut into fine julienne strips*
4 T. *cold pressed* peanut oil
2 T. lime juice
cayenne pepper, *to taste*
salt, *to taste*

Combine vegetables, oil, lime juice, salt, and cayenne *to taste*; toss and *mix well*.

GENE JONES' SOUTHWESTERN CRAB CAKES

1 *small* garlic clove, *minced*
1/4 c. *finely-chopped* green bell pepper
1/4 c. *finely-chopped* red bell pepper
3 T. *unsalted* butter
1/4 c., *plus* 2 T., *crushed* saltine crackers
1 *large* egg, *beaten lightly*
2 T. *minced* scallion
2 t. *fresh* lemon juice
1 t. LEA & PERRINS WORCESTERSHIRE SAUCE
1 pinch of cayenne pepper
1 T. mayonnaise
1/2 lb. *lump* crab meat, *picked over*
1 T. vegetable oil
PILLSBURY ALL-PURPOSE FLOUR - *for coating the crab cakes*
tartar sauce - *as an accompaniment*
lemon wedges - *as an accompaniment*

In a small skillet, cook the garlic and bell peppers in 2 T. of the butter over *moderately-low* heat, *stirring* for 2 minutes, or *until they are softened*. Transfer the mixture to a bowl; add cracker crumbs, egg, scallion, lemon juice, Worcestershire sauce, cayenne pepper, and mayonnaise. *Mix well*. Form the crab mixture into four 1/2-inch thick cakes; coat the cakes with flour. In a large heavy skillet, heat the oil and remaining 1 T. of butter over *moderately-high* heat *until the foam subsides*. Add the crab cakes to the skillet; cook them, *turning them carefully*, for 3-4 minutes on each side, or *until they are golden brown*. Serve crab cakes with tartar sauce and lemon wedges. Makes 4 crab cakes (*serve 2 as a main course*).

DALLAS ⭐ COWBOYS
Super Bowl XXVIII Champions

Stephen Jones with Jessica (23 months) and Jordan (9 months) at home.

Karen Jones and Jordan (10 months) at the circus.

DALLAS COWBOYS
Super Bowl XXVIII Champions

STEPHEN & KAREN JONES
Vice President
Dallas Cowboys Football Club

BIRTH DATES: *Stephen* -- 6-21-64 (Danville, Arkansas); *Karen* -- 8-9-64 (Warren, Arkansas)

COLLEGES: *Stephen* -- University of Arkansas (Chemical Engineering); *Karen* -- University of Arkansas (Business Administration)

GREATEST MOMENT AT SUPER BOWL XXVIII: Winning a Second Straight Super Bowl

ENJOY MOST ABOUT BEING A DALLAS COWBOY: Working in Sports on a Daily Basis

HOBBIES & INTERESTS: *Stephen* -- Hunting, Fishing, Snow-Skiing, Diving, and Spending Time with Family; *Karen* -- Traveling, Exercise, Reading, Being a Mom

FAVORITE AUTHOR: *Stephen* -- John Grisham; *Karen* -- John Grisham; and Sidney Sheldon

FAVORITE TYPES OF MUSIC: *Stephen and Karen* -- All Kinds of Music

FAVORITE SPORTS HERO: *Stephen* -- Roger Staubach; *Karen* -- Jackie Joyner

FAVORITE FOOD: *Stephen* -- Steak, Pizza, and Pasta; *Karen* -- Italian

CHILDREN & AGES: Jessica - 2 yrs.; and Jordan - 1 yr.

9

DALLAS ★ COWBOYS
Super Bowl XXVIII Champions

Jessica and "Papa" at her "2nd" birthday party.

Jessica and Jordan at Cowboys' Training Camp in Austin, Texas.

STEPHEN JONES' TORTILLA SOUP

1 *medium* onion, *chopped*
1 jalapeno pepper, *chopped*
2 cloves garlic, *minced*
2 T. oil
2 lbs. BEEF STEW MEAT or BUTTERBALL BONELESS, SKINLESS CHICKEN BREASTS, *optional*
1 can tomatoes (*14-1/2 oz. can*)
5 oz. Rotel tomatoes and green onions
1 can beef broth (*10-1/2 oz. can*)
1 can chicken broth (*10-3/4 oz. can*)
1 can tomato soup (*10-3/4 oz. can*)
1-1/2 *soup cans full* of water
1 t. ground cumin
1 t. chili powder
1 t. salt
1/2 t. lemon-pepper
2 t. LEA & PERRINS WORCESTERSHIRE SAUCE
3 T. McILHENNY CO. TABASCO SAUCE
4 tortillas, *cut in 1" squares*
1/4 c. *grated* Cheddar cheese

Saute first 5 ingredients in a large kettle. Add remaining ingredients, *except tortillas and cheese*, and simmer for 50 minutes. Add tortillas and cook for 10 minutes. Pour into mugs. Sprinkle with cheese. Serves 6 to 8.

KAREN'S SEAFOOD SPREAD

10 oz. *imitation* crab chunks
8 oz. cream cheese
1/3 c. mayonnaise
1/4 c. chili sauce
juice of 1/2 lemon
1 t. horseradish (*more, if desired*)
2 c. *roughly-chopped* shrimp, *boiled*

Put everything, *except shrimp*, in food processor. Puree *until smooth*. Taste; add more lemon juice or horseradish, *if desired*. Chill until ready to serve. * *Serve with thinly-sliced French bread or buttery crackers.*

DALLAS COWBOYS
Super Bowl XXVIII Champions

Charlotte and Shy Anderson.

DALLAS COWBOYS
Super Bowl XXVIII Champions

CHARLOTTE JONES & D. SHY ANDERSON
Marketing and Special Events Coordinator
Dallas Cowboys Football Club

BIRTH DATES: *Charlotte* -- 7-26-66 (Springfield, Missouri); *Shy* -- 4-3-63 (Little Rock, Arkansas)

COLLEGES ATTENDED: *Charlotte* -- Stanford University (B.A. - Organizational Management, and Human Biology); *Shy* -- University of Arkansas (B.A. - Business)

GREATEST MOMENT AT SUPER BOWL XXVIII: Having Clint Black Come to Celebrate the Cowboys' Second Super Bowl Win at the Victory Party

ENJOY MOST ABOUT BEING A DALLAS COWBOY: Working with My Family and the Other Special People within the Organization

HOBBIES & INTERESTS: *Charlotte* -- Skiing, Hunting, Exercising, and Being a Mom; *Shy* -- Golf, Hunting, and Exercising

FAVORITE AUTHOR: *Charlotte* -- Sidney Sheldon, and Jeffrey Archer; *Shy* -- Michael Crichton, and Tom Clancy

FAVORITE TYPE OF MUSIC: *Charlotte* -- Contemporary; *Shy* -- Country Western

FAVORITE SPORTS HERO: *Charlotte* -- Father, Jerry Jones

FAVORITE FOOD: *Charlotte and Shy* -- Pasta and Mexican

CHILDREN & AGES: Haley Alexis - 15 months; Expecting Second Child at the End of March, 1995

FITNESS & DIET TIP: Running or Walking - at Least Three Times a Week, for 45 Minutes to 1 Hour - to Increase Stamina and Energy while Toning; and Decrease Fat Intake

13

Haley Anderson.

Charlotte, Shy, and Haley Anderson.

DALLAS COWBOYS
Super Bowl XXVIII Champions

CHARLOTTE'S ENCHILADAS

1-1/2 lbs. GROUND BEEF
1/2 t. garlic salt
1/2 t. onion salt
1 t. ground pepper
6 oz. tomato paste
2 to 4 oz. Monterey Jack cheese
1-3/4 *hot* water

1 can cream of mushroom soup
1 can *chopped* green chilies
  (4-oz. can)
8 oz. *light* sour cream
1 pkg. enchilada mix
  (Old El Paso)
8 oz. *shredded* Cheddar cheese

10 to 12 *large* flour tortillas, or 18 corn tortillas (*these must be placed in hot oil for a few seconds until limp*)

* *Serve with refried beans, rice, and tortilla chips!*

Brown ground beef in deep skillet. Season with garlic salt, onion salt, pepper *to taste*; set aside. Heat *separately* enchilada mix, tomato paste, and water. Add **half** of the enchilada sauce to ground beef, plus 4 oz. Cheddar cheese. Put meat mixture into flour tortillas; roll up individually. *Do not overstuff.* Place tortillas in a 13" x 9" pan *seam side down.* Heat *slightly* in separate pan: soup, chilies, and sour cream *until mixed well.* Do not overheat! Pour soup mixture on top of enchiladas. Pour remaining enchilada sauce over the soup mixture and enchiladas. Cover with Cheddar and Monterey Jack cheese. Place in oven at 350 degrees *until cheese melts* (about 20 minutes).

*DEAN FEARING'S TORTILLA SOUP

3 T. corn oil
6 cloves garlic, *finely-chopped*
1 c. *fresh* onion puree
2 c. *fresh* tomato puree
2 t. chili powder
4 T. canned tomato puree
1 *cooked* BUTTERBALL BONELESS, SKINLESS CHICKEN BREAST, *cut into strips*
1 avocado, *peeled, seeded, and cubed*
3 corn tortillas, cut into thin strips and *fried crisp*

4 corn tortillas, *coarsely-chopped*
1 T. *chopped, fresh* epazote (or 1 T. chopped, fresh cilantro)
1 T. cumin powder
2 bay leaves
2 qt. chicken stock

1 c. *shredded* Cheddar cheese
salt and pepper, *to taste*
cayenne pepper, *to taste*

Heat oil in a large saucepan over *medium* heat. Saute tortillas with garlic and epazote over *medium* heat *until tortillas are soft.* Add onion and fresh tomato puree; bring *to a boil.* Add cumin, chili powder, bay leaves, canned tomato puree, and chicken stock; bring *to a boil* again. Then, reduce heat to *simmer.* Add salt and cayenne pepper *to taste*; cook, stirring *frequently*, for 30 minutes. Skim fat from surface, if necessary. Strain; pour into *warm* soup bowls. Garnish each bowl with an equal portion of chicken breast, avocado, shredded cheese, and crisp tortilla strips. Serve *immediately.*

* Executive Chef at The Mansion on Turtle Creek

DALLAS ⭐ COWBOYS
Super Bowl XXVIII Champions

Barry Switzer, Coach of the Dallas Cowboys.

DALLAS COWBOYS
Super Bowl XXVIII Champions

BARRY SWITZER
Head Coach
Dallas Cowboys Football Club

BIRTH DATE: 10-5-37 (Crossett, Arkansas)

COLLEGE: University of Arkansas (B.A. - Business Administration)

HONORS OR AWARDS: Graduated from High School in 1955 with an Appointment to the United States Naval Academy and Offers of Football Scholarships at the University of Arkansas and Louisiana State University; Attended Arkansas, Playing Center and Linebacker Three Years for the Razorbacks; Elected Captain, as Senior, in 1959 (Year Arkansas Reigned as Southwest Conference Champion and Gator Bowl Winner); Spent 2 Years in the Army and Then Returned to Arkansas, Serving as B Team Coach and Scout for 2 Years; 1964-1965, Coached Offensive Ends; in 1966, Moved to Oklahoma as Offensive Line Coach; in April, 1967, Named Offensive Coordinator; Took the Responsibil-ities of Assistant Head Coach in 1970; as Head Coach of the University of Oklahoma from 1973 to 1988, Was the Guiding Force Behind One of the Most Dominant College Football Programs of All Time; Amassed a 157-29-4 Career Record, Underscoring the Long-Term Quality of Winning that Switzer Brought to Coaching; His .837 Winning Percentage at Oklahoma is the Fourth Highest Mark in College History, Behind Only Notre Dame's Knute Rockne (.881), Frank Leahy (.864), and Carlisle's George Woodruff (.846); during 16-Year Tenure at Oklahoma, Switzer Won Three National Championships (1974, 1975, and 1985), 12 Big Eight Titles, and Was Successful in 8 of 13 Bowl Contests; Coached One Heisman Trophy Winner, Two Lombardi Award Winners, One Jim Thorpe Award Winner, One Defensive Player of the Year, and Two Butkus Award Winners; as Sooners' Head Coach, Personally Guided the Careers of More than 120 Young Men Who Went on to Be Drafted into the NFL; Personal Achievements Include Awards from Walter Camp Football Foundation, Big Eight Conference, NCAA District V, Washington Pigskin Club, "The Sporting News", "Football News", "Playboy", The Associated Press, and United Press International; Became Head Coach of the Dallas Cowboys, in 1994

CHILDREN & AGES: Greg - 26 yrs.; Kathy - 25 yrs.; and Doug - 22 yrs.

17

Kathy, Greg, and Doug Switzer.

BARRY SWITZER'S KING RANCH CHICKEN

4 to 5 BUTTERBALL BONELESS, SKINLESS CHICKEN
  BREASTS, *cooked and cubed*
1 can cream of mushroom soup
1 can cream of chicken soup
1 can Rotel tomatoes
1 c. *chopped* onions
1 t. chili powder
1 t. garlic salt
1/2 to 3/4 lb. *grated* cheese
1 pkg. Doritos

Saute onions *until tender*. Add soups, tomatoes, cubed
chicken, and seasonings. In a *greased* 9" x 12" pan, layer as
follows: *crushed* Doritos - chicken mixture - and cheese.
Repeat until ingredients are all used. Bake at 350 degrees for
45 minutes.

BARRY'S BLACK BEAN CASSEROLE

2 c. onions, *chopped*
1 /2 c. green pepper, *chopped*
2 cloves garlic, *crushed*
2 t. ground cumin
2 T. vegetable oil
1 can of tomatoes (*14-oz. can*)
3/4 c. ORTEGA GARDEN-STYLE SALSA
2 cans of black beans, *drained* (*15-oz. cans*)
   Progresso or Green Giant
Monterey Jack cheese, *grated* (*8 ounces*)
12 *fresh* corn tortillas, *cut in half*

Saute onions, garlic, and green pepper in vegetable oil. Mix
in salsa, tomatoes, ground cumin, and black beans. Simmer
on *low heat* for 10-15 minutes. In a *greased* 9" x 13" pan, or
oval casserole dish, layer the following ingredients:

> 1/3 black bean mix
> tortillas
> cheese
> tortillas
> 1/3 black bean mix
> cheese

Bake at 350 degrees for 30 minutes. *Serve with green salad.*

19

Super Bowl XXVIII -- Quarterback Troy Aikman.

DALLAS ★ COWBOYS
Super Bowl XXVIII Champions

Super Bowl XXVIII -- Defensive End Charles Haley.

Super Bowl XXVIII.

VETERANS

Tommie and Anchylus Agee.

ANCHYLUS & THOMAS LEE (TOMMIE) AGEE
* *Number 34* *
Fullback -- 6'-0" -- 235 lbs.

BIRTH DATES: *Tommie* -- 2-22-64 (Maplesville, Alabama); *Anchylus* -- 6-18-62 (Union Springs, Alabama)

COLLEGES: *Tommie* -- Auburn University (B.S. -- Criminal Justice); *Anchylus* -- Troy State University (B.S. -- Business Administration)

GREATEST MOMENT AT SUPER BOWL XXVIII: Victory over the Buffalo Bills

FIRST PLAYED ORGANIZED FOOTBALL: Tailback for the Maplesville "Red Devils"

YEARS IN PROFESSIONAL FOOTBALL: 8th Year

ENJOY MOST AS A DALLAS COWBOY: Team Effort / Spirit

HONORS OR AWARDS: *Tommie* -- All-State Honors in Football, Basketball, and Track at Maplesville High School (Alabama); Four-Year Starter at Fullback and Special Teams Captain at Auburn; Tied for Third on the Cowboys in Special Teams Tackles in 1992; Recorded Seven Special Teams Stops - Second among All Offensive Players - in 1993; Has Played in 60 of 64 Games since Becoming a Cowboy; *Anchylus* -- "Who's Who among American High School Students;" Received the George C. Wallace Academic Scholarship for Valedictorian's among High School Students

HOBBIES & INTERESTS: *Tommie* -- Hunting and Fishing; Interested in America's Youth and Problems They Face; Speaker for the Fellowship of Christian Athletes; Anti-Drug Campaign Speaker for Youth; Youth Counselor for Alabama Department of Youth Services; *Anchylus* -- Bowling, Reading, and Interested in America's Youth - Problems They Face

FAVORITE AUTHOR: *Tommie* -- Alex Haley

FAVORITE TYPE OF MUSIC: *Tommie* -- All Varieties; *Anchylus* -- Blues and Jazz

FAVORITE SPORTS HERO: *Tommie* -- William Andrews; *Anchylus* -- Husband Tommie

FAVORITE FOOD: *Tommie* -- Grandma's Pork Chop Casserole; *Anchylus* -- Beef Dishes

CHILDREN & AGES: Tyler Walker -- Born 8-30-92; Torrey LeMarcus -- Born 3-8-94

FITNESS & DIET TIP: Always Begin and End Exercising by Stretching; Eat Regular Nutritious Meals; and Cut Back on Portions (*It Is Not Healthy to Miss Meals!*)

LONG-RANGE CAREER GOALS: Own and Operate a 24-Hour Day Care in an Effort to Help out the Working Parent

25

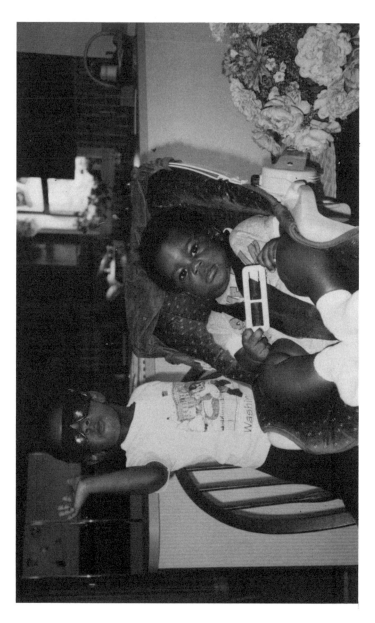

Tyler (2 years) and Torrey (6 months) Agee.

TOMMIE'S MEATLOAF SUPREME

2 lb. *lean* GROUND BEEF
1/2 c. *chopped* onions
1/2 c. *chopped* green pepper
1 T. PILLSBURY FLOUR
1 egg
salt and pepper, *to taste*
1 can tomatoes
ketchup

Combine ground beef, onions, green pepper, flour, egg, salt, and pepper. Shape; press into casserole dish. Bake at 425 degrees for approximately 1 hour. Remove from oven; *drain.* Pour can of tomatoes over the meatloaf. Squeeze ketchup on top. Bake for approximately 30 more minutes. Serve *hot* with meal . . . or *great for sandwiches*!

ANCHYLUS' BAKED POTATO CASSEROLE

6 *medium-size* potatoes
2 T. bacon bits
2 c. sour cream
1 c. Cheddar cheese
butter
salt, *to taste*

Cook and mash potatoes; add butter. Combine bacon bits and potatoes together; place in baking dish. Top with sour cream, cheese, and green onions. Bake at 350 degrees *until cheese is melted and casserole is hot.*

Charlyn (mother), Troy, and Ken (father) Aikman.

Troy and friends in the Bahamas -- March, 1994.

DALLAS ★ COWBOYS
Super Bowl XXVIII Champions

TROY KENNETH AIKMAN
Number 8
Quarterback -- 6'-4" -- 228 lbs.

BIRTH DATE: 11-21-66 -- West Covina, California

COLLEGE: U.C.L.A. (Sociology)

GREATEST MOMENT AT SUPER BOWL XXVIII: Celebrating Second Consecutive Super Bowl Win

FIRST PLAYED ORGANIZED FOOTBALL: When Eight Years Old, as Quarterback for the Suburban "Hornets"

YEARS IN PROFESSIONAL FOOTBALL: 6th Year

HONORS OR AWARDS: All-State Honors at Henryetta High School in Oklahoma; Henryetta Named Street after Aikman; Named Henryettan of the Year for 1992; an All-America, Finished Collegiate Career at U.C.L.A. as Third Rated Passer in NCAA History (Led the Bruins to Win both the Aloha Bowl and Cotton Bowl); Heisman Trophy Finalist, Received MVP for Aloha Bowl and Cotton Bowl, Was Awarded the Davey O'Brien Award, Named College Quarterback of the Year in 1988, and Voted UPI and Consensus All-America His Senior Year; Team Co-Captain in 1988; Selected as the #1 Overall Draft Pick for 1989; Three-Time All Pro; Named NFL All-Rookie His First Year; Named to the All-Madden Team for the Fourth Year in a Row; Named Offensive MVP for the Cowboys Three Years in a Row; Recipient of the Jim Thorpe Performance Award in 1992; S. Rae Hickock Professional Athlete for January, 1993; NFL Professional Quarterback of the Year in 1993; Led Dallas Cowboys to Two Super Bowl Championships; Named MVP of Super Bowl XXVII; ESPN's Insider Quarterback of the Year 1993; Currently Striving to Make History with a Third Consecutive Return to the Super Bowl in 1994; Has Been One of Five Finalists for the NFL Man of the Year, which Honors Players for Their Contributions to the Community and Philanthropic Work off the Field; Featured on the Cover of over Thirty Publications in the Past Three Years; Reached 10,000 Passing Yards in His 52nd Career Game, Faster than Any Quarterback in Team History; in 1993, His 99.0 Quarterback Rating Was the Second Highest in Team History and Placed Him Second in the NFL, the Highest Finish by a Dallas Quarterback since Staubach Led the League in 1979; Top Vote Getter, in 1993, among All Players for the Pro Bowl, Earning His First as the Starting Quarterback; Other 1993 Awards Include: NFL's Most Accurate Passer - Led NFL with a 69.1% Completion Rate, Breaking His Own Club Record Set in 1991 - Has the Top Three Single-Season Completion Percentages in Club History - Established a Club Record in Interception Ratio at 1.53%, Topping Staubach's 1.90% in 1971 - Set a New Dallas Career Interception Rate of 3.44% - Finished 1993 Season with 1,191 Career Completions to Rank Third on the Clubs All-Time List behind White and Staubach - Oklahoma Headliner of the Year - Cowboys' Man of the Year Nominee for Last Three Years - Cowboys' Nominee for the Byron White Humanitarian Award for 1994

HOBBIES & INTERESTS: Seadoo's, Water Sports, and Hanging with Friends; Troy Aikman Foundation - Established in 1991

FAVORITE AUTHOR: John Grisham

FAVORITE TYPE OF MUSIC: Country

FAVORITE FOOD: Italian

DALLAS ★ COWBOYS
Super Bowl XXVIII Champions

Troy coaching at the Jay Novacek Football Camp in '94.

Coach Troy at Jay Novacek Football Camp.

TROY AIKMAN'S BREAKFAST PIZZA

1 can of *refrigerated* Crescent dinner rolls
1 lb. *bulk* sausage
1 c. *frozen* hash browns
1 c. *sharp* Cheddar cheese, *grated*
5 eggs
1/4 c. milk
1/2 t. salt
1/4 t. pepper
1/4 c. Parmesan cheese

Separate and place crescent rolls *flat* on an *ungreased* pizza pan; press together as if making a pizza crust. Crumble and brown sausage; *drain*. Spin sausage over crust. Sprinkle with *thawed* has browns; then, Cheddar cheese. Beat eggs with milk, salt, and pepper; pour over top of pizza. Top with Parmesan cheese. Bake for 30 minutes at 375 degrees. Feeds 6 to 8 people.

TROY'S FAVORITE MEATLOAF

2 lbs. GROUND BEEF
1 egg, beaten
2 T. *chopped* green pepper
1 *small* onion, *chopped*
seasoned salt and pepper, *to taste*
1 T. basil
seasoned bread crumbs (*from a stuffing mix*) -- about 1 c.
equal portions of barbecue sauce and milk, *to moisten*
    (about 3/4 c. total - *depends on amount of bread used*)
1/2 to 3/4 c. *each* Cheddar and Monterey Jack cheese,
    shredded

Pour liquid over crumbs *to moisten well*; set aside. Mix rest of ingredients with ground beef; add bread mixture. Adjust more or less crumbs *to your own preference* and add more barbecue sauce *to keep meatloaf moist*. Pat meat into a 1/2" thick rectangle on a square of tin foil. Sprinkle cheeses all over meat (*to within one inch of edges*). Roll up *jelly-roll fashion* and pinch all around to seal. Put *seam-side down* in pan. Bake at 350 degrees about 1 hour, or *until done*.
* *During last half of baking, spread occasionally with more barbecue sauce.*

31

Denise and Bill Bates with replica of Super Bowl trophy.

DALLAS COWBOYS
Super Bowl XXVIII Champions

DENISE & WILLIAM FREDERICK (BILL) BATES
* Number 40 *
Safety -- 6'-1" -- 205 lbs.

BIRTH DATES: *Bill* -- 6-6-61 (Knoxville, Tennessee); *Denise* -- 1-25-60 (Nashville, Tennessee)

COLLEGES: *Bill* -- University of Tennessee (Economics); *Denise* -- University of Tennessee (B.A. -- Interior Design)

GREATEST MOMENT AT SUPER BOWL XXVIII: To Be Able to Play in This Year's Super Bowl (Instead of Watching from the Sidelines) Was the Ultimate Dream Come True; Being from Tennessee, So Close to Atlanta, All My family Was Able to See the Game; and to Know This Event Meant So Much to My Cousin John Graham Will Forever Be Etched in My Heart

PLACES VISITED WHILE AT SUPER BOWL XXVIII: *Underground Atlanta and Ate at the "Cheesecake Factory"*

YEARS IN PROFESSIONAL FOOTBALL: 12th Year

ENJOY MOST AS A DALLAS COWBOY: Having the Opportunity to Continue Playing a Competitive Sport I Love!

HONORS OR AWARDS: *Bill* -- Second-Team All-Southeastern Conference in Junior and Senior Seasons in College; Captain of College Team; NFL Alumni Special Teams Player of the Year in 1983 and 1984; Pro Bowl in 1985; 1985 NFL Man of the Year Finalist; All-Madden Teams in 1987, 1988, 1990, 1991, 1992, and 1993; Bob Lilly Award in 1990, 1991 and 1993; Special Teams Captain since 1990; Led Team in Special Teams Tackles in 1993 with 25; Second among Active Cowboys with 636 Career Regular-Season Tackles; Has More Interceptions in a Dallas Uniform (14) than Any Active Cowboy Player; Father of the Year in 1993 of "Dallas' Best"

HOBBIES & INTERESTS: *Bill* -- Golf, Fishing -- Any Sport There Is to Play!; *Denise* -- Piano, Arts and Crafts (Especially Painting), Kids' Clothing, and President of the "Plano Area Mothers of Multiples"

FAVORITE AUTHOR: *Bill* -- Tom Clancy, and John Grisham; *Denise* -- Sidney Sheldon

FAVORITE TYPE OF MUSIC: *Bill* -- Country, and Old Rock; *Denise* -- Classical Piano, and Old Rock

FAVORITE SPORTS HERO: *Bill* -- Bart Starr and Joe DiMaggio ("He Always Wanted to Hit the Pitcher's Best Pitch"); *Denise* -- Husband Bill

FAVORITE FOOD: *Bill* -- Chicken Stroganoff; *Denise* -- Pasta

CHILDREN & AGES: (Triplets) Graham, Brianna, and Hunter - Born 5-24-89; Tanner - Born 2-18-91

LONG-RANGE CAREER GOALS: Already Have a Business -- "Bill Bates' Cowboy Ranch", a 360-Acre Ranch for Corporate, Business, and Family Recreational Outings; Also, Chamberlin's Prime Chop House, a Restaurant in Dallas; Have Just Published "Shoot for the Star" - an Autobiography, with Hope that This Book Will Inspire People to Shoot for Their Own Dreams

DALLAS ★ COWBOYS
Super Bowl XXVIII Champions

Bill and Denise Bates and family.

Bill Bates' children at training camp in Austin, Texas.

BILL BATES' HOMEMADE SALSA

6 tomatillos
3 tomatoes
1 onion, *chopped*
4 to 8 jalapenos, *chopped*
10 stems of cilantro, *chopped*
juice of 1 lemon
juice of 1 lime
2 cloves garlic, *chopped*
1 T. oil
garlic salt, *to taste*
tortilla chips

In a food processor or blender, *puree* the tomatillos and lemon and lime juices. Next, chop onions, tomatoes, jalapenos, cilantro, and garlic. Mix together with pureed tomatillos. Add oil and garlic salt. Serve *chilled* with tortilla chips.

DENISE'S JALAPENO WRAP-UPS

25 *fresh* jalapeno peppers
3 to 4 BUTTERBALL Boneless, Skinless CHICKEN
  BREASTS
1 lb. bacon
1/4 c. soy sauce
1/4 c. LEA & PERRINS WORCESTERSHIRE SAUCE
50 toothpicks

Cut jalapeno peppers *in half lengthwise*; *seed* peppers. (*A few seeds may be left in - to provide more heat!*) Slice *raw* chicken into 50 *small* pieces. Place one piece of chicken inside each jalapeno half. Wrap with 1/3 of a piece of bacon; *secure with a toothpick*. When all halves are finished, marinate with soy and Worcestershire sauces (*mixed together*) for about 1 hour in the refrigerator. Just before serving, grill or broil in oven for 10 to 15 minutes, or *until chicken is done and bacon is crisp*. (You will need to turn the peppers half-way through cooking.) * Serve warm . . . *and have plenty of ice water nearby to put out the fire!*

Cornerback Larry Brown.

CHERYL & LARRY BROWN
* Number 24 *
Cornerback -- 5'-11" -- 182 lbs.

BIRTH DATES: *Larry* -- 11-30-69 (Los Angeles, California); *Cheryl* -- 5-20-69

COLLEGES: *Larry* -- Texas Christian University (Criminal Law); *Cheryl* -- Prairie View A & M University (Major - Sociology; Minor - Social Work)

FIRST PLAYED ORGANIZED FOOTBALL: As a Ten-Year-Old, Played for the "Hawthornes"

YEARS IN PROFESSIONAL FOOTBALL: 4th Year

ENJOY MOST AS A DALLAS COWBOY: Being on a Winning Team

HONORS OR AWARDS: All-City Selection in Both Football and Track at Los Angeles, California, High School; Named to the All-Southwest Conference and to the Blue/Gray All-Star Game, Earning Most Valuable Player Honors; Selected to the Pro Football Writers, Football News, Pro Football Weekly, and Football Digest All-Rookie Teams in 1991; One of the Youngest Starting Cornerbacks in the League; Has Started 51 of Past 52 Games for Dallas since Being Selected in the 12th Round of the 1991 Draft

HOBBIES & INTERESTS: *Larry* -- Golf, Basketball, Working Out, and Singing; *Cheryl* -- Reading, Swimming, Dancing, and Singing

FAVORITE AUTHOR: *Larry and Cheryl* -- Maya Angelou

FAVORITE TYPE OF MUSIC: *Larry and Cheryl* -- Jazz, and Gospel

FAVORITE SPORTS HERO: *Larry* -- Marcus Allen; *Cheryl* -- Larry Brown

FAVORITE FOOD: *Larry and Cheryl* -- Mexican Food

LONG-RANGE CAREER GOALS: Run Own Business

#24 -- Larry Brown.

Larry in action.

LARRY BROWN'S EASY STRAWBERRY COBBLER

1 stick butter	1 c. milk
1 c. PILLSBURY FLOUR	3 c. strawberries
2 c. C & H GRANULATED SUGAR	
3 t. baking powder	1 c. water
1/2 t. salt	cinnamon, *to taste*

Melt the butter in a 9" x 13" baking dish. Mix the flour, 1 c. sugar, baking powder, and salt in a bowl; stir in the milk *gradually*. Pour into the baking dish. Combine the strawberries, water, and remaining sugar. Pour the strawberry mixture over the batter; sprinkle with cinnamon. Bake at 350 degrees for 45 minutes, or *until golden brown*. Cut in squares. * *Serve topped with whipped cream or ice cream*. Makes 8 servings.

CHERYL'S TEXAS CASSEROLE

2 lb. BEEF ROUND STEAK	2 cans cream of chicken soup
1/3 c. PILLSBURY FLOUR	1 *soup can full* of water
1 t. paprika	"Dumplings" (*see below*)
1/2 c. salad oil	sour cream
1-3/4 c. *small* canned onions	

Coat round steak with flour; sprinkle with paprika. Then, *pound the steak*. Cut steak into 2-inch cubes; brown in *hot* oil in skillet. Place the browned steak cubes in a deep casserole; cover with the onions. Combine 1 can of soup and water; add to skillet in which steak was browned. Bring *to a boil*; pour over the beef. Bake at 300 degrees for 45 minutes, or *until tender*. Top with "Dumplings". Bake at 425 degrees for 25 minutes, or *until dumplings are brown*. Combine remaining soup with the sour cream in a saucepan; heat *through*. Serve with casserole.

Dumplings:

2 c. PILLSBURY FLOUR	1 t. dried onion flakes
4 t. baking powder	1 c. milk
1/2 t. salt	1/4 c. *melted* butter
1 t. poultry seasoning	1 c. bread crumbs
1 t. celery seed	

Sift flour, baking powder, salt, and poultry seasoning together in a large bowl; then, add celery seed, onion flakes, and milk. Stir *just until moistened*. Combine the melted butter and crumbs in a skillet. Drop dough by *rounded* teaspoonfuls into the crumb mixture; roll *until well-coated*.

Linebacker Derrick Brownlow.

DARRICK BROWNLOW
Number 50 *
Linebacker -- 6'-0" -- 235 lbs.

BIRTH DATE: 12-28-68 (Indianapolis, Indiana)

COLLEGE: University of Illinois (Speech Communications)

FAVORITE ACADEMIC SUBJECT: U.S. History

GREATEST MOMENT AT SUPER BOWL XXVIII: Being on the Winning Team (the Atmosphere in the Locker Room after the Game)

FIRST PLAYED IN ORGANIZED FOOTBALL: As Fullback/Linebacker for Cathedral High School in 1984

YEARS IN PROFESSIONAL FOOTBALL: 4th Year

HOBBIES & INTERESTS: Music, Playing Dominos, Movies, and Pool

FAVORITE AUTHOR: Alex Haley

FAVORITE TYPE OF MUSIC: Rhythm and Blues, and Rap

FAVORITE SPORTS HERO: Mike Singletary

FAVORITE TV/MOVIE STAR: Larry Fishbourne

FAVORITE FOOD: Italian (Pasta), and Mexican (Red Chili)

PET PEEVE: Being Lied To

LONG-RANGE CAREER GOALS: To Be Able to Take Care of Myself and My Family

DARRICK BROWNLOW'S OVEN-FRIED CHICKEN

1 c. *crisp* saltine crackers. *crushed*
1/2 t. pepper
1/2 t. paprika
1/4 t. salt
4 BUTTERBALL BONELESS, SKINLESS CHICKEN BREASTS
1/4 c. *melted* butter

Combine cracker crumbs, pepper, paprika, and salt in a shallow dish. Dip chicken breasts in butter; roll in cracker crumb mixture. Place on a baking sheet, *sprayed with Pam*. Drizzle chicken breasts *lightly* with additional butter. Bake at 350 degrees for 50 minutes, or *until done*. Makes 4 servings.

DARRICK'S WHOLE WHEAT PIZZA

1/2 c. *warm* water
1 T. vegetable oil
1 t. C & H GRANULATED SUGAR
1/2 t. salt
1/2 pkg. dry yeast (*about 1 t.*)
1 c. pizza sauce (*see below*)
1 c. *shredded* Mozzarella cheese, *divided* (*4 ounces*)
3/4 c. *fresh* mushrooms, *sliced*
1/4 c. *sliced* green onions
1 green pepper, *sliced into thin rings* (*optional*)
2 T. *grated* Parmesan cheese
crushed red pepper, *optional*

3/4 c. PILLSBURY FLOUR
3/4 c. whole wheat flour
Pam Cooking Spray
1/2 lb. GROUND CHUCK
1/2 t. salt

Combine water, oil, sugar, and 1/2 t. salt in a medium mixing bowl. Sprinkle yeast over mixture, *stirring until dissolved*. Gradually add flour; *mix well* after each addition. Turn dough out onto a *lightly-floured* surface; knead about 4 minutes, or *until smooth and elastic*. Shape into a ball; place in a bowl coated with Pam, *turning to grease top*. Cover; let rise in a *warm* place, free from drafts, for 1 hour, or *until doubled in bulk*. Coat a 12-inch pizza pan with Pam; set aside. Punch dough down. *Lightly* coat hands with Pam; pat dough *evenly* into pizza pan. Bake at 425 degrees for 5 minutes. Combine ground chuck and 1/2 t. salt in a skillet; cook over *medium* heat *until meat is browned*, stirring to crumble. *Drain beef well* on paper towels. Spread 1 c. pizza sauce *evenly* over pizza crust, leaving a 1/2-inch border around edges. Sprinkle 3/4 c. Mozzarella cheese over top. Sprinkle meat over cheese on pizza crust; top with mushrooms, green onions, and green pepper, *if desired*. Bake at 425 degrees for 15 minutes. Sprinkle with remaining 1/4 c. Mozzarella cheese and Parmesan cheese; bake 5 minutes. Sprinkle with crushed red pepper, *if desired*. Makes 10 slices.

Pizza Sauce:

1 can *whole* tomatoes, *undrained* (*28-oz. can*)
1 can tomato paste (*6-oz. can*)
1 *large* onion, *chopped*
3 T. *fresh* parsley, *chopped*
2 cloves garlic, *minced*
1 *small* green pepper, *chopped*
1-1/2 t. dried whole oregano
1/4 t. pepper

Place tomatoes in container of blender; process *until smooth*. Pour into a small Dutch oven. Stir in remaining ingredients; bring *to a boil*. Reduce heat; simmer *uncovered* for 1 hour, or *until sauce is reduced to about 3 cups*. Divide into 1-cup portions. * *Freeze 2 portions for later use*. Makes 3 cups. or enough for three 12-inch pizzas.

DALLAS ⭐ COWBOYS
Super Bowl XXVIII Champions

Super Bowl XXVIII.

Running Back Lincoln Coleman.

DALLAS ★ COWBOYS
Super Bowl XXVIII Champions

LINCOLN COLEMAN
** Number 44 **
Running Back -- 6'-1" -- 249 lbs.

BIRTH DATE: 8-12-69 (Dallas, Texas)

COLLEGE: Notre Dame University / Baylor University

FAVORITE ACADEMIC SUBJECT: Economics

GREATEST MOMENT IN SPORTS: Winning the Super Bowl in 1993

FIRST PLAYED ORGANIZED FOOTBALL: In the Fifth Grade, with the East Dallas Jets

YEARS IN PROFESSIONAL FOOTBALL: 2nd Year

HONORS OR AWARDS: Earned All-State Honors as a Running Back at Bryan Adams High School in Dallas, where He Rushed for 1,521 Yards, as a Senior; Began College Career at Notre Dame, in 1967, and Transferred to Baylor, in 1968; the Bears' Second Leading Rusher, as a Sophomore; 1993 Season Began as a Member of the Dallas Texans of the Arena Football League; Primary Back-Up to Three-Time NFL Rushing Champion Emmitt Smith

HOBBIES & INTERESTS: Bowling, Dominoes, Camping, and Nintendo

FAVORITE AUTHOR: Emmitt Smith (*Ha! Ha!*)

FAVORITE TYPE OF MUSIC: Rhythm and Blues

FAVORITE SPORTS HERO: Earl Campbell

FAVORITE TV/MOVIE STAR: Denzel Washington

FAVORITE FOOD: A Good Roast Dinner

PET PEEVE: Slow People (I Am Impatient)

FITNESS & DIET TIP: One Hour of Physical Activity a Day Keeps Switzer away; and Make Sure Vegetables Are a Part of Your Diet

LONG-RANGE CAREER GOALS: Presently, I Own and Operate a Nursery; Hope to Open a Couple of More

45

#44 -- Lincoln Coleman.

Lincoln helping coach at Jay Novacek Football Camp.

LINCOLN COLEMAN'S JUMPING JACQUES JALAPENO BURGERS

1 lb. GROUND BEEF
1 *small* onion, *diced* (*about 4 T.*)
1 T. cream
1 clove garlic, *crushed*
1/2 t. salt
1/2 t. pepper
4 t. ORTEGA GARDEN-STYLE SALSA
4 t. nacho jalapeno slices, *chopped*
1/2 c. *shredded* Cheddar cheese

Mix beef, onion, cream, garlic, salt, and pepper together. Top each of 4 patties with 1 t. salsa, 1 t. nacho jalapeno slices, and 2 T. cheese. Top with remaining 4 patties; *press edges to seal in toppings.* Grill over *medium* coals for 12 minutes. Turn <u>once</u> after 7 minutes. * *Serve on your favorite bun. Spread with, or dip, in extra salsa. This burger can stand alone, or be eaten with lettuce and tomato.*

LINCOLN'S SPANISH ROAST

1 BEEF RUMP ROAST (*5 pounds*)
2 cans pimento strips, *drained*
12 *small* onions
3 green peppers, *cut into strips*
2 stalks of celery, *sliced*
6 *small* carrots, *sliced*
1 *large* can of tomatoes
1 can tomato soup
3 *soup cans full* of water
2 bay leaves
4 *whole* cloves
2 t. salt
20 *small* potatoes

Place roast in a large roaster. Bake at 400 degrees for 30 minutes, or *until brown.* Then, reduce temperature to 350 degrees. Add remaining ingredients, *except potatoes*; *cover.* Bake for 1-1/2 hours, or *until roast is almost done.* Place potatoes around the roast; bake for 30 minutes longer, or *until roast and potatoes are tender.*

Secola and Dixon in limo on wedding night.

DALLAS ⭐ COWBOYS
Super Bowl XXVIII Champions

SECOLA & DIXON VOLDEAN EDWARDS, III
*Number 58 *
Linebacker -- 6'-1" -- 222 lbs.

BIRTH DATES: *Dixon* -- 3-25-68 (Cincinnati, Ohio); *Secola* -- 1-18-68 (Flint, Michigan)

COLLEGES: *Dixon* -- Michigan State University (Building Construction Management); *Secola* -- Michigan State University (Communication - Broadcast Journalism)

PLACES VISITED WHILE AT SUPER BOWL XXVIII: Lots of Good Shopping for the Both of Us!

FIRST PLAYED ORGANIZED FOOTBALL: In the 5th Grade, as a Guard and Tackle in Little League

YEARS IN PROFESSIONAL FOOTBALL: 4th Year

ENJOY MOST AS A DALLAS COWBOY: Winning Attitude among Players and Coaches

HONORS OR AWARDS: *Dixon* -- Earned All-District and Team Most Valuable Player Honors as a Tight End and Defensive Tackle in High School; First Season (1989), as Starting Weak-Side Linebacker, Earned Honorable Mention All-America Honors; Shared the Spartans Defensive Player of the Year Award, as a Senior; Selected with Highest Choice Dallas Has Used on a Linebacker since 1984; Moved into Starting Lineup in 1993 at Strong Linebacker - Made 12 Special Teams Tackles to Lead All Offensive and Defensive Starters; *Secola* -- 1990 "Who's Who in America"; 1991 Governor's Award for Student Achievement

HOBBIES & INTERESTS: *Dixon* -- Automobiles, Music, Carpentry, and Auto Body Mechanics; *Secola* -- Tennis, Reading, and Shopping

FAVORITE AUTHOR: *Dixon* -- Secola Edwards; *Secola* -- Stephen King

FAVORITE TYPE OF MUSIC: *Dixon* -- Rap, Rhythm and Blues, and Hip Hop to the Fang Bang Boogie to Be; *Secola* -- Rhythm and Blues

FAVORITE SPORTS HERO: *Dixon* -- "My Dad"; *Secola* -- Husband Dixon

FAVORITE FOOD: *Dixon* -- Soul Food; *Secola* -- Italian

CHILDREN & AGES: Twins -- Dixon Voldean, IV; and Taylor Sierra Lyn - Born 8-19-91

49

Taylor and Dixon Edwards (3 years).

Super Bowl XXVIII Champions

DIXON EDWARDS' BREAKFAST BURRITO

1 pkg. flour tortillas
6 to 8 *large* eggs
3 to 4 *medium* potatoes (*peeled or unpeeled*), *diced*
salt, *to taste*
pepper, *to taste*
favorite breakfast sausage

Brown sausage and dice; set aside. Cook potatoes *to desired texture*; season *to taste* with salt and pepper. Leave in skillet. Scramble eggs, using salt and pepper *to taste*. Combine meat, potatoes, and eggs in potato skillet. Place 2-3 tortillas between 2 *damp* paper towels; heat *in microwave* for 45 seconds. Fill tortilla; roll burrito style. Enjoy!

SECOLA'S TURKEY TACOS

1-1/2 lbs. to 2 lbs. *ground* turkey
seasoning salt, *to taste*
1-1/2 t. chili powder
1 pkg. taco seasoning mix
1/2 c. water
1 pkg. corn tortillas
2 c. cheese
lettuce
1 *small* onion, *diced*
1 *medium* tomato, *diced*

Brown turkey (*no need to drain; ground turkey can be dry*). Add all ingredients, *except for water, tortillas, and 1/2 c. cheese*; mix *thoroughly* and <u>taste</u>. Add as much water *as needed for desired texture*. Fill in shells. Top with lettuce, tomato, and onion. Makes 12-18 tacos.

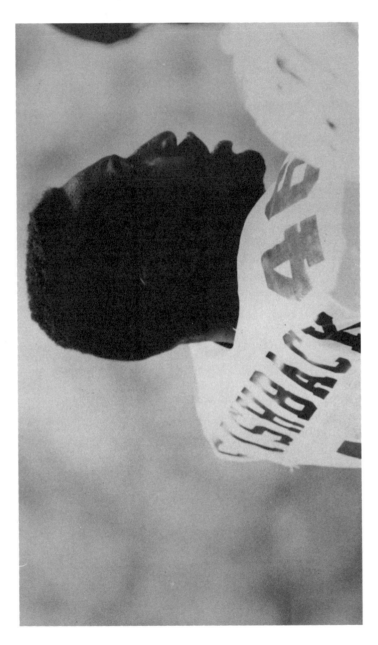

#46 -- Joe Fishbeck.

JOE EDWARD FISHBACK, JR.
* Number 46 *
Safety -- 6'-0" -- 212 lbs.

BIRTH DATE: 11-29-67 (Knoxville, Tennessee)

COLLEGE: Carson-Newman College (Physical Education and Recreation)

FAVORITE ACADEMIC SUBJECT: Math

GREATEST MOMENT IN SPORTS: Being Able to Play in Super Bowl

FIRST PLAYED IN ORGANIZED FOOTBALL: Eight Years Old, for the Baby Roadrunners

YEARS IN PROFESSIONAL FOOTBALL: 5th Year

HONORS OR AWARDS: Earned All-State Honors in Both Football and Baseball at Austin-East High School in Knoxville, Tennessee; Three-Year Starter at Carson-Newman, Earned All-America Honors, as Senior; Runner-up for NAIA's Player of the Year Award; Recipient of the South Atlantic's Defensive Player of the Year Award; Signed as a Free Agent with Dallas in 1993

HOBBIES & INTERESTS: Reading, and Shooting Pool

FAVORITE AUTHOR: Tim Green, and Alex Haley

FAVORITE TYPE OF MUSIC: Oldies

FAVORITE SPORTS HERO: Ronnie Lott

FAVORITE TV/MOVIE STAR: Carroll O'Connor

FAVORITE FOOD: Pork Chops

CHILDREN & AGES: Joe, III - 6 yrs.; and Jalen - 2 yrs.

FITNESS & DIET TIP: Walk a Mile a Day

LONG-RANGE CAREER GOALS: Teaching and Coaching

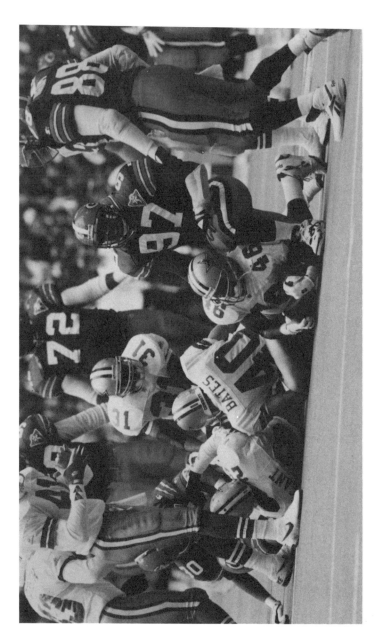

Joe carrying the ball.

JOE FISHBACK'S CANDIED SWEET POTATOES

2 lb. sweet potatoes (*4 medium*)
1 c. DR. PEPPER
3/4 c. C & H GRANULATED SUGAR
1/4 c. butter
1/2 t. salt

Parboil potatoes for 10 minutes. Place in cold water. Peel and slice *crosswise* into casserole. Combine Dr. Pepper, sugar, butter, and salt. Bring *to a boil*. Boil for 10 minutes. Pour over potatoes. Bake at 375 degrees for 45 minutes. Baste potatoes <u>several times</u> with syrup as potatoes bake.

FISHBACK'S PORK CHOPS AND POTATOES CASSEROLE

4 pork chops
1 can cream of mushroom soup
1/2 c. sour cream
1/4 c. water
2 T. *chopped* parsley
4 c. *thinly-sliced* potatoes
salt and pepper, *to taste*

Brown the pork chops in a skillet. Blend the soup with sour cream, water, and parsley. Place *half* of the potatoes in a 2-qt. casserole; sprinkle with salt and pepper. Add *half* of the soup mixture. Add remaining potatoes; sprinkle with salt and pepper. Add remaining soup mixture. Top with pork chops. *Cover*. Bake at 375 degrees for 1-1/2 hours. Makes 4 servings.

Tight End Scott Gailbraith.

DALLAS COWBOYS
Super Bowl XXVIII Champions

SCOTT GALBRAITH
* Number 89 *
Tight End -- 6'-2" -- 255 lbs.

BIRTH DATE: 1-7-67

COLLEGE: University of Southern California (Public Administration)

YEARS IN PROFESSIONAL FOOTBALL: 5th Year

HONORS OR AWARDS: Earned All-Northern California Honors at Highlands High School in North Highlands, California; Earned League MVP Honors in Basketball; Earned First-Team All-PAC-10 Honors, as a Junior and Senior; Earned All-America Honors from Associated Press; Signed with Dallas in November, 1993

#89 -- Scott Gailbraith.

SCOTT GALBRAITH'S SPANISH POTATO OMELET

1-1/2 lb. *cooked* potatoes
3 T. olive oil
4 T. butter or margarine
1 *medium* onion, *chopped*

8 eggs
1/2 c. *sliced* pimento-stuffed
    olives
1/8 t. pepper

Peel and dice potatoes. Heat 2 T. oil and 2 T. butter in a 10-inch seasoned skillet, or omelet pan, over *medium* heat. Add potatoes and onion; saute *until potatoes are brown*. Remove from skillet. *Wipe skillet clean*; add remaining oil and 1 T. butter. Heat. Beat eggs *until light*; mix in olives, potato mixture, and pepper. Pour into the skillet. Cook over *low* heat, running a spatula *around the edges occasionally* to allow uncooked egg to go to bottom, *until omelet is almost firm*. Loosen *around edges*; invert plate over the top of skillet. Turn omelet onto the plate. Clean out any bits that stick to the skillet; add remaining butter. Slide omelet back into skillet. Cook over *low* heat *until lightly browned*. Invert onto a serving plate, or serve from skillet. Makes 6 servings.

SCOTT'S COCONUT POUND CAKE

1-1/2 c. *softened* butter or margarine
3 c. C & H GRANULATED SUGAR
1 t. coconut flavoring
5 eggs
3 c. PILLSBURY ALL-PURPOSE FLOUR
3/4 c. 7UP
1-1/2 c. *flaked* coconut

Glaze: 3/4 c. C & H GRANULATED SUGAR
6 T. 7UP
3/4 t. coconut flavoring

Combine butter, sugar, and flavoring in a large bowl; beat *until light and fluffy*. Add eggs, *one at a time*, beating well after each addition. Add flour *alternately* with 7UP; *mix well*. Fold in coconut. Spoon into a *well-greased* 19-inch Bundt pan. Bake at 350 degrees for 1 hour, or *until done*. Cool in pan on a wire rack for 10 minutes. Remove cake from pan. Combine 3/4 c. sugar and 6 T. 7UP in a small saucepan; bring *to a boil*. Boil for 3 minutes. Remove from heat; stir in coconut flavoring. *Punch holes in top of cake with a toothpick*. Carefully spoon glaze over *warm* cake. Cool *completely*. *Cover tightly*; let stand overnight *before slicing*.

DALLAS ★ COWBOYS
Super Bowl XXVIII Champions

#29 -- Kenny performing the "Shark Dance".

DALLAS ★ COWBOYS
Super Bowl XXVIII Champions
ARIS & KENNETH (KENNY) GANT
Number 29
Cornerback -- 5'-11" -- 189 lbs.

BIRTH DATES: *Kenny* -- 4-18-67 (Lakeland, Florida); *Aris* -- 11-2-71 (Tuskegee, Alabama)

COLLEGES: *Kenny* -- Albany State College (Criminal Justice); *Aris* -- Albany State College

FIRST PLAYED ORGANIZED FOOTBALL: As an Eight-Year-Old, Played for the Lakeland "Gators" in Lakeland, Florida

YEARS IN PROFESSIONAL FOOTBALL: 5th Year

ENJOY MOST AS A DALLAS COWBOY: The Introduction of the Starting Teams at the Beginning of the Game

HONORS OR AWARDS: Four-Year Starter for the Golden Rams of Albany State College; Earned All-Southern Intercollegiate Athletic Conference Honors for Three Years; Earned a Game Ball Award for Special Teams Play versus Cincinnati, in 1991; Led All Dallas Players in Special Teams Tackles with 25, in 1991; Five Times Player of the Game, in 1992; in 1992, Received Stallion Award; for the Second Consecutive Season, Led All Non-Starters in Tackles with 43, and Tied for Second in Passes Defensed with 11, in 1993; Known for Performing "Shark Dance"

HOBBIES & INTERESTS: *Kenny* -- Driving Go-Carts, Laughing, and Signing Autographs; *Aris* -- Singing, Shopping, and Traveling

FAVORITE AUTHOR: Kenny -- Richard Wright; *Aris* -- Alice Walker

FAVORITE TYPE OF MUSIC: *Kenny* -- Rhythm and Blues, and Jazz; *Aris* -- Rhythm and Blues

FAVORITE SPORTS HERO: *Kenny* -- Deion Sanders; *Aris* -- Michael Jordan

FAVORITE FOOD: *Kenny* -- Chicken, and Grits; *Aris* -- Steak

CHILDREN & AGES: Destynee Michelle - 21 mon.

LONG-RANGE CAREER GOALS: Become an Actor; and Love My Daughter and Wife More and More Each Day

61

DALLAS ★ COWBOYS
Super Bowl XXVIII Champions

Safety Kenny Gant.

Kenny Gant entertaining at Jay Novacek Football Camp.

KENNY GANT'S SOUTHWESTERN GRITS

1-1/2 c. grits
6 c. *boiling* water
1-1/2 sticks butter
1 lb. *grated* American cheese
2 t. savory salt
2 t. salt
dash of hot sauce
3 eggs, *well-beaten*

Cook grits in *boiling* water in a saucepan for 15 minutes. Stir *frequently*. Add butter, cheese, savory salt, salt, hot sauce, and eggs; *mix well*. Turn into 2 *greased* casseroles. Bake for 30 minutes at 350 degrees. Makes 12 servings.

ARIS' BARBECUED ROUND STEAK

1-1/2 lb. ROUND STEAK (*1-1/2" thick*)
2 T. oil or shortening
1 garlic clove, *minced*
3/4 c. vinegar
1 T. C & H GRANULATED SUGAR
1 t. paprika
2 T. LEA & PERRINS WORCESTERSHIRE SAUCE
1/2 c. catsup
1 t. salt
1 t. *powdered* mustard
1/2 t. pepper

Cut steak *across the grain* into 1-inch slices. Heat oil in a skillet; brown steak in the oil. Place steak in a casserole. *Pour off oil*. Place garlic clove, vinegar, sugar, paprika, Worcestershire sauce, catsup, salt, mustard, and pepper in the skillet. Simmer for 3 minutes. Pour over steak. *Cover*. Bake at 350 degrees for 1 hour. *Uncover*. Bake for 30 minutes longer. Makes 4 servings.

Jason and Brill Garrett on their honeymoon in the California wine country of Napa Valley.

BRILL & JASON GARRETT
** Number 17 **
Quarterback -- 6'-2" -- 195 lbs.

BIRTH DATES: *Jason* -- 3-28-66 (Abington, Pennsylvania); *Brill* -- 12-8-65 (Chicago, Illinois)

COLLEGES: *Jason* -- Princeton University (A.B. -- History); *Brill* -- Princeton University (A. B. -- Woodrow Wilson School); Harvard University (J.D. -- Law School)

GREATEST MOMENT AT SUPER BOWL XXVIII: Running out on the Field before the Game and the Post-Game Locker Room Celebration

PLACES VISITED WHILE AT SUPER BOWL XXVIII: The Underground, the Coca-Cola Museum, and Buckhead

SPECIAL FOOD EATEN WHILE AT SUPER BOWL XXVIII: Seafood at Checkers, and Cajun at "A Taste of New Orleans"

FIRST PLAYED ORGANIZED FOOTBALL: In Second Grade, Played Center for the Meadowwood "Eagles"

YEARS IN PROFESSIONAL FOOTBALL: 4th Year

HONORS OR AWARDS: All-League Safety and Quarterback at University High School in Chagrin, Ohio; Lettered in Basketball and Baseball, Earning All-League Honors in Basketball; Honorable Mention All-America Selection at Princeton, as a Senior; Established NCAA Division 1-AA Records for Single-Season Completion Percentage (68.2%) and Lowest Percentage of Passes Intercepted (1.0%) at Princeton; Named the Ivy League Player of the Year in 1988; Elevated to Back-Up Duty as Quarterback Following the Final Preseason Game at Chicago in 1993

HOBBIES & INTERESTS: *Jason and Brill* -- Movie Watching, Skeeball, Reading, Traveling, and Whack-a-Mole

FAVORITE AUTHOR: *Jason* -- Ernest Hemingway; *Brill* -- F. Scott Fitzgerald

FAVORITE TYPE OF MUSIC: *Jason* -- Folk, Soul, Rhythm and Blues, and Rock; *Brill* -- All Types

FAVORITE SPORTS HERO: *Jason* -- Brian Sipe; *Brill* -- Michael Jordan

FAVORITE FOOD: *Jason* -- Pasta Primevera with Chicken in a Pesto Sauce; *Brill* -- Quesadillas

FITNESS & DIET TIP: Do Some Sort of Exercise Every Day -- Use Variety and Do Things You Enjoy -- You'll Keep Coming Back; and Drink Water -- *You Can Never Be Too Hydrated*!

Jason and wife Brill on their wedding day, May 21, 1994.

JASON GARRETT'S CILANTRO PESTO
POTATO SALAD

2 lbs. *red, new* potatoes, *cooked and cooled*
1/2 lb. green beans, *cut into 1-inch pieces*
1/2 c. *lightly-packed, fresh* parsley
1/2 c. *lightly-packed, fresh* cilantro leaves
1/2 c. *grated* Parmesan cheese
3/4 c. *low-fat, plain* yogurt
2 T. orange juice
1 t. *grated* orange peel
1 clove garlic
salt and *freshly-ground* pepper, *to taste*
1/2 c. pecan halves, *toasted and coarsely-chopped*

Cut potatoes into 3/4-inch pieces. Place in large bowl. Steam beans *until tender* (5-10 minutes). Rinse with *cold* water; drain, and add to potatoes. In blender or food processor, combine parsley, cilantro, cheese, yogurt, orange juice, orange peel, and garlic. Process *until smooth*. Pour dressing over potato mixture; mix *gently*. Season *to taste* with salt and pepper. *Cover*; refrigerate up to 4 hours. Serve, garnished with pecans. Makes 6 servings.

BRILL'S PICO DE GALLO

1 *large* tomato, *diced* into 3/4-inch pieces
1 *small* red onion, *chopped*
2 jalapeno chilies, *finely-chopped* (*including some seeds*)
3 T. *chopped, fresh* cilantro leaves
salt, *to taste*

In small bowl, mix all ingredients together. Makes about 2 cups.

Karen and Charles Haley at Super Bowl Victory Party in Atlanta, January, 1994.

Karen, C.J., and Charles at Fort Worth Zoo - May, '94.

KAREN & CHARLES LEWIS HALEY
* *Number 94* *
Defensive End -- 6'-5" -- 250 lbs.

BIRTH DATES: *Charles* -- 1-6-64 (Gladys, Virginia); *Karen* -- 10-10-64 (Richmond, Virginia)

COLLEGES: *Charles* -- James Madison University (B.S. - Social Science); *Karen* -- James Madison University (B.S. - Public Administration and Political Science; M.P.A. - Public Administration)

FIRST PLAYED ORGANIZED FOOTBALL: As a Linebacker at William Campbell High School (Virginia)

YEARS IN PROFESSIONAL FOOTBALL: 9th Year

ENJOY MOST AS A DALLAS COWBOY: Young Team with a Bright Future

HONORS OR AWARDS: Starred in Football, Basketball, and Track at William Campbell High School in Naruna, Virginia; Led Team with 130-or-More Tackles in Each of His Final Three Seasons at James Madison University; Division II All-America Recognition as a Senior; Three-Time Pro Bowler; One of NFL's Premier Pass Rushers; in 1993, Led the Cowboys in Quarterback Pressures (28) for the Second Straight Season, while Missing a Fair Amount of Playing Time Due to Injuries; in NFC Title Game, He Accounted for 6 Tackles, 3 Sacks, 5 Quarterback Pressures, and 2 Forced Fumbles; in 2 Games against the Buffalo Bills (One was Super Bowl XXVIII), Haley Totaled 9 Tackles, 9 Quarterback Pressures, 1 Forced Fumble, and Half a Sack

HOBBIES & INTERESTS: *Charles* -- Playing Cards and Dominoes, Motorcycle Riding, and Listening to Music; *Karen* -- Reading Books

FAVORITE AUTHOR: *Charles* -- All Black Authors; *Karen* -- Alice Walker, Terry McMillan, and Maya Angelou

FAVORITE TYPE OF MUSIC: *Charles and Karen* -- All Types, Especially Rhythm and Blues

FAVORITE FOOD: *Charles* -- Any Type of Southern Cooking; *Karen* -- All Types, Especially Mexican

CHILDREN & AGES: Princess Kay - Born 11-18-88; Charles, Jr. "C.J." - Born 10-11-90; and Brianna - Born 1-15-94

FITNESS & DIET TIP: Hard Work Never Hurt Anybody; and Get Away from the Table and/or Kitchen after Eating

LONG-RANGE CAREER GOALS: Coaching; and Be Self-Employed

69

DALLAS ⬦ COWBOYS
Super Bowl XXVIII Champions

Brianna, Karen, C. J., and Princess on Mother's Day, 1994.

CHARLES HALEY'S CHILI CON CARNE

1 T. Crisco shortening, or Crisco oil
1 c. *chopped* onion
1 c. *chopped* green bell pepper
1 lb. GROUND BEEF - ROUND
1 can tomatoes (*28-oz. can*)
1 can tomato sauce (*8-oz. can*)
1 T. chili powder
1 t. salt
1/4 t. pepper
dash of *hot* pepper sauce (*optional*)
1 can kidney beans (*30-oz. can*)

Heat Crisco shortening or oil in a large saucepan on *medium* heat. Add onions and green peppers. Saute *until softened*. Add meat; brown *lightly*. Stir in <u>undrained</u> tomatoes, tomato sauce, chili powder, salt, pepper, and *hot* pepper sauce, *if desired*. Bring *to a boil*. Reduce heat; simmer for 45 minutes. Add <u>undrained</u> kidney beans. Bring *to a boil* to heat beans. Makes eight one-cup servings.

KAREN'S HOT 'N SPICY
BLACK-EYED PEAS AND RICE

6 c. water
1 lb. *dried* black-eyed peas
1 c. turkey ham, *diced* (*8 ounces*)
1 c. celery, *chopped*
1 *large* onion, *chopped*
1 t. garlic powder
1 t. chili powder
1/2 t. cayenne pepper
1/2 t. black pepper
4 c. *cooked* rice (*without salt or fat*)
1 can tomato paste (*6-oz. can*)

Put first nine ingredients in large, deep cooking pot. *Cover*; simmer about 1-1/2 hours, *until peas are tender*. Add more water, as needed. Stir in rice and tomato paste. *Cover*. Let stand, to heat thoroughly, before serving.

Alvin and Alexis on her baptism day - May '94.

DALLAS COWBOYS
Super Bowl XXVIII Champions

JAMISE & ALVIN CRAIG HARPER
* Number 80 *
Wide Receiver -- 6'-3" -- 208 lbs.

BIRTH DATES: *Alvin* -- 7-6-67 (Frostproof, Florida); *Jamise* -- 10-7-68 (Murfreesboro, Tennessee)

COLLEGES: *Alvin* -- University of Tennessee / Knoxville (Psychology); *Jamise* -- University of Tennessee / Knoxville (B.S. -- Finance)

SPECIAL PEOPLE MET AT SUPER BOWL XXVIII: Michael Jordan, Magic Johnson, and Jesse Jackson; and Being with Family and Friends

PLACES VISITED WHILE AT SUPER BOWL XXVIII: Underground Atlanta, Coca-Cola Museum, and Martin Luther King, Jr., Memorial

FIRST PLAYED ORGANIZED FOOTBALL: As an Eight-Year-Old, Played Wide Receiver for the Frostproof "Cowboys"

YEARS IN PROFESSIONAL FOOTBALL: 4th Year

ENJOY MOST AS A DALLAS COWBOY: Being a Role Model to Many Young Children; and Enjoy Helping Those Less Fortunate

HONORS OR AWARDS: Earned All-America Honors at Frostproof High School; Set Florida State High Jump Record with Leap of 7' 1"; at Tennessee - Won High Jump Title in 1989 SEC Indoor Meet with a Personal Best Jump of 7' 2-1/2"; Set 1990 Indoor High Jump Record with 7' 3-1/2"; Two-Time All-Southeastern Conference Pick; Most Valuable Player at the Senior Bowl; Set New School Record for Touchdown Receptions, as a Senior, at University of Tennessee; Third on All-Time Receiving List; in 1992, Was Team's Fourth Leading Receiver and Ranked Third on the Squad in Touchdown Receptions; Distinguished Himself with the Spectacular Catch and the Big Play in both the NFC Championship Game and in Super Bowl XXVII; after Super Bowl Victory, Honored in Hometown (Frostproof) - Receiving Key to the City -- and on 2-27-93 Having Proclaimed "Alvin Harper Day" in the Town; in 1993 Postseason, Became the NFL's All-Time Leader in Receiving Yards Per Catch - Has a Career Playoff Average of 25.4 Yards Per Catch; in Regular Season in 1993, Led the NFC in Average yards Per Reception with a 21.6 Yard Mark

HOBBIES & INTERESTS: *Alvin* -- Video Games, Golf, Bowling, and Pool; *Jamise* -- Reading, Swimming, Helping the Homeless, and Breast Cancer Awareness

FAVORITE TYPE OF MUSIC: *Alvin* -- Jazz, and Rapp; *Jamise* -- Rhythm and Blues

FAVORITE FOOD: *Alvin* -- Chicken and Seafood (Lobster and Crab Legs); *Jamise* -- Pasta (Spaghetti); and Secola Edwards' Cinnamon Streusel Cake

CHILDREN & AGES: Alexis Chanel - Born 3-10-94

LONG-RANGE CAREER GOALS: To Establish a Shelter for Needy or Homeless Persons

Jamise and Alvin outside of Planet Hollywood (London, England) in August, 1993.

After becoming a Back-to-Back World Champion, Alvin also became a father on March 19, 1994.

ALVIN HARPER'S EASY TEXAS SCAMPI

1/4 c. onion, *finely-chopped*
4 garlic cloves, *crushed*
4 sprigs *fresh* parsley, *chopped*
3/4 c. butter
2 lbs. *fresh* shrimp, *medium-size* (*peeled and deveined*)
1/4 c. dry white wine
2 T. lemon juice
salt, *to taste*
pepper, *to taste* (*freshly-ground*)

Saute onion, garlic, and parsley in butter *until onion is tender*. Reduce heat to *low*. Add shrimp. Cook, *stirring frequently*, for approximately 5 minutes. Remove shrimp (*with a slotted spoon*) to a serving dish. Keep warm. Add wine, lemon juice, salt, and pepper to butter mixture. Simmer for 2 minutes. Pour mixture over shrimp. Serve <u>at once</u>. Makes 4 servings.

JAMISE'S FETTUCCINE WITH SPINACH SAUCE

1 pkg. Fettuccine (*16-oz. package*)
1 pkg. *frozen, chopped* spinach (*10-oz. package*)
1/4 c. butter or margarine
1 c. Ricotta cheese
1/4 c. *grated* Parmesan cheese
1/4 c. whipping cream
1/2 t. salt
1/8 t. ground nutmeg

Cook fettuccine (*according to package directions*). *Drain well.* Rinse with *warm* water; drain again. Set aside. Cook spinach (*according to package directions*). *Drain*; set aside. Melt butter in a large skillet over *medium* heat. Add spinach, cheese, whipping cream, salt, and nutmeg; stir *well*. Combine spinach mixture and *warm* noodles. Toss *gently*. Makes 8 to 10 servings.

Hillary Hellestrae (2 years).

DALLAS COWBOYS
Super Bowl XXVIII Champions

BROOKE & DALE ROBERT HELLESTRAE
** Number 70 **
Guard/Center -- 6'-5" -- 275 lbs.

BIRTH DATES: *Dale* -- 7-11-62 (Phoenix, Arizona); *Brooke* -- 11-28-63 (Phoenix, Arizona)

COLLEGES: *Dale* -- Southern Methodist University (Physical Education); *Brooke* -- Phoenix College

GREATEST MOMENT AT SUPER BOWL XXVIII: Being World Champions for the Second Year in a Row!

PLACES VISITED WHILE AT SUPER BOWL XXVIII: Atlanta Was Fun -- We Got Together with Friends Who Live There, and Enjoyed Seeing the Sights with Both Families

FIRST PLAYED ORGANIZED FOOTBALL: As an Eight-Year-Old, for the Boys' Club Football Team -- the "Banditos"

YEARS IN PROFESSIONAL FOOTBALL: 10th Year

ENJOY MOST AS A DALLAS COWBOY: Being Part of This Team That Has Improved Each Year -- Rewarded by Going to the Second Super Bowl

WIFE'S OCCUPATION: Owns "Cookies by Design" Shop in Scottsdale, Arizona

HONORS OR AWARDS: *Dale* -- All-State Pick in Football and Basketball at Saguaro High School in Scottsdale, Arizona; Earned All-Southwest Conference Honors, as a Senior, in 1984; Participated in Cotton, Sun, and Aloha Bowls; Handles All of the Dallas' Deep-Snapping Chores on Punts and Placekicks, Delivering Deep Snaps That Have Been Consistently Perfect for Four Straight Seasons; Dallas Has Not Had Punt Blocked since Dale's Arrival as a Cowboy

HOBBIES & INTERESTS: *Dale* -- Golf, Basketball, Softball, Pool, and Volleyball; *Brooke* -- Golf, Racquetball, Most Outdoor Sports, and Singing

FAVORITE AUTHOR: *Dale* -- John Grisham; *Brooke* -- Evelyn Christenson, Gary Smalley, and Frank Peretti

FAVORITE TYPE OF MUSIC: *Dale* -- Country and Western; *Brooke* -- Bits of Everything

FAVORITE SPORTS HERO: *Dale* -- Walt Frazier; *Brooke* -- Brooks Robinson ("I Was Named after Him!")

FAVORITE FOOD: *Dale* -- Steak, Lobster, and Mexican; *Brooke* -- Ice Cream

CHILDREN & AGES: Hillary Royce -- Born 2-17-92; Expecting Second Child in February, 1995

LONG-RANGE CAREER GOALS: First Goal -- Coaching; and Second -- Expand "Cookies by Design"

Dale and Hillary in Scottsdale, Arizona, this past off-season.

Brooke and Hillary at Laguna Beach in summer, 1994.

DALE HELLESTRAE'S FANTASTIC CHICKEN ENCHILADA CASSEROLE

1 pkg. corn tortillas (*18 count*)
1 *finely-chopped* onion
2 cans of *shredded* chicken
2 *large* cans *chopped or diced* green chilies
3 c. *grated* Cheddar cheese (*approximately - enough to cover each layer*)
2 cans cream of chicken soup
1 c. sour cream
2 *soup cans full* of milk

Fry all of the tortillas so they are just cooked on both sides (*not crispy*). Combine the rest of the ingredients (*except the grated cheese*). THINK LASAGNA! In *lightly-buttered* 9" x 13" glass dish, put one layer of tortillas (*approximately* 6), so they are *just overlapping*. Spread some of the mixture on top (*enough to cover the tortillas*). The mixture will ooze between the tortillas. Cover layer with cheese. Continue layering in this order until you have used all of the ingredients, *ending the top layer with sprinkled cheese*. Bake for 45 minutes at 350 degrees; then, for 20 minutes at 325 degrees. *Cover* with foil only for the first 30 minutes. When baking time is finished, insert a knife through the center to check for softness. Let casserole sit on top of the oven for 10 minutes or so, *to set up a little before serving*. IT'S GREAT!

BROOKE'S CHICKEN TAMALE PIE

1 pkg. corn muffin mix (*8-1/2 to 12-oz. size*)
1/2 c. *shredded* Cheddar cheese
1 can cream of mushroom soup
1 t. chili powder
1 garlic clove, *minced*
1 can *chopped* green chilies (*4-oz. can*)
1/2 c. *chopped* green onions
1 c. *whole-kernel* corn
1-1/2 c. *shredded* BUTTERBALL BONELESS, SKINLESS CHICKEN BREASTS

Garnish with: additional cheese, green onions, and *diced* tomatoes

Preheat oven to 350 degrees. In bowl, combine muffin mix (*according to package directions*) and cheese; set aside. In saucepan, stir remaining ingredients *until blended*. Heat *thoroughly*. Spoon muffin mixture into *greased* 2-qt. casserole dish. Spoon *hot* mixture over muffin mixture to *within 1/2" of edges*. Bake for 25 minutes, or *until cornbread is golden and puffy*. Garnish with additional cheese, green onions, and diced tomatoes. Serves 6.

Chad Hennings and son Chase (9 months) swimming on a hot summer day in Texas.

DALLAS ★ COWBOYS
Super Bowl XXVIII Champions

TAMARA (TAMMY) & CHAD HENNINGS
Number 95
Defensive Tackle -- 6'-6" -- 286 lbs.

BIRTH DATES: *Chad* -- 10-20-65 (Elberon, Iowa); *Tammy* -- 12-11-66 (Salida, Colorado)

COLLEGES: *Chad* -- United States Air Force Academy (B.S. -- Financial Management); *Tammy* -- Americana Beauty Academy (Trade School)

FIRST PLAYED ORGANIZED FOOTBALL: Quarterback, in Junior High

YEARS IN PROFESSIONAL FOOTBALL: 3rd Year

ENJOY MOST AS A DALLAS COWBOY: Being a Part of a Team That Has a Winning Tradition

HONORS OR AWARDS: Two-Time All-State Football Player and State-Champion Wrestler in Brenton Community High School; in 1985, Earned Honorable Mention All-America and Second-Team All-WAC Honors as a Sophomore; in 1986, Earned First-Team All-WAC Recognition While Named Honorable Mention All-America; Two-Time Academic All-America NCAA Scholarship Winner; Japan Bowl MVP; 1987 Western Athletic Conference Defensive Player of the Year Honors; 1987 All-America and Outland Trophy Winner; Finished 1993 Season with 17 Tackles and 5 Quarterback Pressures

HOBBIES & INTEREST: *Chad* -- Reading, Watching Movies, and Public Speaking; *Tammy* -- Golf, Reading, Being in the Mountains, and Spending Time with Family

FAVORITE AUTHOR: *Chad* -- Tom Clancy, and Frank Peretti; *Tammy* -- Ann Rice

FAVORITE TYPE OF MUSIC: *Chad* -- Old Rock; *Tammy* -- Instrumental, and Jazz

FAVORITE FOOD: *Chad* -- Pizza; *Tammy* -- Mexican (Enchiladas from the 1992 "Dallas Cowboys Wives' Cookbook"!)

CHILDREN & AGES: Chase Hoover Hennings - 1 yr.

FITNESS & DIET TIP: Never Give Fitness Up -- Always Be Doing Something; and Follow Your Head, Not Your Stomach

LONG-RANGE CAREER GOALS: Buy a Ranch; and Raise Kids

81

DALLAS ⬥★⬥ COWBOYS
Super Bowl XXVIII Champions

Chad, Chase, and Tammy Hennings on July 4 at a parade.

Tammy and Chase in Texas -- June, 1994.

DALLAS ★ COWBOYS
Super Bowl XXVIII Champions

CHAD HENNINGS' SUPER HOT BOWL OF GREEN CHILI

1 can tamales, *sliced 1-inch thick*
1 can *Mexican-style* tomatoes
1 can pinto beans
1 can black beans
1 can *cream-style* corn
1 can *cut* green beans
1 can *chopped* green chilies
1 can jalapenos
1 to 2 c. water (*depending on desired thickness*)
1 pkg. tortillas
shredded Cheddar cheese

Mix all ingredients in a crock pot. Cook for 3 to 4 hours (*or all day*). Serve with *shredded* Cheddar cheese and tortillas.
* *Corn bread is also great with this!*

TAMMY'S BLACK BEAN TORTILLA BAKE

2 c. onions, *chopped*
1-1/2 c. green pepper, *chopped*
1 can tomatoes (*14-1/2 oz. can*)
3/4 c. picante sauce
2 cloves garlic
2 t. cumin
1 can black beans (*15-oz. can*)
1 can kidney beans (*15-oz. can*)
12 corn tortillas
2 c. Monterey Jack cheese, *shredded*

tomatoes
lettuce
olives
sour cream

Bring first 6 ingredients *to a boil* in a skillet; simmer for 10 minutes. Stir beans into the mixture. Layer in 13" x 9" x 2" pan in this order: tortillas - sauce - cheese. Bake at 350 degrees for 30 to 35 minutes. Top with tomatoes, lettuce, olives, and sour cream.

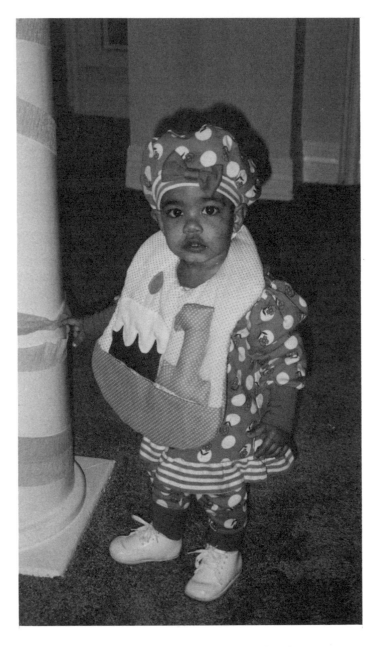

Briana celebrating her 1st birthday -- January 9, 1994.

LISA & CLAYTON A. HOLMES
* Number 47 *
Cornerback -- 5'-10" -- 181 lbs.

BIRTH DATES: *Clayton* -- 8-23-69 (Florence, South Carolina); *Lisa* -- 3-21-69 (Lenoir City, Tennessee)

COLLEGES: *Clayton* -- Carson-Newman College (Management); Lisa -- Carson-Newman College (Double Major - Psychology and Human Services)

GREATEST MOMENT AT SUPER BOWL XXVIII: Having Our Families Together for the First Time

FIRST PLAYED ORGANIZED FOOTBALL: As a Twelve-Year-Old, the Quarterback and Safety for the Tran-South "Volunteers"

YEARS IN PROFESSIONAL FOOTBALL: 3rd Year

ENJOY MOST AS A DALLAS COWBOY: Being Back on the Field Playing, after Spending 1993 Rehabilitating from Knee Surgery

HONORS OR AWARDS: *Clayton* -- Earned All-Conference Honors as a Quarterback and Defensive Back in High School; Set South Carolina State Record in the Long Jump; Junior College All-America Quarterback at North Greenville; Two-Time NAIA All-America at Cornerback at Carson-Newman; South Atlantic Conference's Defensive Player of the Year, as a Senior; Fastest Member of Dallas Cowboys with a 4.23 Forty-Yard Dash; Sat out the Entire 1993 Season after Tearing Ligaments in Right Knee in a Preseason Game

HOBBIES & INTERESTS: *Clayton* -- Music, Dancing, Nintendo, Hanging with the Guys, Golf, and Basketball; *Lisa* -- Being a Mother, Swimming, and Dancing

FAVORITE TYPE OF MUSIC: *Clayton and Lisa* -- Soul, Rap, and Rhythm and Blues

FAVORITE SPORTS HERO: *Clayton* -- Walter Payton; *Lisa* -- Magic Johnson

FAVORITE FOOD: *Clayton* -- New York Strip Steak; Lisa -- Chicken Parmesan

CHILDREN & AGES: Dominique (Clayton's Son) - 7 yrs.; and Kenya Briana - 20 mon.

LONG-RANGE CAREER GOALS: *Clayton* -- Finish School; and Own and Manage a Hotel; *Lisa* -- Finish School; Own Day Care or Shelter for Underprivileged Children; and a New Goal -- To Have Another Child Soon -- Hopefully, a Boy!

Clayton and Lisa Holmes at the Super Bowl Ring Ceremony in July, 1994.

47 -- Cornerback Clayton Holmes.

CLAYTON HOLMES' SOUTHWESTERN PORK CHOPS

1 T. chili powder
1 T. vegetable oil
1 t. ground cumin
1/4 t. ground cayenne pepper
1/4 t. salt
1 *large* clove garlic, *finely-chopped*
8 *center loin* pork chops

Mix all ingredients together, *except pork chops*. Spread chili powder mixture <u>evenly</u> *on both sides* of pork chops. *Cover*; refrigerate for at least 30 minutes. *Cover*; grill over *medium* coals (approximately 10 to 12 minutes) turning <u>frequently</u>, *until no longer pink when cut near the bone.*

LISA'S SPINACH DIP

2 blocks *hot pepper* Jack cheese (*grated*)
1 pkg. cream cheese, *softened* (*8-oz. package*)
1 pkg. *chopped* spinach
2 tomatoes, *chopped*
1 onion, *chopped*
2 T. milk

Preheat oven to 400 degrees. Cook spinach; drain. Mix remaining ingredients together. Bake *until golden around the edges. * Best if served with tortilla chips.*

Michael and daughter Myesha.

DALLAS ★ COWBOYS
Super Bowl XXVIII Champions

SANDY & MICHAEL JEROME IRVIN
Number 88 *
Wide Receiver -- 6'-2" -- 205 lbs.

BIRTH DATES: *Michael* -- 3-5-66 (Ft. Lauderdale, Florida); *Sandy* -- 1-2-66 (Miami, Florida)

COLLEGES: *Michael* -- University of Miami (Major - Business Management; Minor - Communications)

YEARS IN PROFESSIONAL FOOTBALL: 7th Year

HONORS OR AWARDS: Earned All-State Honors at St. Thomas Aquinas High School; Fine Basketball Player -- Won Several Slam-Dunk Contests in the Florida Area while in College; Holds Miami Career Records for Catches, Receiving Yards, and Touchdown Receptions; 11 Touchdown Catches in 1986 - Hurricanes' Record; Involved in Two of the Cowboys' Three Longest Plays in 1990 - Giving Him Four of Dallas' Eight Longest Plays since 1988; Other than Quarterbacks, No Other Cowboys Player Has Been Involved in More than One of Those Big Plays; in 1988, Became First Cowboys Rookie Wide Receiver to Start a Season-Opener since Bob Hayes in 1965; in 1990, Led Dallas in Yards Per Catch - and Had the Team's Longest Reception; in 1991, a Career-Best Season with Single Season Club Record Numbers for Receptions and Receiving Yards, Led NFC in Catches, and Led the NFL in Yardage; Eclipsed Bob Hayes' Club Record for 100-Yard Receiving Games with 7, in 1991; Earned Consensus All-Pro Recognition; Named the MVP of the Pro Bowl in First Appearance in Hawaii; Finest Game of the Year -- 10-Catch, 169-Yard Outing versus Atlanta, with a 58-Yard TD Reception; Registered the Top Three Single Season Receiving Performances in Dallas' History (with 1,523 Yards, in 1991 - 1,396 Yards, in 1992 - and 1,330 Yards, in 1993); Turned in the Top Three Single Season Totals for Receptions - with 93 in 1991, 78 in 1992, and 88 in 1993; Established New Team Record in 1992 for Consecutive Games of Owning, or Sharing, the Team Lead for Receptions with 8 Straight Games; Three Consecutive Pro Bowl Seasons in 1991, 1992, and 1993; in 1993, Finished Second in the NFL in Receiving Yardage, and Third in Receptions; Collected Five 100-Yard Receiving Games and Now Has Sixteen 100-Yard Games in 14 of the Club's 19 Games in 1993; for the Second Straight Season, Irvin Led the Cowboys in Postseason Receptions (16) and Receiving Yardage (215); Nicknamed "The Playmaker" - a Handle That Fits!

HOBBIES & INTERESTS: Michael -- Playing Video Games; Host of the Michael Irvin Show - a Weekly Television Show That Runs throughout the Football Season; Sandy -- Spending Time with Michael, Movies, and Going Dancing and Dinner

FAVORITE TYPE OF MUSIC: *Michael* -- Hip Hop (Educated Rap); *Sandy* -- Luther Vandross

FAVORITE SPORTS HERO: *Sandy* -- Husband Michael

FAVORITE FOOD: *Michael and Sandy* -- Seafood

CHILDREN & AGES: Myesha Beyonca - 4-1/2 yrs.

89

Michael and Sandy Irvin.

Wide Receiver Michael Irvin.

IRVIN'S COCONUT CREAM PIE

Pastry: 1-1/4 c. PILLSBURY ALL-PURPOSE FLOUR
1/2 t. salt   1/3 c. shortening   3 to 4 T. *cold* water

In medium mixing bowl, stir together flour and salt. Cut in shortening *until pieces are the size of small peas*. Sprinkle tablespoon of *cold* water over part of the mixture; *gently* toss with a fork. Push to side of bowl. Repeat until all is moistened. Form dough into a ball. On *lightly-floured* surface, flatten dough with hands. Roll dough from center to edge, forming a circle about 12" in diameter. Line a 9" pie plate with the pastry. Trim pastry to 1/2" beyond edge of pie plate. Flute edge; *prick pastry*. Bake at 450 degrees for 10-12 minutes, or *until golden*. Cool <u>thoroughly</u> on rack.

Filling:

1 c. C & H GRANULATED SUGAR
1/2 c. PILLSBURY ALL-PURPOSE FLOUR,
    or 1/4 c. cornstarch
1/4 t. salt
3 c. milk
4 eggs
3 T. butter or margarine
1-1/2 t. vanilla extract
1 can *flaked* coconut (*3-1/2 oz. can*)

In saucepan, combine sugar, flour, and salt. Gradually stir in milk. Cook and stir the mixture *until thickened and bubbly*. Reduce heat. Cook and stir for 2 minutes more. Remove saucepan from heat. Separate egg yolks from whites; *set whites aside for meringue*. <u>Gradually</u> stir 1 cup of the *hot* mixture into yolks. Return egg mixture to saucepan; *bring to a <u>gentle</u> boil*. Cook; stir 2 more minutes. Remove from heat. Stir in butter and vanilla. Stir in 1 c. of coconut. Pour *hot* mixture into *baked* pastry shell.

Meringue: 4 egg whites
                     1 t. vanilla
                     1/2 t. cream of tartar
                     1/2 c. C & H GRANULATED SUGAR

In a medium mixer bowl, beat the egg whites, vanilla, and cream of tartar at *medium* speed for about 1 minute, or *until <u>soft</u> peaks form*. *Gradually* add the sugar, *about 1 T. at a time*, beating at *high* speed about 5 minutes more, or *until mixture forms <u>stiff</u>, glossy peaks and sugar is dissolved*. <u>Immediately</u> spread meringue over pie, *carefully sealing to edge of pastry to prevent shrinkage*. Sprinkle meringue with the remaining coconut.

Bake at 350 degrees for 12 to 15 minutes, or *until meringue is golden*. Cool. *Cover*; chill to store.

DALLAS ★ COWBOYS
Super Bowl XXVIII Champions

"With visions of sugar plums" -- Jim and Tammy Jeffcoat and Family.

TAMMY & JAMES WILSON (JIM) JEFFCOAT, JR.
* Number 77 *
Defensive End -- 6'-5" -- 280 lbs.

BIRTH DATES: *Jim* -- 4-1-61 (Long Branch, New Jersey); *Tammy* -- 1-21-63 (Columbus, Ohio)

COLLEGES: *Jim* -- Arizona State University (B.S. -- Communications; M.B.A. -- Business Administration); *Tammy* -- University of Arizona

PLACES VISITED WHILE AT SUPER BOWL XXVIII: Martin Luther King, Jr., Home and Monument

FIRST PLAYED ORGANIZED FOOTBALL: In High School, as an Offensive Tackle and Defensive End for the Matawan "Huskies"

YEARS IN PROFESSIONAL FOOTBALL: 12th Year

HONORS OR AWARDS: *Jim* -- Received Key to Hometown City; High School Jersey (#79) Retired; New Jersey Sportswriters' Association Unsung Hero Award in 1991; Received All-PAC 10 Honors, College Defensive Lineman of the Year, and Honorable Mention All-America Honors in 1981-1982; Outstanding Defensive Player of 1983 Fiesta Bowl; Named to the All-Time Fiesta Bowl Team in 1991; ASU Hall of Fame; Led the NFL's No. 1 Ranked Defense in Sacks with 10.5 in 1992; Has Played in 110 Straight Games for the Cowboys for the Team Lead in That Department; Leads Team in Career NFL Sacks with 86-1/2; Has Started More NFL Games (126) than Any Current Cowboys Player; over Past Five Seasons, His 360 Tackles Lead All Defensive Linemen; *Tammy* -- Miss Arizona, Second Runner-Up

HOBBIES & INTERESTS: *Jim* -- Fishing, Reading, Writing, Bowling, and Computer Buff; and Working with Special Olympics, Make-A-Wish Foundation, Leukemia Society, and Boys' Clubs; *Tammy* -- Physical Fitness, Weightlifting, and Crafts

FAVORITE AUTHOR: *Jim* -- John Grisham; *Tammy* -- Terry McMillan, Frank Peretti, and Paul Meir

FAVORITE TYPE OF MUSIC: *Jim* -- Rhythm and Blues; *Tammy* -- Rhythm and Blues, Jazz, and Contemporary Christian

FAVORITE SPORTS HERO: *Jim* -- Ed Jones; *Tammy* -- Arthur Ashe

FAVORITE FOOD: *Jim* -- Chicken; *Tammy* -- Italian, and Seafood

CHILDREN & AGES: Jaren James -- Born 10-1-87; Twins: Jackson Dean and Jacqueline Nicole -- Born 12-26-90

FITNESS & DIET TIP: Don't Eat Too Much! Drink a Lot of Water; and Substitute Low-Fat Food Whenever Possible

LONG-RANGE CAREER GOALS: Career in Real Estate Development

DALLAS ★ COWBOYS
Super Bowl XXVIII Champions

"Sweet Success of a Repeat" -- Jackson (3 years), Jaren (6 years), and Jacqueline (3 years).

Jeffcoat children enjoying '94 spring Texas Bluebonnets.

JIM JEFFCOAT'S FANCY TOSTADAS

1 can *refried* beans (*16-oz. can*)
dash of McILHENNY CO. TABASCO SAUCE
1/4 c. *sliced* green onion
4 oz. Monterey Jack cheese, *grated*
1 tomato, *chopped*
3 c. *shredded* lettuce
3 green onions, *chopped*
1 avocado, *chopped*
3 T. Italian salad dressing (*Thousand Island is good, also*)
1 lb. GROUND BEEF
1 *small* onion, *chopped*
1/8 t. garlic powder
1 can green chilies (*4-oz. can*)
1 can *mild* enchilada sauce
1/2 c. tomato juice
7 to 8 *fried* tortillas

In small bowl, combine refried beans, Tabasco, green onions, and Monterey Jack cheese. *Cover*; bake for 25 min. at 325 degrees. In salad bowl, combine tomato, lettuce, onion, and salad dressing. Brown ground beef, onion, and garlic in skillet; *drain grease*. Add green chilies, enchilada sauce, and tomato juice. *Mix well*; let simmer for 20 min.
To serve: Fry tortillas in 1/2" of oil in small skillet. Turn once. Top with *hot* refried bean mixture, meat sauce; then, salad. * *Can top with cheese or taco sauce*. Serves 4.

TAMMY'S HOT CHEESY SEAFOOD DIP

1 lb. process cheese, *cut into 1-inch cubes*
1 pkg. cream cheese (*3-oz. package*)
1/4 c. butter or margarine
1/4 t. hot sauce
1 can *small* shrimp, *drained, rinsed, chopped* (*4-1/2 oz. can*)
green onions, *chopped (with tops)*
tortilla chips

Combine process cheese cubes, cream cheese, and butter in top of a double boiler. Bring water *to a boil*. Reduce heat to *low*; cook, <u>stirring frequently</u>, until cheese melts. Stir in hot sauce, small shrimp, and green chilies. Transfer mixture to a chafing dish. Sprinkle with onions. Serve warm with tortilla chips. Makes approximately 4 cups.

John and Jacque Jett, and Bugsy -- Christmas, 1993.

JACQUE & JOHN JETT
Number 19
Punter -- 6'-0" -- 184 lbs.

BIRTH DATES: *John* -- 11-11-68 (Richmond, Virginia); *Jacque* -- 1-18-71 (Lenoir, North Carolina)

COLLEGES: *John* -- East Carolina University (B.S.B.A. - Finance); *Jacque* -- East Carolina University (B.A. - Economics)

FAVORITE ACADEMIC SUBJECT: *John and Jacque* -- Statistics

GREATEST MOMENT IN SPORTS: Stanford's Kick-Off Return to Win the Game (when the Band Member Was Run Over)

FIRST PLAYED ORGANIZED FOOTBALL: As a Ten-Year-Old, the Quarterback for the Fleeton "Eagles"

YEARS IN PROFESSIONAL FOOTBALL: 2nd Year

WIFE'S OCCUPATION: Part-Time Sales Representative

HONORS OR AWARDS: Starred in Football and Baseball at Northumberland High School in Heathsville, Virginia; Earned First-Team All-State Honors as an Outfielder and Pitcher; Four-Year Letterman at East Carolina; Established as the Top Punter in School History, Setting a Pirates' Career Mark for Punting Average (40.1); Honorable Mention All-America (Sporting News) and Second-Team All-South Independent Selection, in 1991; Finished 1993 Season Ranked Third in the NVC in Net Punting Average with a 37.7 Mark; Highest Net Punting Average by a Dallas Player since 1964; Averaged Better than 50 Yards Per Punt in Three Games in 1993

HOBBIES & INTERESTS: *John and Jacque* -- Fishing, Water Skiing, Hunting, Golf, and Being Outdoors

FAVORITE TYPE OF MUSIC: *John* -- Country (Garth Brooks, and George Strait)

FAVORITE SPORTS HERO: *John* -- Fred Lynn

FAVORITE TV/MOVIE STAR: *John* -- Clint Eastwood; *Jacque* -- Meg Ryan

FAVORITE FOOD: *John* -- Grilled Dolphin; *Jacque* -- Macaroni and Cheese

FITNESS & DIET TIP: Exercise at Least Four Times a Week; and Cut out the Fat Grams

LONG-RANGE CAREER GOALS: Go Back to Virginia and Run Father's Boat Dealership when He Retires

Punter John Jett in Alaska.

JOHN JETT'S CHILI-SPAGHETTI

2 lbs. GROUND BEEF
2 *medium* onions, *chopped*
2 cloves garlic, *minced*
1 green pepper, *chopped*
4 cans *whole* tomatoes, *undrained* (*16-oz. cans*)
1 can tomato sauce (*20-oz. can*)
1 can kidney beans, *undrained* (*15-1/2 oz. can*)
1 pkg. spaghetti (*12-oz. package*)
1/4 c. *chopped, fresh* parsley
2 to 3 T. chili powder
1 T. *minced, fresh* marjoram, or 1 t. *dried, whole* marjoram
1 T. *minced, fresh* oregano, or 1 t. *dried, whole* oregano
2 t. salt
1 t. *ground* cumin
1 t. red pepper

Cook ground beef, onions, garlic, and green pepper in Dutch oven *until browned*; stir, while browning, to crumble meat. *Drain off liquid.* Add remaining ingredients; *mix well.* *Cover*; reduce heat, and simmer for 2 hours, stirring *occasionally*. Makes 10 to 12 servings.

JACQUE'S SOUTHWESTERN SHRIMP

1 lb. shrimp
1 can *chopped* mushrooms (*4-oz. can*)
2 T. vegetable oil
3 *medium* onions, *sliced*
1 clove garlic, *minced*
1 c. *sliced* celery
1/2 green pepper, *sliced*
1 T. PILLSBURY FLOUR
1 can tomatoes (*No. 2 can*)
1 bay leaf
1/2 t. oregano
1-1/2 t. chili powder
2 pimentos, *sliced*
1 t. salt
1/8 t. pepper
corn chips

Shell and devein shrimp. Drain mushrooms. Heat oil in a large frying pan; add onions, garlic, celery, and green pepper. Cook *until onions and celery are tender*. Sprinkle with flour; cook, *stirring constantly*, until mixture is *lightly-browned*. Add tomatoes, bay leaf, oregano, chili powder, mushrooms, pimentos, salt, and pepper; cook for *at least 10 minutes*. Add shrimp; bring *to a boil*. Reduce heat; simmer for about 3 minutes. Serve on corn chips. Makes 4 servings.

99

DALLAS ★ COWBOYS
Super Bowl XXVIII Champions

\# 48 -- Fullback Daryl 'MOOSE" Johnson in Home Run Derby at Arlington Stadium.

DARYL PETER ("MOOSE") JOHNSTON
** Number 48 **
Fullback -- 6'-2" -- 238 lbs.

BIRTH DATE: 2-10-66 (Youngstown, New York)

COLLEGE: Syracuse University (B.A. -- Economics)

GREATEST MOMENT AT SUPER BOWL XXVIII: Beating My Hometown Team Again

FIRST PLAYED ORGANIZED FOOTBALL: In 1975, as a Running Back for the Lew-Port "Chargers" -- 80-lb. Team

YEARS IN PROFESSIONAL FOOTBALL: 6th Year

ENJOY MOST AS A DALLAS COWBOY: Close Friendships with Teammates

HONORS OR AWARDS: Named Western New York Player of the Year, in 1983, while Playing for Lewiston-Porter High School in Youngstown, New York; Graduated First in Class of 290 Students with a 4.0 Grade-Point Average; All-America and All-East First-Team Pick, in 1988; Co-Captain of the 1989 Syracuse Orangemen; All-Madden Team, in 1992; in 1992, Selected for the Ed Block Courage Award, for Demonstrating Unusual Courage in Dealing with Injuries; in 1993 -- First Fullback Selected to the Pro Bowl - Earned All-Pro Honors from "Sports Illustrated" - and Finished 5th in NFC in Receptions among Running Backs; the Cowboys' Lead Blocker in the Past Four Seasons

HOBBIES & INTERESTS: Jet Skiing, Snow Skiing, and Golf

FAVORITE AUTHOR: Tom Clancy

FAVORITE TYPE OF MUSIC: Alternative

FAVORITE SPORTS HERO: Larry Csonka

FAVORITE FOOD: Italian

FITNESS & DIET TIP: Nutrition Is as Important as Exercise; and Don't Eat Big Meals Late at Night

LONG-RANGE CAREER GOALS: To Make a Smooth Transition into Next Career

10th-year high school reunion -- John Garrett, Daryl Johnston, Pete Sikoski, and Todd Freischlag (left to right).

DARYL JOHNSTON'S STUFFED MUSHROOMS

1 lb. mushrooms
2 c. crabflakes
1/2 stack of Ritz Crackers (*about 17*)
1 stick butter, *melted*
1/4 c. *fresh, chopped* parsley
2 c. *shredded* Mozzarella cheese
1/2 c. bread crumbs
1/4 t. black pepper
3/4 t. cayenne pepper

Clean mushrooms; remove stems. Combine all ingredients, after processing crabflakes and Ritz Crackers *in a food processor*. Stuff mushroom caps with one teaspoon of filling. Bake for 10 minutes at 350 degrees. Top with Mozzarella cheese. Return to oven *until cheese melts*.

JANICE'S ECLAIR CAKE

Pastry Shell: 1 c. *boiling* water
1 stick margarine
1 c. PILLSBURY FLOUR
4 eggs

Melt margarine in *boiling* water. Remove from stove; stir in flour. Let cool about 5 minutes. Beat in <u>by hand</u> 4 eggs, *one at a time*. Spread on *greased* cookie sheet. Bake at 350 degrees for 35 minutes, or *until golden brown*. Let cool.

Filling: 1 pkg. cream cheese (*8-oz. package*)
3 pkgs. *instant* vanilla pudding
(*3-3/8 oz. packages*)
5 c. milk
1 *large* container Cool Whip
Hershey Chocolate Syrup

Beat *softened* cream cheese with 1 c. milk for approximately 2 minutes. Add 3 pkgs. instant vanilla pudding and 4 cups milk; beat for 2 minutes on *low speed* with an electric mixer. Spread over *cooled* pastry shell. Cover with Cool Whip. Drizzle Hershey Chocolate Syrup over Cool Whip. Refrigerate before serving.

103

Maneesha and Robert enjoying the festivities at the annual Michael Jordan Celebrity Golf Classic.

MANEESHA & ROBERT LEE JONES
* *Number 55* *
Linebacker -- 6'-2" -- 237 lbs.

BIRTH DATES: *Robert* -- 9-27-69 (Blackstone, Virginia); *Maneesha* -- 7-2-72 -- (York, Pennsylvania)

COLLEGES: *Robert* -- East Carolina University (Criminal Justice); *Maneesha* -- West Virginia University / East Carolina University / University of North Texas (Psychology)

SPECIAL PEOPLE YOU MET WHILE AT SUPER BOWL XXVIII: Stevie Wonder, Gary Busey. Charlie Pride, Charlie Daniels, and Rev. Jesse Jackson

FIRST PLAYED ORGANIZED FOOTBALL: In Junior High, for the Nottaway "Cougars"

YEARS IN PROFESSIONAL FOOTBALL: 3rd Year

ENJOY MOST AS A DALLAS COWBOY: Winning; and Being Associated with Team Chaplain and Wife, John and Carol Weber

HONOR OR AWARDS: *Robert* -- Unanimous All-America for Four Years; Finalist - Dick Butkus Award; in East-West Shrine Game; MVP of Peach Bowl (1991 ECU versus NC State); First-Round Draft Pick out of E.C.U.; Honor Roll at E.C.U.; NFC Defensive Rookie of Year and All-Rookie Team, in 1992; Second Leading Tackler, in 1992; Super Bowl Champ as a Rookie; in 1993, the First Player with Back-to-Back Double-Digit Tackle Games since September, 1991; Starting Middle Linebacker for Cowboys, in 1994; *Maneesha* -- Honor Roll (High School); Dean's List in College; and Best Award Ever - #1 Mom and Wife!

HOBBIES & INTERESTS: *Robert* -- Playing Video Games, Remote Control Cars, and Being with Family; *Maneesha* -- Native American Dancing, Working Out, Watching Football, and Reading the Bible

FAVORITE AUTHOR: *Robert* -- John Grisham; *Maneesha* -- Annie Orlund

FAVORITE TYPE OF MUSIC: *Robert* -- Rhythm and Blues, and Rap; *Maneesha* -- Rhythm and Blues, Soul, Reggae, and Gospel

FAVORITE SPORTS HERO: *Robert* -- Michael Jordan; Maneesha -- Husband Robert; and Jeff Blake (Quarterback - Cincinnati Bengals, and Brother); and Willie Anderson (San Antonio Spurs)

FAVORITE FOOD: *Robert* -- Pork Chops, and Seafood; *Maneesha* -- Shrimp

CHILDREN & AGES: Cayleb Seth - 1-1/2 yrs.

FITNESS & DIET TIP: Get in Shape; Lift Hard and Stretch Well; and Work Out at Home in the Off-Season

LONG-RANGE CAREER GOALS: Counsel Youth with Substance Abuse Problems; and Have <u>Many</u> Healthy Children

Cayleb Jones takes his two girlfriends (Brianna Marion and Brianna Holmes) out on the town in his limo!

Robert and Cayleb (18 months) enjoy Wildwater Kingdom (PA) with brother-in-law Jeff Blake and children, Princess and Emory.

DALLAS COWBOYS
Super Bowl XXVIII Champions

ROBERT JONES' CHILI BEANS & MAC CASSEROLE

2 T. vegetable oil
2 *medium* onions, *chopped*
1-1/2 lb. *lean* GROUND BEEF
1 to 2 T. chili powder
1-1/2 c. *sharp* Cheddar cheese, *grated*
2 cans of kidney beans, *undrained* (*47-oz. cans*)
3 garlic cloves, *minced*
1 can *crushed* tomatoes (*28-oz. can*)
3/4 c. *uncooked, elbow* macaroni
1/2 c. *sharp* Cheddar cheese, *grated*

Saute onion and brown beef; *drain excess fat.* Add chili powder, garlic, 1-1/2 c. cheese, beans, tomatoes, and *uncooked* macaroni. Spoon *moist mixture* into 9" x 13" pan. *The noodles will absorb the moisture.* Top with remaining 1/2 c. Cheddar cheese. Bake at 350 degrees for 1 hour. *Serves 2 Dallas Cowboys . . . or 8 average people*!

MANEESHA'S NOODLE-CRAB CASSEROLE

1 pkg. *wide* noodles (*6-oz. package*)
2 cans cream of mushroom soup (*10-oz. cans*)
1 lb. crab meat
1 green pepper, *seeded and chopped*
2 t. curry powder
1/4 c. dry sherry
1 c. dry bread crumbs
1 c. *sharp* Cheddar cheese, *grated*

Cook noodles (*according to package directions*); *drain well.* Place noodles in *lightly-greased* 9" x 13" pan. Warm soup in saucepan. Stir in crab, green pepper, and curry powder. *Mix gently, but well.* Stir in sherry; then, spoon mixture over noodles. Top with bread crumbs; then, with cheese. Bake at 350 degrees for 30 minutes. Serves 6 to 8.

DALLAS ⭐ COWBOYS
Super Bowl XXVIII Champions

Kennard children: Derek (13 years), Denisha (8 years), and Devon (3 years).

DALLAS ★ COWBOYS
Super Bowl XXVIII Champions

DENISE & DEREK CRAIG KENNARD
* Number 60 *
Guard -- 6'-3" -- 300 lbs.

BIRTH DATES: *Derek* -- 9-9-62 (San Mateo, California); *Denise* -- 2-3-62 (Bakersfield, California)

COLLEGES: *Derek* -- University of Nevada-Reno (Criminal Law); *Denise* -- Stockton's Private Business College

FAVORITE ACADEMIC SUBJECT: *Derek* -- Criminal Law; *Denise* -- Business

FIRST PLAYED IN ORGANIZED FOOTBALL: Nose Guard for Southside Vikings in Stockton (Pop Warner)

YEARS IN PROFESSIONAL FOOTBALL: 9th Year

HONORS OR AWARDS: All-America in High School; Starred at Edison High School in Stockton, Shooting Several Episodes of the HBO Series "First and Ten" during the Summer of 1986, along with O. J. Simpson, Marcus Allen, and Mike Sherrard; Two-Time All-Big Sky Conference Selection and a Division 1-AA All-America, as a Senior, for the Wolfpack in 1983; NFL Honorable Mention All-Pro at Center, in 1988; Earned Second-Team All-Pro Honors, in 1992; Signed as an Unrestricted Free Agent -- April, 1994, by Dallas

HOBBIES & INTERESTS: *Derek* -- Golf, Fishing, and Swimming; *Denise* -- Sewing, Crafts, and Shopping

FAVORITE AUTHOR: *Derek* -- John Grisham; *Denise* -- Terry McMillan

FAVORITE TYPE OF MUSIC: *Derek and Denise* -- Rap, Rhythm and Blues, and Jazz

FAVORITE SPORTS HERO: *Derek* -- Muhammad Ali

FAVORITE TV/MOVIE STAR: *Derek* -- Steve Segal

FAVORITE FOOD: *Derek* -- Cajun, Seafood, and Ribs; *Denise* -- Soul Food, and Mexican

CHILDREN & AGES: Derek, Jr. - 12 yrs.; Denisha - 8 yrs.; and Devon Jay - 3 yrs.

PET PEEVE: Messy Home and Messy Person; Unorganized People

FITNESS & DIET TIP: Drink Plenty of Water (One Gallon per Day); and Curb Appetite

LONG-RANGE CAREER GOALS: Open up a Group Home for Boys; and Counselor for Juvenile Delinquents

Denise and Derek Kennard.

Derek Kennard coaching in the rain at Jay Novacek Football Camp.

DEREK KENNARD'S MENUDO

2 lbs. tripe
2 pigs feet, *cut into 4*
1/4 t. salt
3 bay leaves
1 T. red pepper, *crushed*
2 T. garlic powder, or 4 cloves garlic
1 t. cumin
1 t. oregano
1/2 sweet basil
1 T. Menudo seasoning
1 can hominy
1 can tomato sauce

Cook pigs feet for 30 minutes. Cut tripe to *bite-size* pieces; add to pigs feet. Cook tripe *until tender*. Add other ingredients. Cook on *low* heat for 30 minutes. Serve *as soup*.

DENISE'S SHRIMP SALAD

1 lb. *cooked* shrimp, *deveined*
1 red bell pepper
1 green bell pepper
1 *large* tomato
1 *large* onion
2 or 3 lemons
seasoning salt, *to taste*
pepper, *to taste*
garlic powder, *to taste*

Cut shrimp, red bell pepper, green bell pepper, tomato, and onion into *bite-size* pieces. Put all ingredients into a bowl. Add seasoning salt, pepper, and garlic powder; blend together seasonings *to taste*. Cut lemons in *half*; squeeze juice into bowl with ingredients. Blend together. Refrigerate *until chilled*. Then, serve.

Running Back Derrick Lassic.

DERRICK OWENS LASSIC
* Number 25 *
Running Back -- 5'-10" -- 188 lbs.

BIRTH DATE: 1-26-70

COLLEGE: University of Alabama (Criminal Justice)

YEARS IN PROFESSIONAL FOOTBALL: 2nd Year

HONORS OR AWARDS: High School Standout in Both Track and Baseball; Selected New York State's Player of the Year (North Rockland High School - Haverstraw, New York) -- Rushing for 1,787 Yards, Including Nine Straight Games of 100 or More Yards, and 31 Touchdowns, as a Senior; in Addition to Running Skills -- Caught 31 Passes for 586 Yards; Received All-State Honors; Earned a Junior Heisman Trophy from the New York Downtown Athletic Club; Played in Four Bowl Games during College Career at Alabama; Earned the Sugar Bowl MVP Award; Despite Starting Only One Season for the Crimson Tide, Finished Career Ranked 11th on Alabama's All-Time Rushing List - with 1,696 Yards; Only Offensive Back Selected from Alabama, in 1993; First Rookie Running Back in NFL History to Start a Season Opener for a Defending Super Bowl Champion; First Offensive Rookie to Start for Dallas in Season Opener since Troy Aikman Started at Quarterback, in 1989

25 -- Derrick Lassic.

DERRICK LASSIC'S MOIST SUPPER CAKE

1-1/4 c. *boiling* DR. PEPPER
1 c. *quick-cooking* oats
1/2 c. shortening
1/2 c. C & H GRANULATED SUGAR
1 c. C & H BROWN SUGAR
2 eggs
1-1/3 c. PILLSBURY FLOUR
1/2 t. salt
1 t. baking soda
1/2 t. nutmeg

Pour Dr. Pepper over oats. Stir; let stand 15 to 20 minutes. Meanwhile, cream shortening and sugar (add sugars gradually); *cream well*. Add eggs, beating *until mixture is fluffy*. Sift flour with salt, baking soda, and nutmeg. Add flour mixture to creamed mixture; *mix well*. Add oatmeal mixture; *mix thoroughly*. Pour into 9" x 9" x 2" pan, *greased and floured*. Bake at 375 degrees for 40-45 minutes, or *until cake tests done*. Remove from oven. Spread topping over *hot* cake; place under broiler. Broil *until bubbly and lightly brown*. Serve warm. Makes 12 to 16 servings.

Topping: 1/3 c. *melted* butter
                1/2 c. C & H BROWN SUGAR
                1/4 c. *light* cream
                1 c. *fine-grated* coconut.

Mix butter with brown sugar; add cream and coconut. Spread over *hot* cake, before placing under broiler.

LASSICK'S SOMBRERO SPREAD

1 lb. GROUND BEEF
1 c. *chopped* onion
1/2 c. *hot* catsup
3 t. chili powder
3 t. salt
2 cans kidney beans (*8-oz. cans*)
1 c. *sharp* American cheese, *shredded*
1/2 c. *stuffed* olives, *sliced*
corn chips

Brown ground beef and 1/2 c. onions in a skillet. Stir in the catsup, chili powder, and salt. *Mash the beans with liquid* in a bowl; then, stir into the beef mixture. Stir in the cheese. Place in a *chafing dish*. Sprinkle with remaining onion and olives. Serve with corn chips.

115

78 -- Leon Lett.

LEON LETT
* Number 78 *
Defensive Tackle -- 6'-6" -- 285 lbs.

BIRTH DATE: 10-12-68 (Fair Hope, Alabama)

COLLEGE: Emporia State University (Sociology)

GREATEST THRILL ABOUT BEING A PRO ATHLETE: Draft Day

FAVORITE ACADEMIC SUBJECT: English

YEARS IN PROFESSIONAL FOOTBALL: 4th Year

HONORS OR AWARDS: Starred in Football and Basketball at Fair Hope, Mississippi, High School; Received an Honorable Mention NAIA All-America, All-NAIA District 10, and All-CSIC Honors, in 1989; Twice Named District 10 Player of the Week, as a Junior, in College; First Person from Emporia State to Make a Cowboys' Roster; Nicknamed "Big Cat" by Teammates for His Agility; Led All Defensive Linemen in Batted Passes, in 1992; Finished 1992 Tied for Second on the Team with 19 Quarterback Pressures, Including at Least One Pressure in the Final Seven Regular Season Games; in Post Season, Tied for Team Lead with Two Tackles for Losses, and Led Team with Three Forced Fumbles; Established a Record for the Longest Fumble Return in Super Bowl History when He Rambled 64 Yards in the Fourth Quarter with a Buffalo Miscue; Seeing Action in Only 11 Games, Led All Defensive Lineman in Passes Deflected for the Second Straight Season (4 in 1992, and 4 in 1993) - the Other 7 Dallas Linemen Combined for 11 Batted Passes over That Same Period; Despite Being Hobbled during the 1993 Season with a Broken Ankle, Lett Displayed Tremendous Athletic Ability and Versatility in Moving along the Defensive Line to Replace Fallen Teammates

FAVORITE AUTHOR: Alex Haley

FAVORITE TYPE OF MUSIC: Rhythm and Blues

FAVORITE SPORTS HERO: Ed "Too Tall" Jones

FAVORITE TV/MOVIE STAR: Wesley Snipes

FAVORITE FOOD: Italian, Especially Lasagna

CHILDREN & AGES: Shanavia - 7 yrs.

117

Defensive Tackle Leon Lett in action.

DALLAS COWBOYS
Super Bowl XXVIII Champions

LEON LETT'S TEXAS FUDGE

4 c. C & H GRANULATED SUGAR
1-1/3 c. DR. PEPPER
4 oz. *grated, unsweetened* chocolate
4 T. white corn syrup
1/2 c. butter or margarine
2 t. vanilla
1-2 c. *chopped* nuts, *optional*

Place sugar, Dr. Pepper, grated chocolate, and corn syrup in a heavy saucepan. Cook *very slowly*, stirring <u>constantly</u>, until sugar and chocolate is *thoroughly dissolved*. Continue cooking on *low-medium* heat until temperature is *236 degrees*, or *soft-ball stage is reached*. Remove from heat; cool *at room temperature* to lukewarm (*110 degrees*). Add butter and vanilla. Beat *until the candy loses its shiny look*. Add nuts, *if desired*. Pour into *slightly-buttered* pans. When *cold*, cut into squares. Makes 36 pieces (*2-1/2 inch*).

LEON'S MEXICAN CORNBREAD

1-1/2 c. cornmeal
1 c. canned *cream-style* corn
1 c. buttermilk
1/2 c. vegetable oil
2 eggs, *beaten*
1 T. baking powder
1 t. salt
1 t. C & H GRANULATED SUGAR
2 jalapeno peppers, *seeded and minced*
1/4 c. *finely-chopped* onion
2 T. *minced* green pepper
1 c. *sharp* Cheddar cheese, *shredded* (*4 ounces*)

Combine all ingredients, *except cheese*, in a large bowl; *stir well*. Pour *half* of mixture into a *greased* 10-inch iron skillet; top with cheese. Add remaining cornmeal mixture. Bake cornbread at 450 degrees for 30 minutes, or *until done*. Makes 10 to 12 servings.

119

DALLAS ★ COWBOYS
Super Bowl XXVIII Champions

Keri and daughter Briana at Daddy's agent's office.

BROCK MARION
* Number 31 *
Safety -- 6'-0" -- 190 lbs.

BIRTH DATE: 6-11-70 (Wheeling, West Virginia)

COLLEGE: University of Nevada (Architecture and Interior Design)

GREATEST MOMENT AT SUPER BOWL XXVIII: Although Injured (against San Francisco 49'ers in Playoffs) and Could Not Play, the Greatest Moment from Last Year's Super Bowl Was Being a Part of the "Back-to-Back" Championship Title

FIRST PLAYED ORGANIZED FOOTBALL: In the Second Grade

YEARS IN PROFESSIONAL FOOTBALL: 2nd Year

HONORS OR AWARDS: Earned Nine Varsity Letters in Football, Basketball, and Track at West High School in Bakersfield, California; All-State Selection, as Senior - Led State with 13 Interceptions; Three-Time All-Conference Selection, Twice All-Big Sky, and Once (First Team) Big West; Only the Second Player from Nevada-Reno Ever Chosen by the Cowboys; Earned Two Awards for Special Teams Player of the Game during Rookie Year

HOBBIES & INTERESTS: Hunting, Fishing, Listening to Music, and Collecting Miniature Jazz Instruments

FAVORITE AUTHOR: Romantic Poets (i.e., Keats, Shelly)

FAVORITE TYPE OF MUSIC: Rhythm and Blues, Rap, and Jazz

FAVORITE SPORTS HERO: Michael Jordan

FAVORITE TV/MOVIE STAR: Sean Connery, and Jack Nickolson

FAVORITE FOOD: Pasta, and Seafood

FAMILY: Keri Deal (*Fiancee*) -- Wedding Date: 3-18-95; Briana Elise -- Born 8-9-93; and Dog - Sheba

FITNESS & DIET TIP: Eat Three Good Meals a Day

PET PEEVE: People Who Talk Too Much

LONG-RANGE CAREER GOALS: Have Own Architectural Firm and Interior Design Offices in Bakersfield, California

DALLAS ★ COWBOYS
Super Bowl XXVIII Champions

Brock and Keri after the presentation of the Super Bowl rings.

#31 -- Brock Marion with Briana on the sidelines after a preseason game in 1994.

BROCK MARION'S BLUE CORN BREAD

1-1/2 c. *blue* cornmeal
3 T. C & H GRANULATED SUGAR (*or more, if you like*)
2 t. baking powder
3/4 c. milk
1 *large* egg, *beaten*
3 T. bacon drippings, *melted*
3 T. *minced* green chilies

Combine dry ingredients together in one bowl. Mix milk, egg, bacon drippings, and chilies in a separate bowl. Add wet mixture to the dry ingredients; mix *just enough to combine*. Pour into 8-inch square or round pan; bake at 350 degrees for about 20 minutes. Do not overbake! * *This bread dries out quickly - best if eaten the same day it is made.*

KERI'S CHILI-CORN SOUFFLE

3 T. butter
3 green onions, *minced*
3 T. PILLSBURY FLOUR
1 c. milk
4 *large* egg yolks
salt and pepper, *to taste*
4 jalapenos, *seeded and minced*
1-1/2 c. *fresh or frozen* corn kernels
1-1/2 t. *chopped, fresh* basil
1 c. Cheddar cheese, *grated*
6 *large* egg whites

Melt butter in a large saucepan; saute onions *until soft*. Stir in flour; cook approximately 2 minutes. Stir in milk; whisk *until smooth and thickened* (6 to 7 minutes). Cool *slightly*. Add egg yolks; blend. Stir in salt and pepper *to taste*, jalapenos, corn, basil, and Cheddar cheese. Beat egg whites *until stiff, but not dry*. Fold into chili-corn mixture in *three parts*. Pour into deep *buttered* gratin or quiche dish. Bake at 450 degrees for 20 minutes. Serve!

67 -- Defensive Tackle Russell Maryland.

DALLAS COWBOYS
Super Bowl XXVIII Champions

RUSSELL MARYLAND
Number 67 *
Defensive Tackle -- 6'-1" -- 279 lbs.

BIRTH DATE: 3-22-69 (Chicago, Illinois)

COLLEGE: University of Miami (B.A. -- Psychology)

FIRST PLAYED ORGANIZED FOOTBALL: In 1982, as a Ninth Grader for the Whitney Young "Dolphins" as Offensive Tackle and Defensive End

YEARS IN PROFESSIONAL FOOTBALL: 4th Year

HONORS OR AWARDS: Starred as Two-Way Lineman in High School; Undefeated in "Big Man's 60-Yard Dash" - which Was Open to Those Who Competed in the Field Events, in which He Competed on the Track Team in the Shot Put; Played on Two-Time National Champions Miami Team, in 1987 and 1989; Two-Time First-Team All-America at Miami; Winner of 1990 Outland Trophy; First Player Selected in 1991 NFL Draft; in 1991 -- Named NFL Rookie of the Year by Edelstein Pro Football Letter; and Earned All-Rookie Honors from Pro Football Writers of America, Pro Football Weekly, and College & Pro Football Newsweekly; Selected to First Pro Bowl after Just Three Seasons in the NFL, in 1993; Ranked Second on the Team in Tackles among Defensive Linemen with 56 Stops, in 1993

HOBBIES & INTERESTS: Listen to Music

FAVORITE AUTHOR: Alex Haley

FAVORITE TYPE OF MUSIC: All Types of Good Music -- Especially Rhythm and Blues, and Rap

FAVORITE SPORTS HERO: Walter Payton

FAVORITE FOOD: Spaghetti ("Because It's Easy to Cook")

FITNESS & DIET TIP: "If Your Gut Sticks out Farther than Your Chest, Then You've Got Problems"; and Eat Lots of Spaghetti!

LONG-RANGE CAREER GOALS: To Be Successful!

125

Russell Maryland and Jerry Jones.

RUSSELL MARYLAND'S SPANISH RICE

1/4 lb. *sliced* bacon, *diced*
1 *medium* green pepper
1 *medium* onion, *minced*
2 c. *packaged precooked* rice
2 cans tomato sauce (*8-oz. cans*)
1 t. salt
dash of pepper
1/2 t. *prepared* mustard
1 can consomme
tomato wedges

Cook the bacon in a saucepan *until brown*; remove from saucepan. Cut green pepper in *half*; mince *half* of the green pepper and add to saucepan. Add onion and rice; cook, stirring, *until lightly browned*. Add tomato sauce, salt, pepper, and mustard; *mix well*. Stir in consomme and bring *to a boil*. Reduce heat; *cover*. Simmer *until rice is tender and liquid is absorbed*. Cut remaining green pepper into strips. Garnish the rice mixture with tomato wedges and green pepper strips. * *This dish may be prepared the day before serving, and chilled.* Bake at 325 degrees for 25 minutes; then, garnish. Makes 6 servings.

RUSSELL'S TEXAS RANGER COOKIES

1 c. shortening
1 c. C & H GRANULATED SUGAR
1 c. C & H BROWN SUGAR, *packed*
2 eggs
3 c. *crushed* cornflakes
1 c. oats
1-1/4 t. baking soda
1 t. baking powder
1/2 t. salt
1 c. *chopped* pecans
1 t. vanilla

Cream shortening and sugars together *until smooth*. Add eggs, <u>one at a time</u>, *beating well after each addition*. Stir in cornflakes and oats. Sift baking soda, baking powder, and salt together; add to creamed mixture, *small amount at a time*. Stir in the pecans and vanilla. Drop from a teaspoon onto a *greased* cookie sheet. Bake at 375 degrees for about 10 minutes, or *until brown*. * *One cup of shredded coconut may be substituted for the pecans, if desired.*

Linebacker Geoffrey Myles.

DALLAS ★ COWBOYS
Super Bowl XXVIII Champions

GODFREY MYLES
* Number 98 *
Linebacker -- 6'-1" -- 242 lbs.

BIRTH DATE: 9-22-68 (Miami, Florida)

COLLEGE: University of Florida (Sociology)

FIRST PLAYED ORGANIZED FOOTBALL: In 1975, as a Running Back/Quarterback for the Little League (75-lbs.)

YEARS IN PROFESSIONAL FOOTBALL: 4th Year

ENJOY MOST AS A DALLAS COWBOY: Unity

HONORS OR AWARDS: Earned Second-Team All-State Honors at Carol City High School in Miami; Selected to Florida's 35-Man Super Squad that Met a Team of Georgia Prep All-Stars, in Summer of 1987; Named the "Most Underrated Player in the Country" by The Sporting News, Prior to His Junior Year; All-Southeastern Conference, in 1990; Honorable Mention All-America Pick (1989-1990); Made a Name for Himself as a Hard-Hitting Special Teamer, Collecting Nine Kick Coverage Tackles, in 1992; Picked up First Career Interception in the Regular Season Finale, in 1992; Began 1993 Season with a Knee Injury

HOBBIES & INTERESTS: Music

FAVORITE TYPE OF MUSIC: Rhythm and Blues, and Ballads

FAVORITE SPORTS HERO: Lawrence Taylor

FAVORITE FOOD: Chicken and Yellow Rice

LONG-RANGE CAREER GOALS: To Own a Record Business

DALLAS ★ COWBOYS
Super Bowl XXVIII Champions

98 -- Geoffrey Myles.

Myles in action.

GODFREY MYLES' WESTERN BAKED BEANS

1 lb. pinto beans	3 T. PILLSBURY BROWN SUGAR
6 c. water	pinch of oregano
1/2 c. *chopped* onions	pinch of oregano
1 T. cooking oil	1 t. salt
1 can tomatoes and chilies	1/8 t. pepper

Cook pinto beans in *boiling* water *until tender*. Add water <u>as needed</u>. Pour into a casserole. Saute onions in cooking oil *until tender*; stir in tomatoes and chilies, brown sugar, oregano, salt, and pepper. Then, stir into beans. *Cover.* Bake at 375 degrees for 30 minutes. *Uncover.* Bake for 30 minutes longer. Makes 8 to 10 servings.

GODFREY'S PEANUT BUTTER MERINGUE PIE

3/4 c. *creamy* peanut butter
3/4 c. *sifted* PILLSBURY POWDERED SUGAR
1 *baked* 9" pastry shell
1/2 c. C & H GRANULATED SUGAR
1/3 c. PILLSBURY ALL-PURPOSE FLOUR
1/2 t. salt
1/4 c., *plus 2 T.*, C & H GRANULATED SUGAR

2 c. milk	1/2 t. vanilla extract
3 eggs, *separated*	1/4 t. cream of tartar
1 T. butter or margarine	

Combine peanut butter and powdered sugar. Stir with a fork *until mixture resembles coarse meal.* Spread mixture in *cooled* pastry shell. Set aside. Combine 1/2 c. sugar, flour, and salt in a heavy saucepan. *Gradually* add milk, stirring *until well blended.* Cook over *medium* heat, <u>stirring constantly</u>, *until mixture is thickened and bubbly.* Remove pan from heat. Beat egg yolks *until thick and lemon colored.* *Gradually* stir about 1/4 of hot milk mixture into yolks. Add to remaining hot mixture, <u>stirring constantly</u>. Cook over *medium* heat, <u>stirring constantly</u> (about 4 minutes), *until thickened.* Remove from heat; stir in butter and vanilla. Pour over peanut butter in pastry shell. Combine egg whites (*at room temperature*) and cream of tartar. Beat *until foamy.* *Gradually* add remaining sugar, <u>one tablespoon at a time</u>. Beat *until stiff peaks form.* Spread meringue over *hot* filling, sealing to the edge of pastry. Bake at 350 degrees for 12 to 15 minutes, or *until golden brown.* Cool to room temperature. Makes one 9" pie.

Nate and Dorothy Newton and son, Nate, III.

DALLAS COWBOYS
Super Bowl XXVIII Champions

DOROTHY & NATHANIEL (NATE) NEWTON, JR.
Number 61
Offensive Guard -- 6'-3" -- 325 lbs.

BIRTH DATES: *Nate* -- 12-20-61 (Orlando, Florida); *Dorothy* -- 12-20-61 (New Orleans, Louisiana)

COLLEGES: *Nate* -- Florida A & M University - Negro League (Physical Education); *Dorothy* -- University of Southwestern Louisiana - Lafayette, Louisiana (Accounting and Sociology)

GREATEST MOMENT AT SUPER BOWL XXVIII: Celebrating with Coach Johnson, Because It Was the Last Time; Being Able to Take My Family and My Wife's Family to the Super Bowl; and for God's Blessing of Another Super Bowl Victory

PLACES VISITED WHILE AT SUPER BOWL XXVIII: "Magic City" - for the First and Last Time

SPECIAL PEOPLE MET WHILE AT SUPER BOWL XXVIII: *Nate* -- Mr. and Mrs. C. Antoine (Dot's Uncle and Aunt); *Dorothy* -- O. J. Simpson

SPECIAL FOOD EATEN WHILE AT SUPER BOWL: Cheese Potatoes

FIRST PLAYED ORGANIZED FOOTBALL: Defensive End for the Windermere Recreation Department

YEARS IN PROFESSIONAL FOOTBALL: 9th Year

HONORS OR AWARDS: *Nate* -- Played on Offensive and Defensive Lines, Winning Four Letters at Florida A & M; Team Captain and Named All-Conference (Senior); Named Cowboys' Most Valuable Offensive Player by Pro Football Weekly and Only Dallas Offensive Lineman to Earn All-Pro Votes from Associated Press, in 1990; Last Year, Made All-Madden Team for the Fourth Straight Year; All-Pro, Pro Bowl, and Hall of Fame (Jone High School - Orlando, Florida), in 1992; 1993 Season Marked the Second Straight Pro Bowl year for Newton; Has Started 103 Games as a Cowboy - More than Any Other Offensive Player for Dallas; *Dorothy* -- College on Academic and Volleyball Scholarship

HOBBIES & INTERESTS: *Nate* -- Reading; *Dorothy* -- Playing Competitive Volleyball, Softball, and Reading Love Stories

FAVORITE AUTHOR: *Nate* -- Louis L'Amour; *Dorothy* -- Alex Haley

FAVORITE TYPE OF MUSIC: *Nate* -- All Music; *Dorothy* -- Rhythm and Blues

FAVORITE SPORTS HERO: *Dorothy* -- Husband Nate

FAVORITE FOOD: *Nate* -- Italian; *Dorothy* -- Mexican

CHILDREN & AGES: Nathaniel, III (Tre) - Born 10-15-89

133

DALLAS ⭐ COWBOYS
Super Bowl XXVIII Champions

Nate Newton, III, is the pilot.

61 -- Nate, Jr., and Nate, III, having a good time in Hawaii after the Super Bowl.

DALLAS ★ COWBOYS
Super Bowl XXVIII Champions

NATE NEWTON'S CHICKEN ENCHILADAS WOOLUM

1 chicken hen (*about 4 lbs.*), or *large* fryer (*3-1/2 lbs., plus*)
1 can condensed cream of chicken soup
1 can condensed cream of mushroom soup
1 can Rotel tomatoes with green chilies (*10-1/2 oz. can*)
1 pkg. Doritos (*6-1/2 oz. package*)
2 *chopped* onions
sharp Cheddar cheese, *grated* (*about 3/4 lb.*)

Cook chicken in water to which has been added 2 t. salt and 1 t. black
pepper. Remove *cooked* chicken; cut into *bite-size* pieces. Set aside. *Drain*
tomatoes; cut or mash into *small* pieces, but save the juice. Combine soups,
tomatoes, and half of the tomato juice in a saucepan; heat until mixture is
hot, stirring *frequently* to avoid burning. *Cover* bottom of a 9" x 12"
casserole or pan with Doritos. Add the chicken on top of the Doritos; pour
the sauce over both. Add a layer of chopped onions; then cover the top with
grated cheese. Bake 45 minutes at 350 degrees. Serves 6 to 8.

DOROTHY'S MEXICAN DIP WOOLUM

2 cans bean dip (*10-oz. cans*)
3 *ripe* avocados
2 T. lemon juice
1/4 t. salt
1/4 t. pepper
1/2 c. mayonnaise
1 carton sour cream (*8 ounces*)

1 bunch green onions, *chopped with tops*
1 can *sliced* ripe olives (*6-oz. can*)
1 lb. GROUND BEEF
8 oz. *sharp* Cheddar cheese
2 T. Ortega Garden-Style Salsa
chopped tomatoes (*optional*)
1 pkg. taco seasonings mix

Mash avocados, lemon juice, salt, pepper, and salsa together; set aside.
Combine sour cream, mayonnaise, and taco seasoning. Chop onions,
including tops (*use at least 1 cup*). Brown ground beef. Grate Cheddar
cheese. *To assemble*: Spread Bean Dip over tray. Then, layer as follows:
ground beef - avocado mixture - sour cream with taco seasoning - onions -
olives - cheese. *You may also add chopped tomatoes.*

NEWTON'S MEXICAN CASSEROLE WOOLUM

1-1/2 lbs. GROUND BEEF
2 *medium* onions, *chopped*
2 cloves garlic, *minced*
1 can *whole* tomatoes, *undrained and chopped* (*16-oz. can*)
1 can Rotel tomatoes, *undrained* (*10-oz. can*)
2 cans *chopped* green chilies, *drained* (*4-oz. cans*)
1 pinch cumin
1 doz. corn tortillas
vegetable oil
4 c. *grated* Colby cheese
1 carton commercial sour cream (*8 ounces*)

Combine ground beef, onion, and garlic in a large skillet. Cook *until meat
is browned*, stirring to crumble meat. Add tomatoes and salt. Reduce heat;
simmer *uncovered* for 25 to 30 minutes. Stir in green chilies. Fry tortillas,
one at a time, in 1/4" of *hot* oil; cook about 5 seconds on each side, or *just
until softened*. Layer half each of the tortillas, meat mixture, and cheese in
a *greased* 13" x 9" x 2" baking dish; repeat layers. Bake at 350 degrees for
10 to 15 minutes, or *until cheese melts*. Serve with sour cream, if desired.
Makes 6 servings.

135

Being outdoors is a big part of Jay and Yvette's lives -- here they're elk hunting in Colorado.

DALLAS COWBOYS
Super Bowl XXVIII Champions

YVETTE & JAY MCKINLEY NOVACEK
* Number 84 *
Tight End -- 6'-4" -- 235 lbs.

BIRTH DATES: *Jay* -- 10-24-62 (Martin, South Dakota); *Yvette* -- 5-5-63 (Cozad, Nebraska)

COLLEGES: *Jay* -- University of Wyoming (Major -- Industrial Arts; *Yvette* -- University of Nebraska / Lincoln (B.S. -- Agricultural Economics)

GREATEST MOMENT AT SUPER BOWL: Scoring the First Touchdown in Super Bowl XXVII

PLACES VISITED WHILE AT SUPER BOWL XXVIII: Went to Norman Bruce's Ranch, outside Atlanta, to Ride Cutting Horses!

FIRST PLAYED ORGANIZED FOOTBALL: In the 7th Grade, for the Gothenburg "Swedes" Junior High Team in Nebraska

YEARS IN PROFESSIONAL FOOTBALL: 10th Year

HONORS OR AWARDS: *Jay* -- All-State Quarterback at Gothenburg (Nebraska) High School; University of Wyoming Record Holder in Decathlon and Pole Vault; Won Western Atlantic Conference Championship in Decathlon, in 1984; Competed in Decathlon at 1984 U.S. Olympic Trials; All-America at University of Wyoming; Won Team Event and Had Highest Individual Score in NFL-National Cutting Horse Association Super Stakes, in 1991, Following with a Third-Place Showing, in 1992; Last Year (1993), Selected to Pro Bowl for Third Straight Season -- Starting Tight End for NFC Squad; Won 1993 NFL Alumni Tight End of the Year Award; Has Caught More Passes (230) than Any Other NFL Tight End; Only Dallas Tight End to Have 50 Receptions or More in Four Straight Seasons; *Yvette* -- Graduated *Magna Cum Laude*

HOBBIES & INTERESTS: *Jay* -- Hunting, Fishing, and Cutting Horses; Hosts Two One-Week Football Camps for Youth (8-18) at Commerce, Texas, during the Off-Season; Donates His Time to Happy Hill Farm, Party Smart Campaign, and Drug Abuse Resistance Education Program; *Yvette* -- Cutting Horses, Baking Desserts, and Gives Time and Support to Happy Hill Farm; Both Yvette and Jay Are Members of Sanger Evening Lion's Club and Krum United Methodist Church

FAVORITE AUTHOR: *Jay* -- Louis L'Amour; *Yvette* -- John Grisham

FAVORITE TYPE OF MUSIC: *Jay and Yvette* -- Country

FAVORITE SPORTS HERO: *Jay* -- Mike Beers (Team Roper); *Yvette* -- Phil Rapp (Non-Professional Cutter)

FAVORITE FOOD: *Jay* -- Wild Game; *Yvette* -- Desserts

PETS: Horses -- Sackett, Lady Blue, Lenaetta, and Cola Doc; Dogs -- Marlow, Teal, and Crockett; and Cats -- Chaps and Spurs

FITNESS & DIET TIP: Stretching Is Essential; and Drink Lots of Water

LONG-RANGE CAREER GOALS: Return to Ranch in Nebraska

DALLAS ★ COWBOYS
Super Bowl XXVIII Champions

Since moving to Texas, both of the Novaceks have developed a passion for cutting horses (photos by Jett Photography, Ft. Worth).

These photos were taken during the match cutting at Glen Rose in May, 1994, which introduced several cutters to Happy Hill Farm.

JAY NOVACEK'S BBQ SPICE RUB

2 T. salt
2 T. C & H GRANULATED SUGAR
1 T. C & H BROWN SUGAR
2 t. chili powder
1 t. paprika
1 t. cumin
1/2 t. cayenne pepper
1/2 t. black pepper
1/2 t. garlic powder
1/2 t. onion powder

Jay uses this spice rub on wild game, especially wild hog roast! Rub spice onto meat; wrap in foil. Arrange coals in grill around meat. *Slow-cook* for 3 to 4 hours, *depending on size of roast.* * *Serve with Punk Carter's "A Cut Above" Barbecue Sauce!*

YVETTE'S INDOOR S'MORES

5 c. *miniature* marshmallows
1/3 c. *light* corn syrup
6 T. margarine or butter
1-1/2 c. milk chocolate chips
1 t. vanilla
8 c. Golden Grahams cereal
1 c. *miniature* marshmallows

Measure cereal into a large bowl. Butter 13" x 9" x 2" rectangular pan. Put 5 c. marshmallows, corn syrup, margarine, and chocolate chips in a 3-qt. saucepan over *low* heat, stirring <u>constantly</u>. Remove from heat. Stir in vanilla. Pour over cereal in large bowl. Mix <u>quickly</u> *until completely coated with chocolate.* Stir in 1 c. marshmallows. Form squares by pressing mixture *evenly* in *buttered* rectangular pan with a *buttered* back of spoon. Let stand *for at least 1 hour*, or refrigerate, *if a firmer bar is desired.* Cut into 2-inch squares. Makes 24 squares.

Holly and Rodney Peete at opening of Planet Hollywood in Phoenix, Arizona - March '94.

DALLAS COWBOYS
Super Bowl XXVIII Champions

RODNEY PEETE
Number 9
Quarterback -- 6'-0" -- 193 lbs.

BIRTH DATES: *Rodney* -- 3-16-66 (Mesa, Arizona); *Holly Robinson (Fiancee)* -- 9-18-64 (Philadelphia, Pennsylvania)

COLLEGES: *Rodney* -- University of Southern California (B.A. - Broadcast Journalism); *Holly* -- Sarah Lawrence College / Sorbonne - Paris, France (B.A. - Psychology)

FAVORITE ACADEMIC SUBJECT: *Rodney* -- Geography; *Holly* -- Foreign Languages

FIRST PLAYED ORGANIZED FOOTBALL: Eight Years Old, as Quarterback for the Wildcats (Pop Warner)

YEARS IN PROFESSIONAL FOOTBALL: 4th Year

FIANCEE'S OCCUPATION: Actress / Singer

GREATEST MOMENT IN SPORTS: Overcoming the Measles to Beat U.C.L.A., in Senior Year, and Advance to the Rose Bowl

HONORS OR AWARDS: All-America Honors as Quarterback at Shawnee Mission (Kansas) High; Arizona High School Athlete of the Year; as a Junior; First-Team All-America and All-PAC 10 Selection, as a Senior, at Southern Cal; Concluded College Career as Trojans' All-Time Leader in Pass Attempts, Completions, and Passing Yardage; All-Pac 10 Third Baseman for U.S.C. Baseball Squad, in 1988; Sixth-Round Draft Choice of Detroit Lions, in 1989; Named to 1989 Football Digest All-Rookie Team; Five Seasons in Detroit as Starting Quarterback; Started All 47 Games He Played during His Career; Started 10 of First 12 Games of the 1993 Season for the Lions, Posting a 62.3 Percent Completion Rate (Second Highest in Club History); Passed for over 1,000 Yards in Each of His Five NFL Seasons, while Running for a Total of 886 Yards and 13 Touchdowns (Career Rushing Average of 5.2 Yards)

HOBBIES & INTERESTS: *Rodney* -- Golfing, and Fishing; *Holly* -- Traveling

FAVORITE TYPE OF MUSIC: *Rodney* -- Rhythm and Blues

FAVORITE SPORTS HERO: *Rodney* -- Jackie Robinson; *Holly* -- Rodney Peete

FAVORITE TV/MOVIE STAR: *Rodney* -- Holly Robinson

FAVORITE FOOD: *Rodney* -- Seafood; *Holly* -- Fried Shrimp

9 -- Quarterback Rodney Peete and Nikki

RODNEY'S TUCSON LEMON CAKE

1-1/2 c. C & H GRANULATED SUGAR	1 c. buttermilk
1/2 c. margarine or butter, *softened*	1/4 c. poppy
3 eggs	seed
2-1/2 c. PILLSBURY ALL-PURPOSE FLOUR	
1 t. baking soda	2 T. *grated*
1/2 t. salt	peel
"Lemon Glaze" (*see below*)	1 T. lemon juice

Pre-heat oven to 325 degrees. *Grease and flour* 12-cup Bundt cake or tube pan (10" x 4"). Beat sugar and margarine in large bowl on *medium* speed *until light and fluffy*. Beat in eggs, <u>one at a time</u>. Mix flour, baking soda, and salt together; beat into sugar mixture <u>alternately</u> with buttermilk until well-blended. Stir in poppy seed, lemon peel, and lemon juice. Spread in pan. Bake *until wooden pick inserted in center comes out clean* (50 to 55 minutes). *Immediately poke holes in top of cake* with long-tined fork. Pour about 2/3 of "Lemon Glaze" over top. Cool for 20 minutes. *Invert on <u>heatproof</u> serving plate*; remove pan. Spread with remaining glaze.

Lemon Glaze: 2 c. C & H POWDERED SUGAR
1/4 c. margarine or butter, *melted*
2 T. *grated* lemon peel
1/4 c. lemon juice

Mix together all ingredients. Spread on cake.

HOLLY'S SPECIAL GRILLED CORN WITH CHILE-LIME SPREAD

1/2 c. margarine or butter, *softened*   3 T. lime juice
1/2 t. *grated* lime peel   1-2 t. *ground* red chilies

Mix all ingredients, *except corn*. Remove large *outer* husks from each ear of corn; turn back *inner* husks and remove silk. Spread each ear with about 2 t. butter mixture; reserve remaining mixture. Pull husks up over ears; tie with fine wire to secure. Grill corn 3" from *medium* coals, <u>turning frequently</u> *until done* (20 to 30 minutes). Serve with remaining butter mixture. Makes 6 servings.

Jim and Brenda Schwantz.

BRENDA & JIM SCHWANTZ
* Number 52 *
Linebacker -- 6'-2" -- 232 lbs.

BIRTH DATES: *Jim* -- 1-23-70 (Arlington Heights, Illinois); *Brenda* -- 4-14-71 (Chicago, Illinois)

COLLEGES: *Jim* -- Purdue University (B.A. - 1992); *Brenda* -- Purdue University

FAVORITE ACADEMIC SUBJECT: *Jim* -- Math; Brenda -- English

GREATEST MOMENT IN SPORTS: Receiving a Scholarship to Attend Purdue University, which Enabled Me to Accomplish Many Goals for Myself

FIRST PLAYED IN ORGANIZED FOOTBALL: Freshman Year in High School, as Tight End for the Vikings

YEARS IN PROFESSIONAL FOOTBALL: 2 Years (Both with Chicago Bears); Traded to Dallas 9-1-94

HONORS OR AWARDS: Second Team All-Big 10; Team MVP; and Kiwanis Citizenship Award

HOBBIES & INTERESTS: *Jim* -- Golf; *Brenda* -- Reading, and Jogging

FAVORITE AUTHOR: *Jim* -- Michael Crichton; *Brenda* -- Dean R. Koontz

FAVORITE TYPE OF MUSIC: *Jim and Brenda* -- Country

FAVORITE SPORTS HERO: *Jim* -- Walter Payton, Michael Jordan, and Mike Singletary

FAVORITE TV/MOVIE STAR: *Jim* -- Tommy Lee Jones, and Harrison Ford; *Brenda* -- Sean Connery

FAVORITE FOOD: *Jim and Brenda* -- Italian

CHILDREN & AGES: Ashlynne Marie - Newborn

FITNESS & DIET TIP: Change up Your Workout Periodically; and Stay away from Fast Food

145

Jim Schwantz with new daughter Ashlynne Marie.

JIM SCHWANTZ'S CHICKEN ENCHILADAS SUPREME

2 c. *cooked, chopped* BUTTERBALL BONELESS, SKINLESS
  CHICKEN BREASTS
1 can *chopped, mild* green chilies (*4-oz. can*)
1 can green chile salsa (*7-oz. can*)
oil
1/2 t. salt
2 c. *heavy* cream
12 corn tortillas
1-1/2 c. *grated* Monterey Jack cheese

Combine chicken, green chilies, and green chile salsa; *mix well*. Mix salt and cream in a medium-size bowl. Heat about 1/2" oil in small skillet. Dip each tortilla into *hot* oil for about 5 seconds, *just to soften*; drain on paper towels. Dip each fried tortilla into bowl containing salt and cream, *coating each side*. Fill each tortilla with chicken mixture. Roll and place in *ungreased* flat baking dish. Pour remaining cream over enchiladas; sprinkle with cheese. Bake *uncovered* at 350 degrees for 20 to 25 minutes. Serves 6.

BRENDA'S CAULIFLOWER SALAD WITH GUACAMOLE DRESSING

1 head *raw* cauliflower (*about 2 lbs.*)
1/2 c. *thinly-sliced* green pepper
1/2 c. *thinly-sliced* red pepper
3/4 c. *homemade* oil and vinegar dressing
1 head romaine lettuce
1 *large* cucumber, *sliced*
4 tomatoes, *sliced*
guacamole dressing

Thinly slice cauliflower; combine with green and red peppers. Add oil and vinegar dressing; *toss gently*. Refrigerate *at least 2 hours*. *To serve*: Line a large platter with *crisp* romaine lettuce; mound cauliflower mixture in center; and overlap *alternate* slices of tomatoes and cucumbers around the edge. Serve with guacamole dressing. Serves 12.

Linebacker Darrin Smith.

DARRIN ANDREW SMITH
* Number 59 *
Linebacker -- 6'-1" -- 227 lbs.

BIRTH DATE: 7-15-70 (Miami, Florida)

COLLEGE: University of Miami (B.A. - Management; M.B.A. - Marketing)

FAVORITE ACADEMIC SUBJECT: Management

FIRST PLAYED IN ORGANIZED FOOTBALL: Seven Years Old, as a Linebacker

YEARS IN PROFESSIONAL FOOTBALL: 2nd Year

HONORS OR AWARDS: All-State Selection, as a Senior, at Norland High School in Miami; Led Team in Tackles as a Senior Linebacker, after Playing on the Offensive Line, as a Junior; University of Miami's First National Football Foundation and College Hall of Fame Scholar-Athlete Recipient; One of Ten Student-Athletes to Receive the National Association of Academic Advisors Achievement Award, in 1993; Two-Time All-America, All-Big East Selection, and Semi-Finalist for the Butkus Award during Final Two Years at Miami; Shared Big East Defensive Player of the Year Honors, in 1991, with Syracuse Defensive Tackle; Consensus All-Rookie Selection at Outside Linebacker Position, in 1993

HOBBIES & INTERESTS: Reading, and Listening to Music

FAVORITE AUTHOR: Napoleon Hill

FAVORITE TYPE OF MUSIC: Rhythm and Blues, and Rap

FAVORITE SPORTS HERO: Muhammad Ali

FAVORITE TV/MOVIE STAR: Wesley Snipes

FAVORITE FOOD: Chinese

PET PEEVE: Cold Weather

FITNESS & DIET TIP: Drink Plenty of Water throughout the Day; and Stay Away from Fried Foods as Much as Possible

LONG-RANGE CAREER GOALS: Entrepreneur; and Motivational Speaker

149

Darrin "in flight" -- a weekend in the Bahamas.

Darrin Smith with Grandmother Ethel Smith -- at his cousin's wedding in the Bahamas.

DARRIN SMITH'S SPICY BEEF & NOODLES

1 lb. BEEF ROUND-TIP STEAKS, *cut 1/8" to 1/4" thick*
1 to 2 jalapeno peppers, *minced*
1 T. vegetable oil
1 pkg. *beef-flavored* instant Ramen noodles (*3-oz. package*)
1/4 c. LEA & PERRINS STEAK SAUCE
1 c. bean sprouts
1/4 c. *unsalted* peanuts
2 T. *chopped* cilantro, or parsley

Cut steaks *crosswise* into 1-inch wide strips; cut each strip *in half*. Toss beef and jalapeno peppers with oil; *mix lightly*. Break noodles into 3 or 4 pieces; *reserve seasoning packet*. Cook noodles (*according to package directions*); <u>drain and rinse</u>. Meanwhile, heat large skillet over *medium* heat. Stir-fry beef (*1/2 at a time*) for 30 to 60 seconds. Remove beef from pan; keep warm. Add noodles, steak sauce, bean sprouts, peanuts, and cilantro; sprinkle with reserve seasoning. Heat mixture *until hot*, stirring *occasionally*. Return beef to skillet; *mix lightly*. Makes 4 servings.

DARRIN'S BUTTERMILK POUND CAKE

3 c. *sifted* PILLSBURY ALL-PURPOSE FLOUR
1/2 t. baking soda
1/2 t. baking powder
3/4 t. salt
1 c. butter
2 c. C & H GRANULATED SUGAR
4 eggs
1 t. vanilla
1 t. lemon extract
1 c. buttermilk
C & H CONFECTIONERS SUGAR

Sift the flour, baking soda, baking powder, and salt together *twice*. Cream the butter with sugar in a bowl *until light and fluffy*. Add the eggs, <u>one at a time</u>, beating *well* after each addition; then, blend in flavorings. Add the flour mixture *alternately* with buttermilk, beating *until smooth after each addition*. Pour into a *greased, floured and brown paper-lined* 10-inch tube pan. Bake in a 350-degree oven for about 1 hour and 10 minutes, or *until a toothpick inserted in the center comes out clean*. Remove from the pan; cool. Dust with confectioners sugar.

Running Back Emmitt Smith with Super Bowl trophy #2.

DALLAS COWBOYS
Super Bowl XXVIII Champions

EMMITT J. SMITH, III
*Number 22 *
Running Back -- 5'-9" -- 209 lbs.

BIRTH DATE: 5-15-69 (Pensacola, Florida)

COLLEGE: University of Florida (Major - Therapeutic Recreation)

GREATEST MOMENT AT SUPER BOWL XXVIII: The "One Drive" - Touchdown in Second Half

HONORS OR AWARDS: Concensus All-America Running Back and Prep Player-of-the-Year by Parade Magazine and USA Today as a Senior at Escambia, Florida, High School; Posted Third Highest Career Rushing and Scoring Totals in National High School History with 8,804 Yards and 106 Touchdowns; All-America and Three-Time All-Southeastern Conference Selection at Florida, Establishing 58 School Records in 3 Seasons, Including Career-Rushing Mark of 3,928 Yards; Surpassed the 1,000-Yard Rushing Mark in 7th Game, Earlier than Any Player in College Football History; Became Second Freshman to Finish in Top 10 in Heisman Trophy Balloting; Earned Freshman-of-the-Year Honors from UPI and The Sporting News; in 1989, Set School Single-Game Rushing Mark with 316 Yards on Way to a School-Record 1,599 Yards Rushing for the Season; in 3 Seasons, Became 5th Leading All-Time Rusher in SEC History - Leading Gators in Receiving in Two-of-Three Seasons; in 1990, Started Team-High 52 Straight Games, Including Playoffs; Earned Consensus First-Team All-Pro Honors and All-NFC Honors from UPI and Football News; Joined Jimmy Johnson (1990) and Jerry Jones (1991) as Recipients of "Big D" Award from Dallas All Sports Association, in 1992; Led NFL in Rushing in 1991 - Becoming First Cowboys Player to Lead League in Rushing; Became Youngest Player in NFL History and 28th Overall to Rush for over 1,500 yards in a Season; in 1992, Became 9th NFL Player to Win Consecutive Rushing Titles, and 1st since 1983-'84; Set New Dallas Rushing Record with 1,713 Yards while Leading NFL Setting New Cowboys' Standards for Rushing Touchdowns (18) and Total Touchdowns (19); Became First Player to Win Rushing Title and Super Bowl in the Same Season; Posted 10th Best Rushing Season in NFL History; Is First NFL Player, since 1984-'85, with Consecutive 1,500-Yard Rushing Seasons; Joins Bob Hayes as Only Dallas Player with 3 Straight 10-Touchdown Seasons; Is First Player in Team History with 3 Straight Seasons with 10-or-More Rushing Touchdowns; His 2,048 Yards from Scrimmage Set New Dallas Record, Led NFC, and Was Second in NFL; in 1992, Established a Dallas Mark for Rushing Attempts with 373, and Rushing-Receiving Attempts from Scrimmage with 432; in 1992, Earned Third Straight Pro Bowl Appearance - Second Straight as Starter; and Became First Dallas Player to Start Two Straight Pro Bowls since 1982-83; Only Fourth Player in Team History to Make Pro Bowl in His First Three Seasons in the League; Became First Cowboy Player to Rush for 100 Yards in a Super Bowl; Some of 1993 Honors and Awards -- Associated Press, The Sporting News, Pro Football Writers of America, Miller Lite, the ESPN "ESPY" Awards, Pro Football Weekly and Pro Football Digest - 1993 National Football league MVP; United Press International, Pro Football Weekly and College and Pro Football Newsweekly - NFL Offensive Player of the Year; Bert Bell Award Recipient from the Maxwell Club - as Player of the Year; Consensus All-Pro; NFL Alumni Running Back of the Year; Super Bowl XXVIII MVP; Only the Fourth Player to Win Three Straight Rushing Titles - and the First since Earl Campbell in 1978-'80; First Dallas Player to Start Three Straight Pro Bowls since Randy White in 1981-'83; Joins Mel Renfro as the Only Other Player in Team History to Make the Pro Bowl in His First Four Seasons in the NFL; Did All of This Despite Missing Two Games and Three Starts Because of Contract Negotiations in 1993

HOBBIES & INTERESTS: Golf, Fishing, and Dominos; in 1992, Started Emmitt Smith Charity Golf Tournament - Played Each March in Pensacola, with Money Going to Help Numerous Groups in Pensacola Area; Works with Salvation Army, American Lung Association, and Boxers against Drugs

153

#22 -- Emmitt Smith, Super Bowl XXVIII MVP.

Super Bowl XXVIII Champions

EMMITT SMITH'S BARBECUED SPARERIBS

1 onion, *chopped*
2 T. C & H BROWN SUGAR
1 t. paprika
1 t. salt
1 t. dry mustard
1 t. chili powder
2 dashes of hot sauce
3 T. LEA & PERRINS WORCESTERSHIRE SAUCE
1/4 c. vinegar
1 c. tomato juice
1/4 c. catsup
1/2 c. water
3 T. spareribs
1 *fresh* lemon, *thinly-sliced*

Mix onion, brown sugar, paprika, salt, mustard, chili powder, hot sauce, Worcestershire sauce, vinegar, tomato juice, catsup, and water in a saucepan; simmer for 15 minutes. *Cover*; set aside. Cut spareribs into serving pieces; place on rack in a shallow baking pan. Place a lemon slice on each serving piece. Bake at 450 degrees for 30 minutes. Pour the sauce over the spareribs. Reduce temperature to 350 degrees; *cover*. Bake for 1-1/2 hours longer, basting frequently. Makes 6 servings.

EMMITT'S EASY PECAN TARTS

2 eggs
1 c. *firmly-packed, light* C & H BROWN SUGAR
2 T. butter or margarine, *melted*
1 T. water
1 t. vanilla extract
pinch of salt
1 c. *chopped* pecans
8 *unbaked, prepared* tart shells (*2-inch*)
whipped cream, *optional*
pecan halves, *optional*

Combine eggs, brown sugar, butter, water, vanilla, and salt in a medium mixing bowl; *beat well*. Stir in chopped pecans. Spoon pecan mixture into prepared tart shells. Bake at 425 degrees for 15 to 17 minutes. Garnish with whipped cream and pecan halves, *if desired*. Makes 8 servings.

155

Cornerback Kevin Smith.

DALLAS COWBOYS
Super Bowl XXVIII Champions

KEVIN REY SMITH
Number 26
Cornerback -- 5'-11" -- 180 lbs.

BIRTH DATE: 4-7-70 (Orange, Texas)

COLLEGE: Texas A & M (Recreation, Parks, and Tourism)

GREATEST MOMENT IN SUPER BOWL: Having the Opportunity to Play in Such a Big Game . . . and Winning!

YEARS IN PROFESSIONAL FOOTBALL: 3rd Year

HONORS OR AWARDS: Earned Second-Team All-State Honors, while Leading the West Orange Stark High School Team to a 15-0 Record and a Second Consecutive Texas 4-A State Championship; Big Part of Aggies Squad That Compiled a 27-3-1 Record, Including 1991 SWC Title; Played in Three Bowl Games during Football Career; Scored Six Special Teams/Defensive Touchdowns in Four Years at Texas A & M -- Making Big Plays when Given the Opportunity; Set a SWC Record for Career Interceptions with 20, Tied the Conference Mark for Career Touchdowns on Interceptions with 3, and Set Texas A & M Career Records for Interceptions Yards (289) and Passes Defensed (32); Started 38 Straight Games to End Collegiate Career; Cornerstone of an Aggies' Secondary -- Named the Best in the Country by The Sporting News Prior to the Season, with the Aggies Leading the Nation in Defense and Finishing Second in the Country in Pass Defense, in 1991; Semifinalist for Jim Thorpe Award - Given to the Nation's Best Defensive Back; Earned Consensus All-America Honors, in 1991; for the Third Straight Year - All-SWC Recognition, in 1991; Played in Japan Bowl and East-West Shire Game following Senior Year; in 1990, Earned SWC Defensive Player of the Week Mention; Picked off Nine Passes -- Second Most in a Season in Texas A & M History -- to Lead the SWC, and Finish Fourth in the Nation; Cowboys First Pick in 1992 Draft - Selected with the Highest Choice Ever Used on a Defensive Back from Texas A & M; First Aggie Player Drafted by Dallas since 1985; Only the First Defensive Back Selected in the First Round by Dallas - Chosen with the Highest Pick the Cowboys Have Ever Used on a Defensive Back; Has Uncanny Knack for Finding the Ball -- 4.5 Speed and Big Play Ability; One of Two Cowboys' Rookies Starting on the Dallas Defensive Unit in Super Bowl XXVII; in 1992, the Youngest Player on the Roster at Age 21; in 1992 NFC Championship Game, a Very Visible Factor in the Dallas Secondary - Collected a Career-High 8 Tackles (7 Solos), while Returning a Fumble Recovery 11 Yards; Led Cowboys in Interceptions, in 1993, with Six; Tied for Second in the NFC in Interceptions, while Finishing Seventh Overall in the NFL; the Team's Leader in Passes Defensed with 13, and Tied for Team Lead in Forced Fumbles with Three; Became First Cowboy Defender, since 1990, to Be Named NFC Defensive Player of the Week

157

DALLAS ✦ COWBOYS
Super Bowl XXVIII Champions

#26 -- Kevin Smith in action.

KEVIN SMITH'S CRAB TETRAZZINI

2 T. butter or margarine
2 T. PILLSBURY FLOUR
1/2 t. paprika
1/2 t. salt
1/8 t. pepper
1 c. *thin* cream
1 t. *instant, minced* onion
2 T. sherry
1/2 c. sour cream
1 egg yolk, *beaten*
1/2 lb. crab meat
2 t. lemon juice
1/3 c. *finely-chopped* almonds
spaghetti

Melt the butter in a saucepan over *low* heat; stir in flour, paprika, salt, and pepper. Stir in the cream and onion; cook over *low* heat, stirring constantly, until sauce comes *to a boil*. Remove from heat. Stir in sherry and sour cream; then, the egg yolk. Stir in the crab meat; heat *through*. Add lemon juice and *half* of the almonds. Fill 6 *individual* casserole dishes about *half* full with *cooked* spaghetti (*according to package directions*). Spoon crab meat mixture over spaghetti. Sprinkle with remaining almonds. Bake at 400 degrees for 15 minutes.

KEVIN'S CHERRY NUT SURPRISES

2-1/2 c. PILLSBURY ALL-PURPOSE FLOUR
1 T. *dry* milk
1 t. baking powder
1/4 t. salt
3/4 c. butter or margarine, *softened*
1 c. C & H GRANULATED SUGAR
1 egg, *unbeaten*
1/4 c. DR. PEPPER
1 t. vanilla
1/2 c. maraschino cherries, *well-drained and finely-chopped*
2 c. *flake* coconut
1 c. almonds, *blanched and chopped*

On wax paper, sift together flour, dry milk, baking powder, and salt. Cream butter and sugar together; add egg and mix *until light and fluffy*. Mix in Dr. Pepper and vanilla. Add Flour mixture about half at a time, *mixing well* after each addition. Stir in cherries, coconut, and nuts. Drop *by teaspoonfuls* (about two inches apart) on *greased* cookie sheet. Bake at 350 degrees for 10 to 12 minutes. Remove from baking sheet to cooling rack immediately. * *For crisp cookies, do not store in tight container*. Makes 6 doz. cookies.

DALLAS ★ COWBOYS
Super Bowl XXVIII Champions

Center Mark Stepnoski with girlfriend Dawn Waters on vacation in
Pittsburgh -- July, '94.

MARK MATTHEW STEPNOSKI
* Number 53 *
Center -- 6'-2" -- 264 lbs.

BIRTH DATE: 1-20-67 -- Erie, Pennsylvania

COLLEGE: University of Pittsburgh (Communications)

GREATEST MOMENT AT SUPER BOWL XXVIII: Spending Time with Johnny Colt (Bass Player) and Steve Gorman (Drummer) of the Black Crowes

FIRST PLAYED ORGANIZED FOOTBALL: As a Fourth Grader, Played Both Offensive and Defensive Line for the St. James "Panthers"

YEARS IN PROFESSIONAL FOOTBALL: 6th Year

ENJOY MOST AS A DALLAS COWBOY: The Lifestyle and Friendships

HONORS OR AWARDS: Star Football Player at Cathedral Prep High School in Erie, Pennsylvania; Member of National Honor Society; Named High School Football All-America by "USA Today" and "Parade" Magazine, in 1984; in 1986, Earned Third-Team All-America Honors and Made Football News Sophomore All-America Team; Won First-Team All-America Honors, in 1988; Named an Outland Trophy Finalist and Lombardi Award Semi-Finalist; Two-Time Academic All-America -- Kodak All-America and Walter Camp All-America; One of Eleven National Football Foundation and Hall of Fame Scholar-Athletes in 1988; Last Season, Named to the A.P. All-Pro Team (Second Team), while Also Collecting All-NFC Recognition from the U.P.I. and The Football News; Only the Second Dallas Center to be Selected to the Pro Bowl (in 1992 and 1993)

HOBBIES & INTERESTS: Music, Reading, and Traveling

FAVORITE AUTHOR: Tom Clancy

FAVORITE TYPE OF MUSIC: Classic Rock

FAVORITE SPORTS HERO: Julius Erving

FAVORITE FOOD: Seafood

FITNESS & DIET TIP: Even a Little Bit of Exercise Is Better than Nothing; and Monitor Fat and Salt Intake

LONG-RANGE CAREER GOALS: Early Retirement

161

#53 -- Mark Stepnoski with Troy Aikman (on left) and Daryl Johnston (on right) at the Super Bowl parade.

MARK STEPNOSKI'S ZESTY CLAM DIP

2 cans *chopped* clams, *drained* (*6-oz. cans*)
1 bottle chili sauce
1 can mushrooms, *drain* (*4-oz. can*)
1/2 c. celery, *chopped*
dash of lemon juice
dash of A.1. STEAK SAUCE
horseradish, *to taste*

Mix all ingredients together. Chill. * *Serve with crackers.*

STEPNOSKI'S EASY SEAFOOD PASTA

1/2 lb. spaghetti
1/2 to 3/4 lb. *imitation* crab (*sea legs*)
1 c. *cooked* broccoli
1/4 lb. mushrooms, *sauteed*, or 1 can mushrooms, *drained*
   (*4-oz. can*)
1 tomato, *chopped and seeded*
1/4 lb. margarine or butter
salt and pepper, *to taste*
grated cheese

Cook pasta (*according to package directions*). *Drain*; <u>save</u>
<u>1/2 cup of the water</u>. Add water to margarine; melt. Add
pasta and rest of ingredients; heat. Season with salt, pepper,
and grated cheese; serve.

PITTSBURGH KEY LIME PIE

4 egg yolks
1 can Eagle Brand Sweetened Condensed Milk
1/3 c. lime juice
graham cracker crust
whipped cream

Beat egg yolks; add Eagle Brand Milk. Beat for 5 minutes,
until thick. Add lime juice; beat 2 more minutes.
(<u>*Optional*</u>: drop of green food coloring may be added). Pour
into graham cracker crust (*use a prepared crust, or your
favorite recipe*). Refrigerate. * *When serving, add dollop of
whipped cream*!

Guard Ron Stone.

RON STONE
* Number 65 *
Guard -- 6'-5" -- 309 lbs.

BIRTH DATE: 7-20-71

COLLEGE: Boston College (Sociology)

YEARS IN PROFESSIONAL FOOTBALL: 2nd Year

HONORS OR AWARDS: Served as Team Captain, and Blocked Three Punts in Senior Year of High School at West Roxbury, Massachusetts; All-America and All-Big East First-Team Selection, in 1992; Only Boston College Player Selected in the 1993 Draft

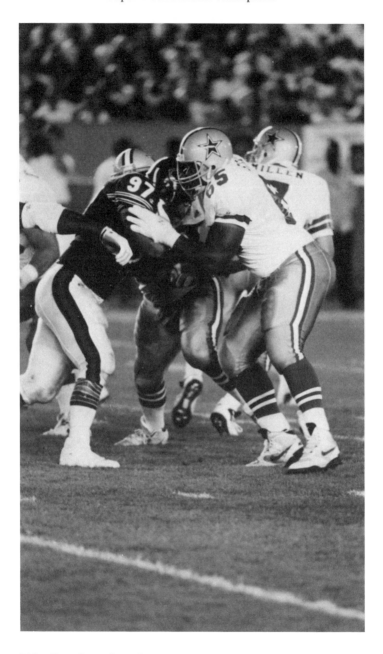

DALLAS ★ COWBOYS
Super Bowl XXVIII Champions

#65 -- Ron Stone in action.

RON STONE'S GUACAMOLE SUBS

1 *small* avocado, *peeled and mashed*
1 T. lemon juice
1 T. mayonnaise
1/4 t. hot sauce
1 garlic clove, *minced*
1 loaf Italian bread (*1-lb. loaf*)
ripe olives, *sliced*
8 slices *cooked* turkey (*1-oz. slices*)
1 *large* tomato, *sliced*
1 c. *chopped* green onions, *with tops*
1 pkg. *sliced* Monterey Jack cheese (*8-oz. package*)

Combine avocado, lemon juice, mayonnaise, hot sauce, and garlic clove; *mix well*. Set aside. Cut bread in half *crosswise*; slice each piece in half *horizontally*. *Lightly* toast bread. Spread with avocado mixture. Top each piece with 2 slices of turkey and tomato. Sprinkle with onions. Top with 2 slices of cheese. Place sandwiches on a baking sheet; broil *just until cheese melts*. Garnish with ripe olives. Serves 4 to 6 people.

RON'S PEANUT BUTTER/OATMEAL COOKIES

1 c. peanut butter
3/4 c. C & H GRANULATED SUGAR
1 egg, *beaten*
1/4 c. water
1 t. ground cinnamon
1 t. vanilla extract
1 c. "Rolled Oats Mix" (*see below*)

Combine peanut butter, sugar, egg, water, cinnamon and vanilla; stir *until smooth*. Add "Rolled Oats Mix", *blending well*. <u>Dough will be stiff</u>. *Cover*; chill for 1 hour. Shape into 1-inch balls; place 3" apart on *greased* cookie sheet. Dip a fork in flour; *flatten cookies to 1/4" thickness*. Bake at 350 degrees for 12 to 15 minutes, or *until slightly browned*. Cool on wire racks. Makes 4 dozen cookies.

Rolled Oats Mix: 4 c. *regular* oats, *uncooked*
4 c. PILLSBURY ALL-PURPOSE FLOUR
1-1/2 c. instant nonfat dry milk powder
3 T. baking powder
1-1/2 t. salt
1-1/2 c. shortening

Combine oats, flour, dry milk powder, baking powder, and salt in a large bowl; cut in shortening with pastry blender *until mixture resembles coarse meal*. Store in a <u>tightly-covered</u> container. Makes approximately 10 cups.

#41 -- Dave Thomas.

DAVE THOMAS
Number 41
Cornerback -- 6'-2" -- 208 lbs.

BIRTH DATE: 8-25-69 (South Carolina)

COLLEGE: University of Tennessee (Sociology)

FAVORITE ACADEMIC SUBJECT: English

GREATEST MOMENT IN SPORTS: Watching Deion Sanders

FIRST PLAYED ORGANIZED FOOTBALL: As a Cornerback and Strong Safety for the Miami Beach High School

YEARS IN PROFESSIONAL FOOTBALL: 2nd Year

HONORS OR AWARDS: Third-Team All-America and All-Conference Selection in Football, as a Senior, at Miami Beach High School; Lettered in Track and Basketball in High School; after Outstanding Career at Butler Community College, Rated Top Junior College Defensive Back and Sixth Best Junior College Player in the Nation by Max Emfinger in 1989; Second in the Nation, as a Sophomore, with 10 Interceptions -- Finishing Junior College Career with 17 Picks; as a Junior, in 1990, Played in All 13 Games as a Back-up for the Volunteers -- Finishing with 17 Tackles, One Pass Defensed, and an Interception Returned 51 Yards (the Longest Interception Return of the Season); in 1993, Training Camp Surprise - Making the Active Roster as an 8th-Round Draft Choice, Became Cowboys' Back-up Cornerback; Finished Season with 8 Special Teams Tackles -- Adding 5 More in the Postseason; Tied Team Lead with 3 Special Teams Tackles in Super Bowl XXVIII

HOBBIES & INTERESTS: Basketball and Track

FAVORITE AUTHOR: Terry McMillan

FAVORITE TYPE OF MUSIC: Janet Jackson

FAVORITE SPORTS HERO: Walter Payton

FAVORITE TV/MOVIE STAR: Bill Cosby

FAVORITE FOOD: Fish

FITNESS & DIET TIP: Keep Running throughout Life; Keep in Good Cardiovascular Shape; Drink Plenty of Water; and Eat No Pork!

LONG-RANGE CAREER GOALS: Work for the C.I.A.

169

DALLAS ★ COWBOYS
Super Bowl XXVIII Champions

Cornerback Dave Thomas in action.

DAVE THOMAS' COCONUT/PECAN CARROT CAKE

2-3/4 c. PILLSBURY CAKE FLOUR, *sifted*
2-1/2 t. ground cinnamon
1-1/2 t. baking soda
1/2 t. salt
1-1/4 c. vegetable oil
2 c. C & H GRANULATED SUGAR
4 eggs, *separated*
1/4 c. *warm* water
3 c. *grated* carrots
"Coconut/Pecan Frosting" (*see below*)

Combine flour, cinnamon, soda, and salt together; set aside. Combine oil and sugar; beat *until smooth*. Combine egg yolks and water; add to oil mixture, beating *well*. Stir in carrots and flour mixture, mixing *until well-blended*. Beat egg whites (*at room temperature*) *until stiff peaks form*. Fold into creamed mixture. Pour batter into three *greased and floured* 9" cake pans. Bake at 350 degrees for 25 to 30 minutes, or *until a pick inserted in center comes out clean*. Cool cake *in pans* for 10 minutes. Remove layers from pans; place on wire racks. Let cool <u>completely</u>. Spread "Coconut/Pecan Frosting" between layers, and on top and sides of cake. Makes one 3-layer cake.

Coconut/Pecan Frosting:

1 can evaporated milk (*13-oz. can*)
1 c. C & H GRANULATED SUGAR
1/2 c. butter or margarine
2 egg yolks
1 c. *chopped* pecans
1 c. *flaked* coconut
1 t. vanilla extract

Combine milk, sugar, butter, and egg yolks in a heavy saucepan. Bring *to a boil*. Cook over *medium* heat for 12 minutes, or *until thickened*, <u>stirring constantly</u>. Remove from heat. Add pecans, coconut, and vanilla. Stir *until frosting is cool and of spreading consistency*. Enough frosting for one 3-layer cake.

171

DALLAS ★ COWBOYS
Super Bowl XXVIII Champions

Tasha and Tony Tolbert on vacation in the Cayman Islands.

Tasha with Tony's mother, sister, and aunt at Super Bowl XXVIII.

DALLAS COWBOYS
Super Bowl XXVIII Champions

SATASHA (TASHA) & TONY LEWIS TOLBERT
*Number 92 *
Defensive End -- 6'-6" -- 263 lbs.

BIRTH DATE: *Tony* -- 12-29-67 (Englewood, New Jersey); *Tasha* -- 3-29-68 (Germany)

COLLEGE: *Tony* -- University of Texas / El Paso (B.S. -- Criminal Justice); *Tasha* -- University of Texas / El Paso (B.S. -- Biology)

SPECIAL PEOPLE MET WHILE AT SUPER BOWL XXVIII: *Tasha* -- Jesse Jackson

FIRST PLAYED ORGANIZED FOOTBALL: In the Sixth Grade, Played Defensive Tackle for Englewood County Team

YEARS IN PROFESSIONAL FOOTBALL: 6th Year

HONORS OR AWARDS: *Tony* -- Earned All-Conference Recognition at Dwight Morrow High School in Englewood, New Jersey; in 1988, Earned All-Western Athletic Conference and Honorable Mention All-America Honors - Leading the Miners in Sacks and Tackles for a Loss; since 1990, Piled up More Quarterback Sacks (29) than Any Other Dallas Defender; Has Been Team's top Tackler among Defensive Linemen in Each of the Past Three Seasons, Averaging 81.3 Per Season; Registered a Season-High 12-Tackle Performance in Road Games at Philadelphia and Washington, in 1992; Led Cowboys in Sacks, in 1993, with 7.5; in 1993, Finished First among All Team Defensive Linemen in Tackles (84); *Tasha* -- Valedictorian at Medical Assisting School

HOBBIES & INTERESTS: *Tony* -- Buying Music; *Tasha* -- Bike Riding, and Bowling

FAVORITE AUTHOR: *Tony* -- Alex Haley; *Tasha* -- Terry McMillan, and Frank Peretti

FAVORITE TYPE OF MUSIC: *Tony* -- Rhythm and Blues, and Rap; *Tasha* -- Rhythm and Blues, and Gospel

FAVORITE SPORTS HERO: *Tony* -- Muhammad Ali

FAVORITE FOOD: *Tony and Tasha* -- Italian, and Soul Food

FITNESS & DIET TIP: Watch What You Eat . . . and Keep Moving

173

Tasha Tolbert's parents, Odell and Billie Kelly of El Paso, Texas.

DALLAS ★ COWBOYS
Super Bowl XXVIII Champions

TONY TOLBERT'S TAMALE PIE

1 lb. GROUND BEEF
1 *large* onion, *chopped*
1 c. bell pepper, *chopped*
1 can *whole-kernel* corn, *drained*
1 can tomato soup
black olives, *optional*
mushrooms, *optional*
cheese for top, *grated* (*optional*)
salt and pepper, *to taste*

Brown meat and drain. Season with salt and pepper. Add onion, bell pepper, corn, soup, olives, and mushrooms; *mix well*. Pour into a baking dish; set aside.

Topping:

2 c. water   3/4 c. cornmeal
1/2 t. salt   1 T. butter

Add cornmeal, water, and salt in saucepan; *mix well*. Thicken over *medium* heat. Add butter; *mix well*. Spread over meat. Bake at 350 degrees for 35 to 40 minutes, or *until topping is done and brown*. Add cheese, if desired. Enjoy!

COUSIN KEM'S GREEN CHILI
ENCHILADA CASSEROLE

12 to 16 corn tortillas
1 can of green chili enchilada sauce (*12-oz. can*)
1 *regular* can cream of chicken or mushroom soup
1 to 2 lbs. GROUND BEEF
1/2 c. onions, *chopped*
1/2 c. cooking oil
1-1/2 c. *grated* cheese
salt and pepper, *to taste*
sour cream, *optional*
guacamole, *optional*

Heat oven to 350 degrees. In large skillet, brown meat; *drain*. Add onions, salt, and pepper; simmer on *low*. In another saucepan, add green chili sauce and can of soup; stir and let simmer for a few minutes. In small skillet, add oil. Heat tortillas. In large casserole dish, dip tortillas in chili sauce *on both sides*. Line bottom of dish with 4 to 5 tortillas, 1/4 of meat mixture, and 1/4 of cheese. Repeat until all tortillas are used. Pour remaining chili sauce on top; add rest of cheese. Bake for 20 to 25 minutes. *Sauce should bubble*. * *Serve with sour cream and guacamole . . . ENJOY!*

175

Pono Tuinei celebrating her 29th birthday with high school classmates from Kamehameha one month after Super Bowl XXVIII.

PONOLANI (PONO) & MARK PULEMAU (TUI) TUINEI
* Number 71 *
Tackle -- 6'-5" -- 305 lbs.

BIRTH DATES: *Mark* -- 3-31-60 (Oceanside, California); *Pono* -- 2-25-   (Honolulu, Hawaii)

COLLEGES: *Mark* -- U.C.L.A. and University of Hawaii; *Pono* -- Santa Ana College (Liberal Arts)

GREATEST MOMENT AT SUPER BOWL XXVIII: Sharing the Experience with Family and Friends Was the Greatest Memory I Will Cherish for a Lifetime; and, Most of All, Seeing Their Smiles after the Dallas Cowboys Won!

FIRST PLAYED ORGANIZED FOOTBALL: In the Ninth Grade, Played Defensive End for Punahou High School

YEARS IN PROFESSIONAL FOOTBALL: 12th Year

HONORS OR AWARDS: *Mark* -- Starred at Punahou High School in Hawaii; Hawaii Prep Lineman of the Year, as a Senior; State Shot Put Champion; All-Star Basketball Player; Defensive Lineman Turned Offensive Lineman, Six Years Ago - One of the Only Players to Play both Offense and Defense in a NFL Game; Has Played in More NFL Games (153) than Any Other Cowboys' Offensive Player; Started All 19 Games during the 1993 Season, Including the Postseason; Voted MVP of the Super Bowl by His Family

HOBBIES & INTERESTS: *Mark* -- Fish Aquariums (Fresh and Salt Water), Golf, Bowling, Darts, Pool, Basketball, Paddle Tennis, Wind Surfing, Jet Skiing, and Tennis; *Pono* -- Music, Sports, Talk Radio, and Playing Bass Guitar

FAVORITE TYPE OF MUSIC: *Mark* -- All Types; *Pono* -- Hawaiian, Jazz, and Oldies

FAVORITE SPORTS HERO: *Mark* -- Muhammad Ali

FAVORITE TV/MOVIE STAR: *Pono* -- Lucille Ball ("I Love Lucy")

FAVORITE FOOD: *Mark* -- Hawaiian Plate Lunch; *Pono* -- Laulau (Authentic Hawaiian Dish); and Poi

FITNESS & DIET TIP: Exercise Daily; Eat Five Small Meals a Day; Never Eat Past 8:00 p.m.; Get Eight Hours Sleep; and Drink Water - without Ice - during Meals (It's Easier on the Digestive System)

LONG-RANGE CAREER GOALS: Get My Golf Handicap Down to Single Digits; Support My Wife in Her Endeavors; and Be "Mr. Mom"

Tackle Mark Tuinei and his mom celebrating Super Bowl Victory #2.

Mark and Pono with Brudda John Grapes (Mr. Met-RX - with no shirt), along with Mark's nieces and nephews attending Super Bowl.

TUI'S TROPICAL CARROTS

4 *medium* carrots, *cut into 3" x 1/4" strips* (*about 2 cups*)
1/2 c. water
3/4 c. *unsweetened* pineapple tidbits, *undrained*
2 t. cornstarch
1/4 t. ground ginger

Combine carrots and water in a small saucepan; *cover* and cook *until carrots are crisp-tender.* Combine pineapple, cornstarch, and ginger in a small bowl; *mix well.* Add pineapple mixture to carrots. Cook over *low* heat, stirring constantly, *until thickened.* Serve immediately. Makes 4 servings.

PONO'S HAWAIIAN TIDBITS

2 T. cooking oil
1 slice *boiled* ham (*3/4-inch slice*)
1 can pineapple chunks, *drained*
1 T. soy sauce
1/4 c. orange marmalade
3/4 c. DR. PEPPER
1/8 t. salt
1/2 t. ground ginger
2 t. cornstarch, *dissolved in 1 T. pineapple juice or water*
toothpicks

Cut ham in 3/4-inch cubes. Heat oil in 10" skillet. Brown ham cubes *evenly.* Drain ham cubes; reserve 2 tablespoons oil for sauce. Place pineapple chunk and cube of ham on toothpick. Make sauce (*in pan in which ham was browned*) by adding the 2 T. oil, soy sauce, marmalade, Dr. Pepper, salt, ginger, and dissolved cornstarch. Simmer for 8 to 10 minutes. Add picks with ham and pineapple. *Cover*; simmer *until hot* (about 10 minutes). * *Serve as* hot *appetizer in chafing dish.* Makes 34 to 36 small tidbits.

#91 -- Matt Vanderbeek (second from right) with friends.

Super Bowl XXVIII Champions

MATT VANDERBEEK
Number 91 *
Linebacker/Defensive End -- 6'-3" -- 243 lbs.

BIRTH DATE: 8-16-67 (Douglas, Michigan)

COLLEGE: Michigan State (Communications)

FAVORITE ACADEMIC SUBJECT: Science

GREATEST MOMENT AT SUPER BOWL: Having Family and Friends Visit

FIRST PLAYED ORGANIZED FOOTBALL: In the Seventh Grade, as Cornerback for the West Ottawa "Panthers"

YEARS IN PROFESSIONAL FOOTBALL: 5th Year

HONORS & AWARDS: All-State Honors, as a Senior, at West Ottawa High School in Holland, Michigan; All-Big 10 at Michigan State, as a Senior; Selected to 1989 Martin Luther King, Jr., Classic and the 1989 Aloha Bowl; in 1993 -- Finished Second on the Team with 22 Special Teams Tackles - Earning One of the Three Dallas Nominations for the Pro Bowl Ballot on Special Teams; and Led the Team in Special Teams Tackles (with 7) during the Postseason

HOBBIES & INTERESTS: Golf, and Sailing

FAVORITE AUTHOR: John Grisham

FAVORITE TYPE OF MUSIC: Country - Hank, Jr.

FAVORITE SPORTS HERO: Mike Tyson

FAVORITE TV/MOVIE STAR: Julia Roberts

FAVORITE FOOD: Pizza

FITNESS & DIET TIP: Jog with a Walkman; and No Sweets

LONG-RANGE CAREER GOALS: Own My Own Business

181

DALLAS ⬟ COWBOYS
Super Bowl XXVIII Champions

Linebacker Matt Vanderbeek celebrating.

DALLAS ★ COWBOYS
Super Bowl XXVIII Champions

MATT'S SPANISH PORK CHOPS

4 pork chops
1 T. oil
1 can tomatoes, *undrained and cut up* (*14-1/2 oz. can*)
1 garlic clove, *minced*
1 t. ground cumin
1/2 lb. Velveeta Mexican Pasteurized Process Cheese Spread
  with Jalapeno Pepper, *sliced*
avocado

Brown pork chops in oil; drain. Combine tomatoes, garlic, and cumin; pour over pork chops. *Cover*; simmer for 35 to 40 minutes, or *until chops are done*. Top with process cheese spread. Continue cooking *until process cheese spread is melted*. Top with *peeled* avocado slices, *if desired*.

VANDERBEEK'S SHRIMP/BLACK BEAN TOSTADAS

1 *small* onion, *finely-chopped*
2 cloves garlic, *minced*
2 T. olive oil
1 can black beans, *drained and rinsed* (*16-oz. can*)
1/3 c. water
1 t. ground cumin
1/4 t. salt
1/2 t. pepper
4 flour tortillas (*8-inch*)
Pam Cooking Spray
1-1/2 c. *cooked* shrimp, *coarsely-chopped* (approximately 1 lb.
  medium-sized, fresh, unpeeled shrimp)
2 T. *fresh* cilantro, *chopped*
2 c. *shredded* Monterey Jack cheese
2 T. *pickled* jalapeno peppers, *sliced*
guacamole dip (*optional*)
ORTEGA GARDEN-STYLE SALSA

Cook onion and garlic in olive oil in a medium skillet over *medium-high* heat. Stir <u>constantly,</u> *until tender*. Combine black beans, water, cumin, salt, and pepper in a blender or food processor; process *until smooth*. Add to onion mixture; cook over *medium* heat (about 3 minutes), or *until thickened*. Stir *occasionally*. Arrange tortillas in a single layer on baking sheet (coated with Pam Cooking Spray). Bake at 350 degrees for 10 minutes, or *until lightly brown*. Spread 1/4 of bean mixture on each tortilla. Top *evenly* with shrimp, cilantro, cheese, and jalapeno peppers. Bake at 375 degrees for 5 minutes, or *until hot and bubbly*. Serve with salsa and guacamole, *if desired*. Makes 4 servings.

DALLAS ★ COWBOYS
Super Bowl XXVIII Champions

James, Dana, and Richard Washington -- "The Gap Ad!"

DANA & JAMES MCARTHUR WASHINGTON
Number 37
Safety -- 6'-1" -- 209 lbs.

BIRTH DATES: *James* -- 1-10-65 (Los Angeles, California); *Dana* -- 2-16- (Whittier, California)

COLLEGES: *James* -- U.C.L.A. (B.A. - History); *Dana* -- U.C.L.A. (Major - Sociology; Minor - Business)

GREATEST MOMENT AT SUPER BOWL XXVIII: Returning a Fumble 46 Yards for a Touchdown, and Then Intercepting a Pass to Set Up Another Score

FIRST PLAYED ORGANIZED FOOTBALL: In the Eleventh Grade, as a Receiver and Defensive Back for the Jordan High "Bulldogs"

YEARS IN PROFESSIONAL FOOTBALL: 7th Year

ENJOY MOST AS A DALLAS COWBOY: Second Super Bowl Ring

HONORS OR AWARDS: *James* -- All-America Honors at Jordan High School (Los Angeles); Four-Year Starter at U.C.L.A.; Honorable Mention All-America Honors (Freshman), and Second-Team All-America (Sophomore); Senior Shriner's Bowl; Three Times Rose Bowl Champ Chancellor's Marshall; Finished 1992 with 95 Total Tackles (Ranking Third on Team), Leading All Dallas Defensive Backs in Tackles, while Tying for Team Leadership in Interceptions; in Super Bowl XXVIII, Finished Second in the MVP Balloting for the Game; Has Recorded an Interception in Three of the Last Five Postseason Games; Involved in All Three Buffalo Turnovers in Super Bowl XXVIII - All Three Leading to Dallas Points; *Dana* -- Chancellor's Marshall, and Homecoming Princess; Took First Place - City Softball Champs (Whittier)

HOBBIES & INTERESTS: *James* -- Making Money; Golf; and Beginning Work on Shelter 37 - a Community Center in South L. A. That Will Feed and House up to 30 Homeless People at a Time; *Dana* -- Reading, Free-Lance Writing, and Educating Young Son

FAVORITE AUTHOR: *James* -- Alex Haley; *Dana* -- Stephen King, and Maya Angelou

FAVORITE TYPE OF MUSIC: *James* -- Blues; *Dana* -- Jazz, and Hip-Hop

FAVORITE SPORTS HERO: *James* -- Jackie Joyner - a Good Friend; *Dana* -- Husband James

FAVORITE FOOD: *James* -- Italian; *Dana* -- Mexican

CHILDREN & AGES: Richard Alexander - Born 3-15-91

LONG-RANGE CAREER GOALS: Become a Successful Real Estate Investor

185

DALLAS ⭐ COWBOYS
Super Bowl XXVIII Champions

James and Richard Washington put on their game faces!

Richard, Dana, and James - "Aloha! Postseason in beautiful Hawaii!"

JAMES WASHINGTON'S RICE CRISPY TREATS

1 c. C & H GRANULATED SUGAR
1 c. *light* caro syrup
1 c. peanut butter
6 c. rice crispies
6 oz. chocolate chips
6 oz. butterscotch chips

Melt sugar and caro syrup together. When melted, add peanut butter; melt together. Once melted, <u>quickly</u> <u>add</u> rice crispies. Stir together *really well*. Press into oblong pan *sprayed with Pam*. Pack in with wax paper! Melt chocolate chips and butterscotch chips together over stove (*add a little milk, if necessary*). Pour over top. Refrigerate *until set*.

DANA'S DELIGHTFUL SEAFOOD SALAD

1 pkg. Lobster Delights, or crab leg meat
3 to 4 *fresh* mushrooms, *sliced*
2 T. olive oil
1/4 t. Italian seasoning
salt and pepper, *to taste*
lettuce
4 wedges *fresh* lemon
1 *small* yellow bell pepper, *sliced*
Parmesan cheese (*optional*)

Mix Lobster Delights (or crab leg meat), mushrooms, bell peppers, olive oil, and Italian seasoning. Salt and pepper *to taste*. Serve on lettuce with a good twist of fresh lemon juice. Sprinkle with Parmesan cheese. Serves 4 (<u>2</u> *in the Washington household!*)

DALLAS ★ COWBOYS
Super Bowl XXVIII Champions

Tackle Erik Williams.

DALLAS COWBOYS
Super Bowl XXVIII Champions

ERIK GEORGE WILLIAMS
* Number 79 *
Tackle -- 6'-6" -- 324 lbs.

BIRTH DATE: 9-7-68 (Philadelphia, Pennsylvania)

COLLEGE: Central State University (Physical Education)

GREATEST MOMENT AT SUPER BOWL XXVIII: When the Score Was 30-13 (Dallas over Buffalo)

FIRST PLAYED ORGANIZED FOOTBALL: In the Ninth Grade, at John Bartram High School

YEARS IN PROFESSIONAL FOOTBALL: 4th Year

ENJOY MOST AS A DALLAS COWBOY: The Winning Tradition

HONORS OR AWARDS: Competed in Shot Put and Discus at John Bartram High School; as a Senior, Small College All-America (1990); in 1990, Most Valuable Player of the Team; First Offensive Lineman from Central State to Ever Be Selected in NFL Draft; Kodak All-America, Sheridan All-America, and NAIA All-America Honors; Earned First-Team All-Pro Honors (Sports Illustrated), and Named to All-Madden Team, in 1992; in 1993, Went to Pro Bowl

HOBBIES & INTERESTS: Fixing Automobiles, and Playing Sega Genesis

FAVORITE AUTHOR: Alex Haley

FAVORITE TYPE OF MUSIC: Rhythm and Blues, and Jazz

FAVORITE SPORTS HERO: Muhammad Ali

FAVORITE FOOD: Seafood, Lobster, Steak, Spaghetti -- Everything!

CHILDREN: Daughter, Shay - Born 6-9-91

FITNESS & DIET TIP: Jogging; and Low-Calorie Intake

LONG-RANGE CAREER GOALS: To Own Many Food Franchises

189

Erik Williams in action.

79 -- Erik Williams.

ERIK WILLIAMS' BEST BAKED HAM

1 *fully-cooked* ham (*6 lbs.*)
whole cloves
1/2 c. C & H BROWN SUGAR, *firmly-packed*
1 t. dry mustard
1 c. DR. PEPPER

Remove tough outer skin from ham; rinse ham with water.
Cut *diamond-shaped* slash marks in fat side of ham. Stud
with whole cloves. Place ham, *fat side up*, in a shallow
roasting pan. *Carefully* pour Dr. Pepper over ham. Bake
uncovered at 325 degrees for 1-1/2 hours, *basting every 15
minutes with pan juices*. Let stand for 15 minutes before
serving. Makes 10 to 12 servings.

ERIK'S STUFFED MEXICAN SHELLS

1 lb. GROUND ROUND
1 *small* white onion, *chopped*
1 *small* can *chopped* green chilies
2 c. *grated* Jack cheese, *divided*
1-1/2 c. ORTEGA GARDEN-STYLE SALSA
1 can tomato sauce
salt and pepper, *to taste*
1 c. water
1 *small* can Durkee French Fried Onion Rings, *divided*
18 *large* pasta shells for stuffing.

Cook pasta shells (*according to package directions*). Preheat
oven to 350 degrees. In a bowl, combine tomato sauce, salsa,
and 1 c. water to make a sauce. Brown meat with onion.
Drain. Add salt and pepper *to taste*. Add green chilies, 1 c.
of cheese, half of the onion rings, and 1/2 c. of prepared
sauce to the ground beef. Stuff shells with meat mixture;
place in a baking dish. Pour remaining prepared sauce over
shells. Bake *uncovered* for 30 minutes. Sprinkle remaining
onion rings and cheese over the top of the shells. Bake 5
minutes more, or *until cheese is melted and sauce is bubbly*.
Serves 6.

#85 -- Kevin Williams in action.

KEVIN WILLIAMS
*Number 85 *
Wide Receiver/Kick Returner -- 5'-9" -- 192 lbs.

BIRTH DATE: 1-25-71

COLLEGE: University of Miami (Criminal Justice)

YEARS IN PROFESSIONAL FOOTBALL: 2nd Year

HONORS OR AWARDS: Rated as One of the Top Five Receivers in the Country, Following Senior Season at Roosevelt High School in Dallas; as a Senior, in 1988, Split Time between Running Back and Wide Receiver, Rushing for 995 Yards on 100 Carries and 10 Touchdowns, while Catching 36 Passes for 757 Yards; Career High School Statistics Are Quite Remarkable -- 21 Receiving TD's; 14 Rushing TD's (17.9 Average); 177 Rushing Attempts for 1,339 Yards (11.4 Average); Kickoff Return Average 25.6, Punt Return Average 33.2; Averaged 17.1 Yards Every Time He Touched the Ball in High School; Fastest Hurricane while at Miami with 4.28 Speed; in College, Had a 430-lb. Squat and a 265-lb. Clean and Jerk; as a Sophomore, in 1991, Drew Heisman Trophy Attention -- Per Attempt Averages for That Season Were: Receiving (15.7 Yards Per Catch); Rushing (10.8); Punt Returns (15.6, Fourth in the Nation); and Kickoff Returns (18.5); Returned a School-Record Three Punts for Touchdowns (One Short of the NCAA Season Record); Registered Three TD Receptions, in 1991, to Go along with a 71-Yard Run against Oklahoma State; Named Kick Returner of the Year by The Sporting News, in 1991, and Punt Returner of the Year by the Football Writers Association of America; Named the Big East Special Teams Player of the Year; Elected to Enter the NFL after Junior Season of Eligibility; as Rookie, in 1993, Touched the Ball 27 Times on Offensive Plays and Scored 4 Touchdowns; Cowboys' Starting Deep Man on Kickoff and Punt Returns

DALLAS ⭐ COWBOYS
Super Bowl XXVIII Champions

Wide Receiver Kevin Williams -- another score!

KEVIN WILLIAMS' TEXAS CHILI

2 lbs. BEEF ROUND STEAK, *full-cut* (*cut into 1/2" pieces*)
1/2 c. A.1. STEAK SAUCE
1 c. *chopped* onion
1 T. margarine
2 cans *peeled* tomatoes, *broken up* (*14-1/2 oz. cans*)
1/4 to 1/3 c. chili powder

Garnish: shredded cheese and *chopped* green onions

Brown steak* pieces (*in batches*) and onion in margarine in large saucepan over *medium* heat. <u>Pour off drippings</u>. Add tomatoes with liquid, steak sauce, and chili powder. Bring *to a boil*; reduce heat. *Cover*; simmer 1-1/2 hours, or *until tender*, stirring *occasionally*. Garnish, as desired. Makes 6 servings.

* May substitute shoulder or chuck eye steak for round steak; simmer for 1 hour, or until tender.

WILLIAMS' APPLE MUFFINS

1 egg, *beaten*
4 T. shortening, *melted*
1/2 c. C & H GRANULATED SUGAR
3 T. dry milk, *optional*
2 c. PILLSBURY ALL-PURPOSE FLOUR
3 T. baking powder
1/8 t. baking soda
1/2 t. salt
1 c. DR. PEPPER
1 c. *raw* apple (*2 medium*), *finely-chopped*

Topping: 2 t. C & H GRANULATED SUGAR
1/4 t. cinnamon

Peel and *finely chop* apple. Beat egg; add sugar, melted shortening, and Dr. Pepper. Sift together dry milk, flour, baking powder, salt, and baking soda. Add to egg mixture, along with chopped apple. Stir <u>only</u> *until all dry ingredients are moistened*. <u>Do not over beat</u>. Fill *greased* muffin cups 2/3 full. Sprinkle small amount of sugar cinnamon mixture over each muffin. Bake at 375 degrees for 20 minutes. Serve *hot*. Makes 2 dozen muffins (*2-1/2 inch*).

#28 -- Darren Woodson.

DALLAS COWBOYS
Super Bowl XXVIII Champions

DARREN RAY WOODSON
* Number 28 *
Safety -- 6'-1" -- 215 lbs.

BIRTH DATE: 4-25-69 (Phoenix, Arizona)

COLLEGE: Arizona State University (Criminal Justice)

GREATEST MOMENT AT SUPER BOWL XXVIII: Being on the Winning Team!

YEARS IN PROFESSIONAL FOOTBALL: 3rd Year

HONORS OR AWARDS: First-Team All-Metro Division AAA Linebacker and Running Back at Maryvale High School in Phoenix, Arizona; Earned First-Team All-City Honors, as a Linebacker, and Second-Team Recognition on Offense, in His Final Season; Served as Team Captain, in Senior Year, Earning Three Letters in Football; All-PAC 10 Second-Team Selection, as a Senior; Honorable Mention All-America, in 1990; Second-Round Draft Choice of the Dallas Cowboys, in 1992; Led the Special Teams with 19 Tackles, in 1992 - in 16 Games Recorded 33 Tackles (28 Solo) -- Second among Dallas' Rookie Tacklers; as a Second-Year Player, in 1993, Earned a Starting Job at Strong Safety and Then, Nearly Won the Team's Individual Tackle Title by Collecting 155 Stops - Just 4 Shy of the Team Leader; the 155 Tackles Were the Most Ever by a Dallas Defensive Back; with Eight Double-Digit Tackle Games in 1993, Only the Second Player to Register at Least Seven Double-Figure Tackle Games in a Season; Led 1993 Cowboys in Fumble Recoveries with Three (while Forcing Another); Team's Leading Tackler in the Playoffs with 27 Total Stops

HOBBIES & INTERESTS: Water Skiing, Basketball, and Hanging Out with Friends and Family

FAVORITE TYPE OF MUSIC: Rhythm and Blues

FAVORITE SPORTS HERO: Walter Payton

FAVORITE TV/MOVIE STAR: Bill Cosby

FAVORITE FOOD: "Anything Mom Cooks"

197

Darren Woodson in action.

Safety Darren Woodson.

DARREN WOODSON'S TEXAS PRALINES

1 c. C & H GRANULATED SUGAR
1 c. *dark* C & H BROWN SUGAR
1 c. DR. PEPPER
4 *large* marshmallows
2 to 3 c. pecan or walnut halves

In heavy saucepan, mix together sugars and Dr. Pepper. Cook over *low* heat, <u>stirring constantly</u>, *until all sugar is dissolved.* Then, cook, stirring occasionally, *until soft ball stage (238 degrees)* is reached. Remove from heat; add marshmallows and nuts together. Beat *hard* for 1 to 2 minutes, *until mixture starts to cream.* Drop on *waxed paper* in *small* balls (about 1 tablespoon at a time). * *The pralines should flatten out around the edges, leaving a mound of nuts in the center.*

WOODSON'S NACHOS DE POLLO

3/4 lb. Velveeta Mexican Pasteurized Process Cheese Spread with Jalapeno Pepper, *cubed*
1 c. *chopped, cooked* BUTTERBALL BONELESS, SKINLESS CHICKEN BREASTS
1/2 c. *chopped* onion
1/2 c. *chopped* green pepper
1/4 c. milk
tortilla chips
1 c. *chopped* tomato

In 2-qt. saucepan, combine process cheese spread, chicken, onions, green peppers, and milk. Stir over *low* heat *until process cheese spread is melted.* Cover serving platter with chips. Top with chicken mixture and tomatoes. Makes 6 to 8 servings. * *2 c. shredded lettuce may also be put over the chicken mixture; then, top with tomatoes.*

DALLAS ★ COWBOYS
Super Bowl XXVIII Champions

Super Bowl XXVIII.

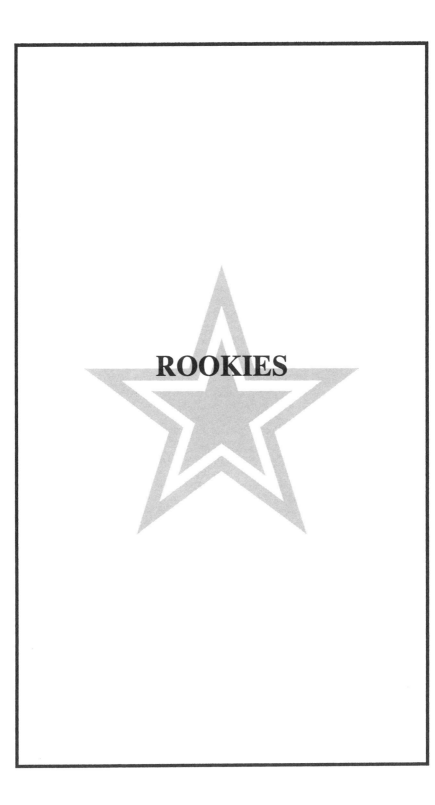

ROOKIES

DALLAS ★ COWBOYS
Super Bowl XXVIII Champions

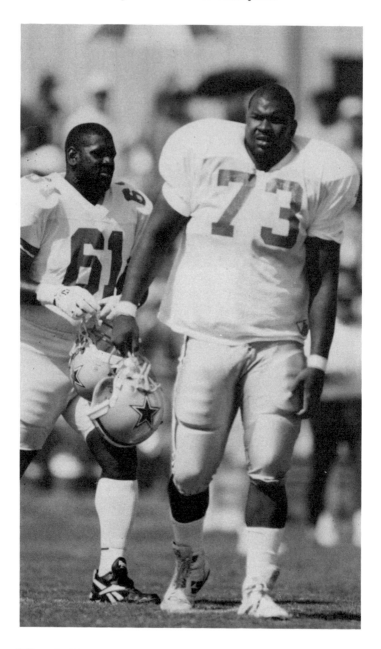

#73 -- Tackle Larry Allen.

JANELLE & LARRY ALLEN
* *Number 24* *
Tackle -- 6'-3" -- 325 lbs.

BIRTH DATES: *Larry* -- 11-27-71 (Los Angeles, California); *Janelle* -- 5-7-71 (Santa Rosa, California)

COLLEGES: *Larry* -- Sonoma State; *Janelle* -- Santa Rosa

FAVORITE ACADEMIC SUBJECT: *Larry* -- Sociology; *Janelle* -- Law

FIRST PLAYED IN ORGANIZED FOOTBALL: Junior Year in High School as Offensive Tackle/Defensive End for the Centennial Apaches

YEARS IN PROFESSIONAL FOOTBALL: Rookie

HONORS OR AWARDS: Lettered in Football, as a Freshman, at Centennial High School in Compton; Consensus All-America Selection; Participated in East-West Shrine Game and the Senior Bowl; Earned All-America Honors Following His Last College Season; Division 2 Lineman of Year; First Player Ever Drafted from Sonoma State when the Cowboys Selected Him in the Second Round

FAVORITE TYPE OF MUSIC: *Larry and Janelle* -- Rhythm and Blues

FAVORITE SPORTS HERO: *Larry* -- Jackie Slater; *Janelle* -- Larry Allen

FAVORITE FOOD: *Larry* -- Steak; *Janelle* -- Chicken

CHILDREN & AGES: Expecting a Child in December

HOW YOU MET SPOUSE: Met at School

FITNESS & DIET TIP: Don't Eat Steak

LONG-RANGE CAREER GOALS: Own Business

LARRY ALLEN'S GRILLED SIRLOIN
WITH TANGY SAUCE

1 *boneless* BEEF SIRLOIN STEAK, *cut 1 inch thick*
1-2 T. LEA & PERRINS WORCESTERSHIRE SAUCE
1/4 c. ketchup
1 *medium* onion, *finely-chopped*
1/4 c. water   1 t. dry mustard
1/4 c. margarine or butter   1/4 t. cayenne pepper
1 T. vinegar   few drops hot pepper sauce
1 t. lemon pepper seasoning

Combine all ingredients, *except steak*, in small saucepan. Bring *to a boil*; reduce heat and simmer for 10 minutes. Place steak on grid over *medium* coals.* Grill steak for 16 to 20 minutes for *rare to medium*, turning <u>once</u>. Brush *cooked* side <u>frequently</u> with sauce. Carve steak into thin slices; serve with remaining sauce. Makes 4 servings. * *Test about 4 inches above coals for medium with 4-second hand count.*

JANELLE'S SPICY CHICKEN

4 eggs, *beaten*   2 T. chili powder
1/4 c. green chile salsa   2 t. ground cumin
1/4 t. salt   1-1/2 t. garlic salt
2 c. *fine, dry* breadcrumbs   1/2 t. ground oregano
1/4 c. butter or margarine
6 BUTTERBALL Boneless, Skinless CHICKEN BREASTS
lettuce, *shredded*
1 carton sour cream (*8-oz. carton*)
1/4 c., *plus 2 T., chopped* green onions
12 cherry tomatoes
1 avocado, *sliced (optional)*
6 lime wedges, *optional*
ORTEGA GARDEN-STYLE SALSA, *optional*

Combine eggs, 1/4 c. salsa, and salt in a shallow bowl; set aside. Combine breadcrumbs, chili powder, cumin, garlic salt, and oregano in a shallow pan; *mix well*. Dip chicken in egg mixture, and dredge in the breadcrumb mixture; *repeat* and set aside. Melt butter in a 13" x 9" x 2" pan. Place chicken in pan, turning <u>once</u> to coat with butter. Bake *uncovered* at 375 degrees for 30 to 35 minutes. Arrange chicken on a bed of shredded lettuce on a large platter. Garnish each piece with a dollop of sour cream and 1 T. of green onions. Arrange cherry tomatoes on platter. * *Garnish with avocado slices and lime wedges, and serve with additional salsa, if desired.* Makes 6 servings.

CHRIS BONIOL
Number 18
Kicker -- 5'-11" -- 159 lbs.

BIRTH DATE: 12-9-71 (Alexandria, Louisiana)

COLLEGE: Louisiana Tech University (Working on Degree in Civil Engineering)

GREATEST MOMENT IN SPORTS: Had a Lot of Fun Playing Baseball in High School with My Dad as My Head Coach

FIRST PLAYED ORGANIZED FOOTBALL: Receiver, as a Freshman, in High School -- Only Because My Dad Coached

YEARS IN PROFESSIONAL FOOTBALL: Rookie

HONORS OR AWARDS: Starred at Alexandria, Louisiana, Senior High School; Ended Collegiate Career as Louisiana Tech's All-Time Scorer; Named All-Louisiana and Louisiana Freshman of the Year by the Louisiana Sportswriters Association -- after Hitting 17-of-24 Field Goals and 38-of-39 Extra Points, in 1990; Earned All-South Independent Honors

HOBBIES & INTERESTS: Golf, and Occasional Reading

FAVORITE AUTHOR: Robert Fulgham

FAVORITE TYPE OF MUSIC: Country

FAVORITE SPORTS HERO: Coach Jim Valvano (Late North Carolina State Basketball Coach)

FAVORITE TV/MOVIE STAR: Clint Eastwood, and Meg Ryan

FAVORITE FOOD: Chicken and Spaghetti Casserole

FITNESS & DIET TIP: Eat Foods That Are on the Color Spectrum (*Ex.: McDonald's Cheeseburger Isn't on the Spectrum -- Broccoli Is!*)

Don, Linda, Cowboys' Kicker Mike Boniol, and Chris after Louisiana Tech vs. Alabama Game -- 1993.

Young Christopher and Mike Boniol.

18 -- Chris Boniol and best friend Chris Hamler at Louisiana Tech
Football Banquet in Ruston, Louisiana - January '94.

MOM'S CHICKEN AND SPAGHETTI CASSEROLE
(Linda Boniol)

4 BUTTERBALL Boneless, Skinless **CHICKEN BREASTS.** *boiled (2-1/2 to 3 c. cut-up)*
spaghetti *(12 ounces) - cook in the broth, if possible*
1 stick margarine
1-1/4 c. *chopped* onion
4 stalks celery, *finely-chopped*
1 lb. Velveeta cheese
sliced or chopped mushrooms *(4 ounces) - optional*
1/4 c. *chopped* bell pepper
1 can cream of mushroom soup
2 cans *diced* Rotel tomatoes with green chilies (*I use one can of Rotel and one can of regular-chopped tomatoes*)
1/4 c. parsley
1/2 c. Cheddar cheese, *grated for topping*

Cook, debone, and chop chicken. Melt margarine; saute celery, onions, and bell pepper. Add mushroom soup, tomatoes (*undrained*), and Velveeta cheese (*cut in large cubes so it will melt*). Add chopped chicken, mushrooms (*drained*), parsley, and *cooked* spaghetti. Put in 10" x 13" casserole (*spray with Pam*). Top with Cheddar cheese. Bake at 325 degrees for 40 minutes. * *Freezes well; thaw first, or increase baking time.*

GRANDADDY'S CRAWFISH ETOUFFEE
(Lawrence L. Lambert)

2 *large* onions
2 *medium* bell peppers
1 rib celery
2 cloves garlic
1 stick butter
1 T. PILLSBURY FLOUR
salt, *to taste*

2 lbs. crawfish tails (*and fat, if available*)
1/2 c. *hot* water
1 t. cayenne pepper
2 T. *chopped* green onion tops
2 T. *chopped* parsley
rice

Mince onions, bell peppers, celery, and garlic. Saute *chopped* vegetables in butter (*add a little extra margarine, if needed*) until the onions are *clear and soft*. Then add flour, crawfish tails, water, salt, and cayenne pepper. *Stir well. Cover;* and simmer *until tails are tender* (approximately 20 minutes). Add green onion tops and parsley. Stir. Serve over *hot, fluffy* rice. Serves 4 to 6.

DALLAS COWBOYS
Super Bowl XXVIII Champions

SHANTE CARVER
*Number 96 *
Defensive End -- 6'-5" -- 240 lbs.

BIRTH DATE: 2-12-71

COLLEGE: Arizona State (Justice Studies)

YEARS IN PROFESSIONAL FOOTBALL: Rookie

HONORS OR AWARDS: Earned First-Team All-State
Honors, as a Senior, at Lincoln High School (Stockton,
California); the Most Prolific Pass Rusher in Arizona State
History -- Had Already Shattered the School Record for
Quarterback Sacks by the End of His Junior Season; First-
Team All-America Selection by the Football Writers
Association; First-Team All Pacific-10 Conference; Arizona
State's Defensive MVP -- in both Junior and Senior Seasons,
while Sharing the Award, as a Sophomore; Led Team in
Tackles as a Senior; Dallas Cowboys' Top Draft Pick, in 1994

#96 -- Defensive End Shante Carver.

SHANTE CARVER'S CARROT BARS

4 eggs, *beaten lightly*
2 c. C & H GRANULATED SUGAR
1-1/3 c. oil (*scant*)
2 t. baking soda
2 t. cinnamon
2 c. PILLSBURY FLOUR
1 t. salt
3 *small* jars *strained* carrots (*baby food*)
orange juice

Combine the baking soda, cinnamon, flour, and salt together in a separate bowl. Then, assemble -- mixing ingredients *in order listed* -- in a mixing bowl (*no mixer required*). Bake in 11" x 15" jelly roll pan at 350 degrees for 40 minutes. Cool <u>before</u> frosting.

Frosting:
4 T. *soft* butter
4 oz. Philadelphia Cream Cheese (*softened*)
1/2 t. vanilla extract
3-1/2 c. C & H CONFECTIONERS SUGAR
orange juice

Assemble and mix all ingredients -- *thinning, as necessary, with orange juice*.

SHANTE'S CHICKEN SPAGHETTI

12 oz. *cooked* spaghetti
1 can Rotel tomatoes
3 BUTTERBALL BONELESS, SKINLESS CHICKEN
  BREASTS, (*approximately*)
1 T. *grated* onion
Velveeta cheese, *sliced* (*enough to cover top of casserole*)
1 can cream of chicken soup
1 can cream of mushroom soup

Cook chicken breasts -- *saving broth* for thinning, as necessary. when mixing casserole. Cut chicken in *bite-size* chunks. Mix all ingredients, *except cheese*. Put in 8" x 14" casserole dish. Cover <u>completely</u> with cheese. *Cover with foil*. Bake in 350-degree oven for approximately 25 minutes. Remove foil; cook longer, if desired.

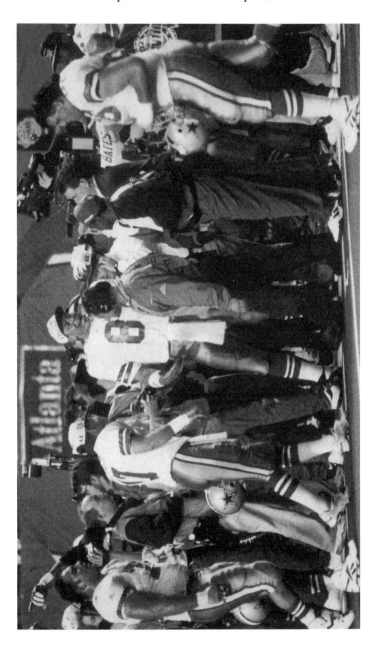

Super Bowl XXVIII.

TRACEY & CORY FLEMING
Number 82 *
Wide Receiver -- 6'-1" -- 207 lbs.

BIRTH DATES: *Cory* -- 3-19-71 (Nashville, Tennessee); *Tracey* -- 11-9-70 (Nashville, Tennessee)

COLLEGE: *Cory* -- University of Tennessee, Knoxville

FAVORITE ACADEMIC SUBJECT: *Cory* -- Psychology

GREATEST MOMENT IN SPORTS: Receiving a Scholarship to Go to a Division-I College from High School; Being the All-Time Touchdown Receiver in Tennessee Volunteers' History; and Being Drafted in 3rd Round in NFL 1994 Draft

FIRST PLAYED IN ORGANIZED FOOTBALL: Six Years Old -- as Quarterback, Running Back, and Safety -- for B & B Bulldogs (1977)

YEARS IN PROFESSIONAL FOOTBALL: Rookie

HONORS OR AWARDS: All-SEC; Earned All-America Honors; and Received Community Service Most Active Award in College

HOBBIES & INTERESTS: *Cory* -- Basketball, Music, and Talking to Kids (Education); *Tracey* -- Cooking, Fashion Design, and Kids

FAVORITE TYPE OF MUSIC: *Cory and Tracey* -- Rap, Rhythm and Blues, Jazz, and Classical

FAVORITE TV/MOVIE STAR: *Cory* -- Larry Fishbourne, and Al Pacino; *Tracey* -- Denzel Washington

FAVORITE FOOD: *Cory* -- Any Food; *Tracey* -- Seafood

CHILDREN & AGES: Tacoria Lavon - 2 yrs.; and Cory Lamont - 1 yr.

LONG-RANGE CAREER GOALS: Recreational Child Psychologist

213

#82 -- Wide Receiver Cory Fleming.

CORY FLEMING'S CHICKEN DIVAN

1 pkg. onion soup mix
1 pt. sour cream
2 pkg. *frozen* broccoli, *cooked*
2 c. *cooked* BUTTERBALL Boneless, Skinless CHICKEN
   BREASTS, *sliced*
1 c. whipped cream
grated Parmesan cheese

Blend onion soup mix with sour cream. Arrange broccoli in a casserole and spoon <u>half</u> of the sour cream mixture over the broccoli. Cover with chicken slices. *Fold the whipped cream into the remaining sour cream mixture*; spread over chicken. Bake at 350 degrees for 20 minutes, or *until bubbly*. Sprinkle with cheese; broil *until brown*. Makes 6 to 8 servings.

TRACEY'S CRUSTY TUNA SURPRISE

1 can cheese soup
1/2 c. milk
2 c. *cooked* rice
1 cans *grated* tuna, *drained*
3/4 c. cornflake crumbs
2 T. *melted* butter

Combine together soup, milk and rice. Place *alternate* layers of tuna and rice mixture in a *greased* casserole. Combine the cornflake crumbs and butter; sprinkle over casserole. Bake at 425 degrees for 15 minutes. Makes 4 servings.

#69 -- Tackle George Hegamin.

DALLAS COWBOYS
Super Bowl XXVIII Champions

GEORGE HEGAMIN
Number 69
Tackle -- 6'-7" -- 355 lbs.

BIRTH DATE: 2-14-73 (Camden, New Jersey)

COLLEGE: North Carolina State University (Business Management)

FAVORITE ACADEMIC SUBJECT: Business Management

GREATEST MOMENT IN SPORTS: Starting in First College Game

FIRST PLAYED IN ORGANIZED FOOTBALL: As a Junior, in Camden High School

YEARS IN PROFESSIONAL FOOTBALL: Rookie

HONORS OR AWARDS: Lettered in Football at Camden (N.J.) High School; Named All-America Honorable Mention by USA Today, as a Senior; Unanimous All-State First-Team Pick as a Defensive Lineman; a Redshirt Freshman, in 1992, Earned Freshman All-America Honors by The Football News and Named to the All-ACC Second Team; First Player from North Carolina State to Be Drafted by Dallas since 1982; Largest Player Selected in the 1993 NFL Draft

HOBBIES & INTERESTS: Listening to Music, Swimming, and Reading

FAVORITE AUTHOR: Malcolm X

FAVORITE TYPE OF MUSIC: Rhythm and Blues

FAVORITE SPORTS HERO: Magic Johnson

FAVORITE TV/MOVIE STAR: Martin Lawrence

FAVORITE FOOD: Soul Food

FITNESS & DIET TIP: Eat to Live - Don't Live to Eat

LONG-RANGE CAREER GOALS: Plan to Purchase an NFL Team after Playing Career Is over

GEORGE HEGAMIN'S FABULOUS MACARONI

1 pkg. *seashell* macaroni (*8-oz. package*)
1/4 c. *chopped* onion
1 jar *diced* pimento, *drained* (*2-oz. jar*)
1 T. butter or margarine
2 c. *shredded* Cheddar cheese (*8 ounces*)
1 can cream of mushroom soup, *undiluted* (*10-3/4 oz. can*)
1/2 c. mayonnaise
1 jar *sliced* mushrooms, *drained* (*2-1/2 oz. jar*)

Cook macaroni (*according to package directions*); *drain*. Saute onion and pimiento in butter *until onion is crisp-tender*. Combine macaroni, onion mixture, and remaining ingredients; *mix well*. Spoon into a *lightly-greased* 2-qt. shallow casserole. Bake at 350 degrees for 30 minutes. Makes 6 servings.

GEORGE'S SPICY CHICKEN

1 egg, *beaten*
3 T. milk
2/3 c. PILLSBURY FLOUR
1/2 t. salt
1/8 t. pepper
1/8 t. paprika
1/4 t. ginger
1/4 t. cloves
1/8 t. nutmeg
2-1/2 lbs. BUTTERBALL Boneless, Skinless CHICKEN
  BREASTS
6 T. margarine

Mix egg and milk. Mix dry ingredients in a plastic bag. Dip chicken in egg mixture; then, shake in the bag *until coated*. Melt margarine in an electric skillet at 340 degrees. Place the chicken in the skillet; *cover*. Cook for 20 minutes. Turn; cook for 20 minutes longer.

DALLAS COWBOYS
Super Bowl XXVIII Champions

WILLARD BERNARD (WILLIE) JACKSON, JR.
Number 81
Wide Receiver -- 6'-1" -- 205 lbs.

BIRTH DATE: 8-16-71 (Gainesville, Florida)

COLLEGE: University of Florida (Telecommunication)

GREATEST MOMENT IN SPORTS: Being Drafted

FIRST PLAYED IN ORGANIZED FOOTBALL: In 6th Grade, as Quarterback

YEARS IN PROFESSIONAL FOOTBALL: Rookie

HONORS OR AWARDS: Earned All-State Honors as a Quarterback, Tailback, Wingback and Defensive Back at P.K. Yonge High School in Gainesville (Florida) and the Team's MVP Award, as a Senior; Second Team All-SEC Pick, as a Sophomore; Selected the Team's Most Outstanding Receiver at Florida; SEC Offensive Player of the Week Honors and the Second Best Yardage Total in Florida Bowl History, His First Season in the Starting Line-Up; First Team All-SEC Honors and Honorable Mention All-America, as a Junior; Though Injured for the Gators, as a Senior, Jackson Finished Second on the Team -- with 49 Receptions for 675 Yards, and 6 Touchdowns -- while Starting Only Nine Games

HOBBIES & INTERESTS: Basketball, and Music

FAVORITE AUTHOR: Langston Hughes

FAVORITE TYPE OF MUSIC: Rhythm and Blues, and Rap

FAVORITE TV/MOVIE STAR: Eddie Murphy, and Martin Lawrence

FAVORITE FOOD: Steak, and Chicken

PET PEEVE: Hypocrisy of All Types

FITNESS & DIET TIP: Be Conscious of What You Eat at All Times

LONG-RANGE CAREER GOALS: To Organize Programs for Youths That Will Help the Community

219

#81 -- Wide Receiver Willie Jackson.

DALLAS ★ COWBOYS
Super Bowl XXVIII Champions

WILLIE JACKSON'S MEXICAN-STYLE PORK RIBS

3 lb. spareribs
1 *large* onion, *sliced*
salt and pepper, *to taste*
1 *large* green pepper, *chopped*
1/2 t. oregano
1 clove garlic, *minced*
1 T. cider vinegar

1 c. tomato juice
1 T. chili powder
1 c. *hot* water
1/2 t. nutmeg
2 T. PILLSBURY FLOUR
2/3 c. *cold* water

Cut the spareribs in serving pieces; brown in a heavy skillet in a *small* amount of bacon drippings. Add onion; cook *until transparent*. Place spareribs and onion in a large casserole. Add salt and pepper *to taste*, green pepper, oregano, and garlic. Mix vinegar and tomato sauce; stir in chili powder. Pour over spareribs; add *hot* water. Bake for 40 minutes at 325 degrees. Mix nutmeg, flour, and *cold* water; add 1/2 t. salt. Stir into liquid in casserole. Bake for 20 minutes longer. Makes 4 servings.

WILLIE'S CHICKEN NACHOS

4 BUTTERBALL BONELESS, SKINLESS CHICKEN BREASTS
1 t. salt
1-1/2 t. ground cumin
1/2 c. *diced* onion
1/4 c. *diced* green pepper
2 T. butter or margarine
1 can *chopped* green chilies, *undrained* (*4-oz. can*)
2/3 c. *chopped* tomato
1 t. ground cumin
1/4 t. salt
1/8 t. pepper
3 doz. *round* tortilla chips, *approximately*
3 c. *shredded* Monterey Jack cheese (*12 ounces*)

3/4 c. sour cream
3 doz. jalapeno pepper slices
paprika (*optional*)

Combine chicken and 1 t. salt in a large saucepan; cover with water. Bring *to a boil*; *cover*, reduce heat, and simmer 5 to 8 minutes. *Drain* chicken, reserving 2/3 cup broth. Place chicken and 1-1/2 t. cumin in container of food processor; process *until coarsely-ground*. Set aside. Saute onion and green pepper in butter in a large skillet *until tender*. Add chicken, reserved broth, and next 5 ingredients. Simmer *uncovered* for about 10 minutes, or *until liquid evaporates*. Place tortilla chips on baking sheets. Spoon about 1 T. chicken mixture on each. Top each nacho with 1 *heaping* T. cheese; broil *until cheese melts*. Remove from oven; top each nacho with 1 t. sour cream and a jalapeno pepper slice. Sprinkle with paprika, *if desired*. Broil 30 seconds. Serve immediately. Makes about 3 dozen.

#99 -- Defensive Tackle Hurvin McCormack.

HURVIN McCORMICK
** Number 99 **
Defensive Tackle -- 6'-5" -- 271 lbs.

BIRTH DATE: 4-6-72 (Brooklyn, New York)

COLLEGE: Indiana University (Sports Management)

GREATEST MOMENT IN SPORTS: In 1991, when Indiana Played Michigan State, and I Had 9 Tackles (4 of Them for Losses) - Beat Them 31-0

FIRST PLAYED ORGANIZED FOOTBALL: Freshman Year in High School, as Defensive End for New Dorp High

YEARS IN PROFESSIONAL FOOTBALL: Rookie

HONORS OR AWARDS: All-City, All-District, and All-Conference Selection during Career at New Dorp High School in Brooklyn; All-America Honorable Mention and All-Big 10 Conference Second-Team Pick; Voted by Peers, in 1993, as Team Captain for Indiana

HOBBIES & INTERESTS: Listening to Music

FAVORITE AUTHOR: John Grisham

FAVORITE TYPE OF MUSIC: Jazz, Rap, Rhythm and Blues, and Reggae

FAVORITE SPORTS HERO: Michael Jordan

FAVORITE TV/MOVIE STAR: Halle Berry

FAVORITE FOOD: West Indian, and Italian

PET PEEVE: Dirtiness

FITNESS & DIET TIP: Work Out Daily

LONG-RANGE CAREER GOALS: Go into Corporate America

HURVIN MCCORMACK'S SAVORY CHEESE TORTELLINI

1/2 lb. Velveeta Pasteurized Process Cheese Spread, *cubed*
1/4 c. milk
1/4 t. ground nutmeg
1 pkg. *cheese-filled* Tortellini, *cooked and drained* (7-oz. pkg.)

Combine Velvetta Process Cheese Spread, milk, and nutmeg in saucepan. Stir over *low* heat *until process cheese spread is melted.* Add tortellini; *mix lightly.*

* *Garnish with tomato rose and fresh basil, if desired.*

HURVIN'S SPICY BEEF AND BLACK BEAN SOUP

1 lb. BEEF CHUCK STEAK OR ROAST, *cut in 1/2-inch cubes*
2 cans black beans, *drained and rinsed*
1 can *double-strength* beef broth, plus 1-1/2 c. water
1 c. ORTEGA GARDEN-STYLE SALSA
1 red bell pepper, *coarsely-chopped*
1 green bell pepper, *coarsely-chopped*
1/2 c. *grated* carrot
1 T. *fresh* cilantro, *finely-chopped* (*optional*)

Brown beef cubes in 1 t. oil over *medium-high* heat in 2-qt. pot. Add beans, broth, water, and salsa to beef. Lower heat and simmer, *covered*, for 45 minutes, or *until beef is tender.* Add peppers and carrots; simmer for 5 minutes longer. Garnish with cilantro, if desired.

DALLAS COWBOYS
Super Bowl XXVIII Champions

TODDRICK McINTOSH
** Number 90 **
Defensive Tackle -- 6'-3" -- 277 lbs.

BIRTH DATE: 1-22-72

COLLEGE: Florida State (Marketing)

FAVORITE ACADEMIC SUBJECT: Math (Calculus)

GREATEST MOMENT IN SPORTS: In 1991, Played Michigan, Got an Interception, and Ran It Back 49 Yards for a Touchdown; Made a Sack and Six Tackles in National Championship

FIRST PLAYED ORGANIZED FOOTBALL: Played Half Back/Strong Safety, in the Fourth Grade, for the Eagles

YEARS IN PROFESSIONAL FOOTBALL: Rookie

HONORS OR AWARDS: Rated As One of the Texas' Top 100 Prospects, as a Senior, at L. V. Berkner High School in Richardson, Texas; Texas Football Magazine Rated Him among the Top 25 Players in the State; Earned All-State Recognition, as a Senior; Capping a Stand-Out Collegiate Career with a National Championship at Florida State, Has the Rare Opportunity to Come Home to Dallas and Earn a Spot on the Defending World Champion Cowboys' Roster

HOBBIES & INTERESTS: Camping, Hunting, Mountain Climbing, and Travel

FAVORITE AUTHOR: Maya Angelou

FAVORITE TYPE OF MUSIC: All Kinds

FAVORITE SPORTS HERO: Muhammad Ali

FAVORITE TV/MOVIE STAR: Denzel Washington

FAVORITE FOOD: Mom's Cooking!

FITNESS & DIET TIP: Drink Eight Glasses of Water a Day

LONG-RANGE CAREER GOALS: Own Sports Marketing Firm

225

#90 -- Defensive Tackle Toddrick McIntosh.

TODDRICK MCINTOSH'S TEX-MEX STRATA

6 slices bread, *toasted*
1 lb. *ground* sausage
12 oz. Cheddar cheese, *grated*
6 oz. jalapeno cheese, *sliced*
6 eggs, *beaten*
2 c. milk

warm tortillas
picante sauce
sour cream

Toast bread. Trim crusts and butter each slice. *Grease* an
8" x 11" baking pan. Place bread slices, *butter-side down*, in
pan. Cook sausage, breaking it up as it cooks; *drain*.
Spread sausage *evenly* over bread slices. Top with Cheddar
cheese; then, with slices of jalapeno cheese. In large bowl,
beat eggs and milk. Pour mixture over cheese. *Cover*;
refrigerate overnight. In the morning, preheat oven to 350
degrees. Keep mixture *covered*; bake for 35 minutes.
Remove cover; bake another 10 minutes, or *until firm*.
Remove from oven. Let stand 10 minutes <u>before serving</u>.
Serve with warm tortillas, picante sauce, and sour cream.
Makes 6 to 8 servings.

* For <u>real</u> Southerners, this dish is great with grits!

PAT'S POUND CAKE

1 box C & H CONFECTIONERS SUGAR
3 sticks butter
5 eggs
1/2 t. baking soda
3 to 3-1/2 c. *sifted* PILLSBURY CAKE FLOUR
1 c. buttermilk, or 8 oz. sour cream
1 t. vanilla extract*

Cream butter and sugar. Add eggs, *one at a time*, beating
well after adding each. Sift flour and baking soda. Add
flour mixture *alternately* with buttermilk or sour cream (*add
1/3 of each at a time*), beating *well* after each addition. Add
vanilla; *mix well*. *Grease and flour* cake pan. Bake in
preheated 325-degree oven for 1-1/2 hours. Allow cake to
cool for 10 minutes; then, transfer cake to cake dish.

** I sometimes use lemon extract, instead of vanilla extract -- or
a combination of both, depending on one's taste.*

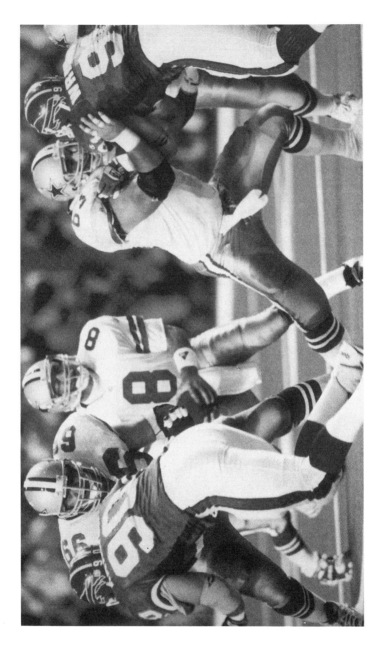

DALLAS ★ COWBOYS
Super Bowl XXVIII Champions

Super Bowl XXVIII.

COACHING STAFF

Axe and Gloria Alexander greeting friends before Super Bowl in the
lobby of Atlanta's HI Crowne Plaza.

DALLAS ★ COWBOYS
Super Bowl XXVIII Champions

GLORIA & HUBBARD LINDSEY ALEXANDER
Assistant Coach
Wide Receivers

BIRTH DATES: *Hubbard "Axe"* -- 2-14-39 (North Carolina); *Gloria* -- 9-9-

COLLEGES: *Axe* -- Tennessee State; *Gloria* -- Tennessee State (Education)

GREATEST MOMENT AT SUPER BOWL XXVIII: Winning Game

PLACES VISITED WHILE AT SUPER BOWL XXVIII: Martin Luther King, Jr., Center

HONORS OR AWARDS: Earned All-America Honors at Center at Tennessee State - Signed as a Free Agent with Dallas; Began Coaching Career with Alma Mater, in 1962; after Seven Seasons as a Very Successful High School Coach in Memphis, Spent Six Seasons as an Assistant at Vanderbilt; Coached Ten Seasons at University of Miami, Developing, in 1987, Three of the School's All-Time Leading Receivers; Three of His Miami Receivers Have Recently Led Their Respective NFL Clubs in Receiving; His Receiving Unit Blossomed into One of the NFL's Finest in 1992 -- Dallas' Starting Receivers Combination of Irvin and Harper Accounted for 113 Catches for 1,958 Yards; in 1993, Irvin Named the Starting Wide Receiver in His Third Consecutive Pro Bowl, Finished as NFL's Second-Ranked Receiver in Yardage, and Was the Third-Ranked Receiver in Catches; Harper Surpassed His Career Highs in Receptions and Finished Second in NFL in Yards Per Catch

HOBBIES & INTERESTS: *Axe* -- Tennis and Exercise; *Gloria* -- Decorating, Computers, Collecting Afro-American Art, and Christmas Decorations

FAVORITE AUTHOR: *Axe* -- James Baldwin; *Gloria* -- Terry McMillan

FAVORITE TYPE OF MUSIC: *Axe* -- Jazz; *Gloria* -- Blues

FAVORITE SPORTS HERO: *Gloria* -- Michael Jordan

FAVORITE FOOD: *Axe* -- Gumbo; *Gloria* -- Seafood

CHILDREN & AGES: Todd - 28 yrs.; Chad - 19 yrs.; and Bard - 14 yrs.

FITNESS & DIET TIP: Work Out at Least Five Days a Week; and Stay away from Fried Foods

231

DALLAS COWBOYS
Super Bowl XXVIII Champions

AXE'S ARROZ CON POLLO
(CHICKEN WITH RICE)

2 BUTTERBALL Boneless, Skinless **CHICKEN BREASTS,** *cut into serving pieces*

4 T. oil	**2 c.** water
1 clove garlic, *chopped*	**2 chicken bouillon cubes**
1 *medium* **onion,** *chopped*	**salt and pepper,** *to taste*
2 *peeled* **tomatoes,** *diced*	**1 c.** rice
1 *small* **can green chilies,** *diced*	

Dry chicken pieces. Fry in oil *until brown on all sides*; put aside. Saute rice in <u>same</u> oil, stirring *until golden brown*. Add garlic, onion, green chilies, and tomatoes. Cook a few minutes. Add chicken. Dissolve bouillon cubes in *hot* water; pour over rice and chicken. *Cover*; cook over *low* heat about 20 minutes, until *liquid is absorbed*. Remove from heat; let stand *covered* for about 15 minutes <u>before serving</u>. Serves 6. * *If made the day before, it will be necessary to add a small amount of water when reheating.*

GLORIA'S MEXICAN PIE

Crust:
2 c. beef broth
1 c. *long grain* rice
1 T. butter
1 t. salt
2 eggs, *beaten*
2 T. *chopped* pimento

Garnish:
halved cherry tomatoes
sliced black olives
sliced avocado
shredded lettuce

Filling:
1 lb. GROUND BEEF
1 garlic clove, *crushed*
1 t. cumin
1/2 t. salt
1/2 c. taco sauce
1 egg, *beaten*
1/2 lb. *grated* Cheddar cheese

Topping:
guacamole
sour cream

<u>For Crust</u>: *Grease* 10" pie plate. Cook rice in broth, butter, and salt *until liquid is absorbed*. Let rice cool *slightly*; stir in eggs and pimento. Press into sides and bottom of pie plate.

<u>For Filling</u>: Preheat oven to 350 degrees. Brown ground beef; *drain*. Stir in garlic, cumin, salt; cook 2 minutes longer. Remove from heat; stir in egg, taco sauce, and <u>half</u> the cheese. Spoon filling into crust; sprinkle remaining cheese on top. Bake for 25 minutes. Remove pie from oven.

<u>Topping and Garnish</u>: Spread guacamole on pie; then, spread sour cream. Return to oven; bake for 5 minutes longer. Garnish *as desired*.

JANE & NEILL ARMSTRONG
Assistant Coach
Coach (Retired)

BIRTH DATES: *Neill* -- 3-9-26 (Tishomingo, Oklahoma); *Jane* -- 4-11-25 (Neosho, Missouri)

COLLEGES: *Neill* -- Oklahoma State University (B.S.); *Jane* -- Oklahoma State University

GREATEST MOMENT AT SUPER BOWL XXVIII: Just Like Super Bowl XXVII - Winning and Seeing Everyone So Happy and Proud to Win Back-to-Back Super Bowls

FIRST PLAYED ORGANIZED FOOTBALL: In High School, for the Tishomingo "Indians"

PROFESSIONAL FOOTBALL OR COACHING EXPERIENCE: Played with Philadelphia Eagles (1947-1951); Canadian Football (1952-1954); Coached Oklahoma State University (1955-1961) and Houston Oilers (1962-1963); Head Coach in Edmonton, Canada (1964-1969); Coached Minnesota Vikings (1969-1977); Head Coach of Chicago Bears (1978-1981); Been with Dallas Cowboys since 1982

ENJOY MOST AS A DALLAS COWBOY: The Association with All the People in the Organization

HONORS OR AWARDS: Football All-America Honors; and President of Student Association

HOBBIES & INTERESTS: *Neill* -- Golf, and Fishing; *Jane* -- Bridge, Volunteering, and Football

FAVORITE AUTHOR: *Neill* -- John Grisham; *Jane* -- Rosmund Pilsner

FAVORITE TYPE OF MUSIC: *Neill* -- Country/Western, Semi-Classical, and Big Band; *Jane* -- Big Band

FAVORITE SPORTS HERO: *Neill* -- Sammy Baugh (Retired); *Jane* -- Nolan Ryan

FAVORITE FOOD: *Neill* -- Black-Eyed Peas, Cornbread, and Chicken Fried Steak; *Jane* -- Grilled Chicken

CHILDREN: Neill, Jr. - 47 yrs.; David - 44 yrs.; Gail - 39 yrs.; and Five Grandchildren

FITNESS & DIET TIP: Stay Flexible; and Practice Moderation

Neill and Jane Armstrong.

DALLAS COWBOYS
Super Bowl XXVIII Champions

NEILL ARMSTRONG'S SOUTH OF THE BORDER ENCHILADAS

6 T. butter
3 *medium* onions, *sliced thin*
2-1/2 c. *shredded, cooked* BUTTERBALL BONELESS, SKINLESS CHICKEN BREASTS
3/4 c. *diced* green chilies
6 oz. cream cheese, *diced*
12 flour tortillas (*6-inch*)
1 c. *heavy* cream
3 c. *shredded* Monterey Jack cheese
ORTEGA GARDEN-STYLE SALSA

Melt butter; saute onions *until limp*. Remove from heat. Stir in chicken, chilies, and cream cheese. Spoon chicken mixture in center of tortilla; roll up and place *seam side down* in *greased* baking dish. Top with cream and cheese. Bake at 375 degrees *until cheese topping bubbles (about 20 minutes)*. * *This dish freezes nicely. Serve with "Awesome Tomatoes" and "Never-Fail Cornbread" (see below)*.

JANE'S AWESOME TOMATOES

Use a *4-sided* cookie sheet. Layer ingredients <u>in order</u>, as follows:
    1/2" thick slices of tomatoes
    finely-chopped celery
    finely-chopped green onions
    Bleu cheese, *crumbled*
    minced parsley
    grated Parmesan cheese

Sprinkle Italian Dressing (*shake well*) over top. *Cover with plastic wrap*; refrigerate several hours, or overnight. Serve <u>directly</u> from cookie sheet. * *You can decorate it with some extra parsley!*

ARMSTRONG'S NEVER-FAIL CORNBREAD

1 c. PILLSBURY FLOUR
2 T. baking powder
1 *large* egg, or 2 *small*
1 c. milk
2 T. canola oil
1 c. cornmeal (*I use yellow*)
2 T. C & H GRANULATED SUGAR

Mix egg, milk, and oil together. Add the dry ingredients. Pour into *well-oiled* muffin tins, or a large *well-greased* iron skillet. Bake in *hot* oven (400 degrees) about 20 minutes. Serves 6. * *This is from my "Bride's Recipe File" - 1946!*

235

Diann, Tony, and Joe Avezzano at Tony's graduation from high school in May, 1994.

Avezzano's daughter, Gail Farden, and grandsons Cole and Taylor.

DALLAS ✯ COWBOYS
Super Bowl XXVIII Champions

DIANN & JOSEPH (JOE) W. AVEZZANO
Assistant Coach
Special Teams

BIRTH DATES: *Joe* -- 11-17-43 (Yonkers, New York); *Diann* -- 3-10-49 (Story City, Iowa)

COLLEGES: *Joe* -- Florida State (Major: Criminology); *Diann* -- Patricia Stevens (Fashion Merchandising)

GREATEST MOMENT AT SUPER BOWL XXVIII: Sharing the Super Bowl Victory with Family and Close Friends

PLACES VISITED WHILE AT SUPER BOWL XXVIII: Celebration Party

SPECIAL PEOPLE MET WHILE AT SUPER BOWL XXVIII: Clint Black

FIRST PLAYED ORGANIZED FOOTBALL: In the Ninth Grade, for the Boys Club

ENJOY MOST AS A DALLAS COWBOY: Enjoying a Good Positive Working Environment for My Family in a Great City

HONORS OR AWARDS: *Joe* -- President of Student Body; Named NFL Special Teams Coach of the Year, in 1991, by the Widest Margin Ever; in 1992, the Dallas Special Teams Led the Entire NFL in Team Punt Return Average; Under Joe's Guidance, Dallas Was Recognized as Perhaps the NFL's Most Productive Team in the Kicking Game for the Second Straight Year; Named NFL's Special Team Coach, in 1993 - for the Second Time in Three Years; *Diann* -- Female Lead in High School Musical All Four Years; Sang Professionally while Living in Pittsburgh

HOBBIES & INTERESTS: *Joe* -- Music, and Weight Training; *Diann* -- Music, and Lifting Weights

FAVORITE TYPE OF MUSIC: *Joe* -- Like All Kinds - Mainly Rhythm and Blues, and Country; *Diann* -- All Music

FAVORITE SPORTS HERO: *Diann* -- Hank Aaron

FAVORITE FOOD: *Joe* -- Italian; *Diann* -- Sushi

CHILDREN & AGES: Tony - 18 yrs.

FITNESS & DIET TIP: Eat Most Anything You Want, But Just Eat a Moderate Amount; and Use It, or Lose It!

237

Joe and Diann with the "Oak Ridge Boys" in Nashville -- June, 1994.

JOE AVEZZANO'S EASY HOT LAYERED MEXICAN DIP

1 lb. GROUND BEEF
1 pkg. taco seasoning mix
1 *small* can *chopped* green chilies
2 c. *shredded* Cheddar cheese
1 can *spicy refried* beans

ripe olives
fresh tomatoes, *chopped*
tortilla chips

Brown ground beef in skillet. Add taco seasoning; *mix well*. Add can of refried beans to the taco meat; stir *until well-mixed*. Spread the mixture in the bottom of an <u>oven-safe</u> casserole dish. In a separate bowl, mix sour cream and green chilies; spread on top of the meat/bean mixture. Top sour cream mixture with shredded Cheddar cheese. Heat in 350-degree oven *until cheese is melted and sides are bubbling* (about 25 minutes). Garnish with ripe olives, chopped fresh tomatoes, or whatever you prefer. Serve with tortilla chips.

DIANN'S MEXICAN CASSEROLE

2 cans *chopped* green chilies
2 lbs. GROUND BEEF, *cooked and drained*
1 *large* onion, *chopped*
1 can *chopped* tomatoes (*10-oz. can*)
1 pkg. *frozen* spinach, *squeezed dry*
1 can cream of mushroom soup
1 can golden mushroom soup
1 *large* carton sour cream
1/4 c. milk
1/2 c. butter, *melted*
1/2 t. garlic powder
12-16 corn tortillas
1/2 lb. *grated* Cheddar cheese

Cook ground beef. Stir in onion, tomatoes, spinach, salt and pepper *to taste*, and one can of green chilies. Combine soups, sour cream, milk, garlic powder, and other can of green chilies. Arrange tortillas in bottom of casserole dish *after they have been softened in butter*. Layer ingredients, as follows: tortillas - meat mixture - soup mixture - cheese. Refrigerate *overnight*. Bake at 350 degrees for 45 minutes.

DALLAS ★ COWBOYS
Super Bowl XXVIII Champions

Robert and Diana Blackwell, with Nate and Lora, in backyard --
August, 1994.

DALLAS COWBOYS
Super Bowl XXVIII Champions

DIANA & ROBERT GLENN BLACKWELL

Video Director

BIRTH DATES: *Robert* -- 12-1-50 (Dallas, Texas); *Diana* -- 5-25-58 (Louisville, Kentucky)

COLLEGES: *Robert* -- Stephen F. Austin State University (B.S. -- Communications); *Diana* -- Moorpark Junior College (A.A.) and California Lutheran College

GREATEST MOMENT AT SUPER BOWL XXVIII: Son, Nathaniel, Got to Attend His First Super Bowl

PLACES VISITED WHILE AT SUPER BOWL XXVIII: *Diana* -- Coca-Cola Museum, and Breakfast at Tiffany's

SPECIAL PEOPLE MET WHILE AT SUPER BOWL XXVIII: *Robert* -- Kevin Costner

ENJOY MOST AS A DALLAS COWBOY: Being Part of a Winning Effort

PROFESSIONAL FOOTBALL EXPERIENCE: Enters Sixth Season as Team's Video Director, after Eight Seasons as an Assistant with Dallas; in Charge of Taping and Editing All Cowboys' Practices and Games; Edits Opponents' Tapes; and Handles All the Teams' Photographic Needs

HONORS OR AWARDS: *Robert* -- Became a Member of the SAR (Sons of the American Revolution); *Diana* -- 1993 Professional Flight Attendant Award; and Two Years Perfect Attendance Award at American Airlines

HOBBIES & INTERESTS: *Robert* -- Fly Fishing, Golf, and My Family; *Diana* -- Coppell Women's Club, Mom's in Touch, Decorating, Crafts, Reading, and Family

FAVORITE AUTHOR: *Robert* -- Mark Twain; *Diana* -- John Grisham

FAVORITE TYPE OF MUSIC: *Robert* -- Classic Rock, and Country; *Diana* -- Pop Rock, and Classic Rock

FAVORITE SPORTS HERO: *Robert* -- Mickey Mantle; *Diana* -- Michael Jordan

FAVORITE FOOD: *Robert* -- Mexican; *Diana* -- Seafood

CHILDREN & AGES: Nathaniel Rivers (Nate) - 7 yrs.; and Lora Ann - 2 months

LONG-RANGE CAREER GOALS: To Be the Best

ROBERT BLACKWELL'S MEXICAN CHICKEN

1 BUTTERBALL CHICKEN, *boned*
2 cans cream of chicken soup
1 can Rotel tomatoes   1 *large* pkg. Doritos, *crushed*
1 can Ranch-Style Beans   1 lb. Cheddar cheese, *grated*

Line 13" x 9" baking dish with *half* of doritos. Add *bite-size* chicken pieces and beans. Blend soup and Rotel tomatoes; pour over top. Sprinkle cheese and remaining Doritos on top. Bake at 350 degrees for 30 minutes.

DIANA'S CHICKEN / SPINACH SOUR CREAM ENCHILADAS

1 *whole* BUTTERBALL CHICKEN
12 tortillas   1 onion, *chopped*
2 jalapenos   1 carton sour cream (*16 ounces*)
1 pkg. *fresh* spinach   dash of cumin
1 t. white vinegar   dash of corriander
2 cloves garlic, *minced*   1 lb. Monterey Jack cheese,
                                    grated

Boil chicken with onion, garlic, and corriander for 2 hours. Remove bone; *retain broth*. Cook spinach 30 minutes with vinegar; *strain*. Mix chicken and spinach; chop *finely*. Dip tortillas, <u>one at a time</u>, into *hot* chicken broth; then, roll chicken/spinach mixture in tortilla (1-1/2" thick). Place *flap down* in enchilada dish. <u>Gently</u> beat sour cream with 2 T. chicken broth *until creamy*. Pour over enchiladas. Heat in 350-degree oven for 30 minutes. Garnish with cheese, paprika, and sliced jalapenos.

BLACKWELL'S TEX-MEX DIP

3 *medium* avocados   2 t. lemon juice
1/2 t. salt   1/4 t. pepper
1 c. sour cream (*8 ounces*)   1/2 c. mayonnaise
1 pkg. taco seasoning mix
2 *large* cans jalapeno bean dip
1 *large* bunch green onions (*1 c. with tops*)
3 *medium* tomatoes, *chopped* (*2 cups*)
2 cans *pitted* black olives, *chopped* (*3-1/2 oz. cans*)
1 pkg. *sharp* Cheddar cheese (*8-oz. package*)
large, round tortilla chips

Pit, peel, and mash avocados. Add lemon juice, salt, and pepper. Combine in bowl. In separate bowl, combine sour cream, mayonnaise and taco seasoning. *To assemble*: spread bean dip; top with avocado mixture; and layer with sour cream and taco mixture. Sprinkle with chopped onions, tomatoes, olives, and lastly, cheese. Serve *chilled*, or *at room temperature*.

DALLAS ⭐ COWBOYS
Super Bowl XXVIII Champions

FREDA & JOHN BLAKE
Assistant Coach
Defensive Line

BIRTH DATES: *John* -- 3-6-61 (Rockford, Illinois); *Freda* -- 4-15-62 (Tulsa, Oklahoma)

COLLEGES: *John* -- University of Oklahoma (B.S. -- Public Relations and Recreation); *Freda* -- Central State University (B.B.A. - Business Management; Minor in Marketing)

FAVORITE ACADEMIC SUBJECT: *John* -- Mathematics; *Freda* -- English

FIRST PLAYED ORGANIZED FOOTBALL: In 1974, as Fullback and Nose Guard for the Clyde Boyd Junior High "Trojans"

GREATEST MOMENT AT SUPER BOWL XXVIII: Last Year's Super Bowl Was an Event That We Both Will Always Cherish - to Begin, the Activities Planned for the Wives Were Great! It Gave Us a Chance to Meet Wonderful People and to see the Beautiful City of Atlanta; It's a Good Feeling to Be a Part of World Champions!

WIFE'S OCCUPATION: Financial Analyst

HONORS OR AWARDS: Highly-Recruited All-State Pick at Charles Page High School in Sand Springs, Oklahoma; Playing Nose Tackle at Oklahoma, from 1980-1983, Earned All-Big Eight Conference Defense Lineman; Was a Big Part of Building a Top-Rated Defense while Coaching at Oklahoma, from 1989-1992; in 1988, Named One of the Outstanding Young Men in America; in First Year as the Cowboys' Defensive Line Coach, Helped Guide Defensive Tackle Russell Maryland to the Pro Bowl

HOBBIES & INTERESTS: *John* -- Fishing, and Hunting; *Freda* -- Interior Decorating

FAVORITE AUTHOR: *John* -- Alex Haley; *Freda* -- Jackie Collins

FAVORITE TYPE OF MUSIC: *John and Freda* -- Jazz

FAVORITE SPORTS HERO: *John* -- Leroy Selmon; *Freda* -- Michael Jordan

FAVORITE TV/MOVIE STAR: *John* -- Clint Eastwood; *Freda* -- Denzel Washington

FAVORITE FOOD: *John* -- Fried Chicken, and Catfish; *Freda* -- Pasta Dishes

FITNESS & DIET TIP: For a Healthy Mind and Body, Forty-Five Minute Work Out -- at Least Three Times a Week; Drink an 8-oz. Glass of Water Eight Times a Day; and Maintain Low-Fat Meals

243

John and Freda Blake in Las Vegas at Caesar's Palace.

John and Freda at class reunion.

THE BLAKE'S FAMOUS SOUTHWEST CORNBREAD

1 c. PILLSBURY FLOUR	jalapeno peppers, *optional*
1 c. cornmeal	1 *medium* onion, *diced*
4 t. baking powder	chili powder, *optional amount*
1 can *cream-style* corn	1 t. salt
1/4 c. shortening, *melted*	1 egg
1 lb. GROUND ROUND	1 c. milk
1 pkg. Cheddar cheese	

In mixing bowl, combine flour, cornmeal, salt, egg, baking powder, and melted shortening; set aside. In a skillet, brown the ground round. *Drain*; add chili powder *to taste*. Set aside. In a bowl, grate 1 pkg. Cheddar cheese; set aside. Dice 1 onion; set aside. In large *greased* casserole dish, layer half of cornbread mixture, meat, onion, Cheddar cheese; then, the remainder of the cornbread mixture. Bake at 350 degrees for 1 hour. Right before finished baking, brown top for just a short time on broil. * *Recommended to serve with pot of pinto beans and green salad, red wine, or even a pitcher of Margarita's. YUM!*

SIZZLING SALSA STEAK SANDWICH

4 BEEF STRIP LOIN STEAKS, *cut 1/2-in. thick*
4 *oblong-shaped* rolls, *split and toasted*
1/2 c. ORTEGA GARDEN-STYLE SALSA

1/2 c. sour cream	leaf lettuce
1/2 c. green onions, *chopped*	*cracked* black pepper

Mix salsa, sour cream, and green onions together to make sandwich spread. Season both sides of steak with cracked black pepper. Grill steaks over *medium* coals for 6 to 7 minutes (*turn once after 4 minutes*); or pan fry over *medium-high* heat for 6 minutes, turning *occasionally*. Spread rolls with 2 tablespoons of spread per side. Top with lettuce leaf and sizzling steak. Close sandwich and serve immediately. Makes 4 servings.

Joe and Joyce Brodsky.

The Brodsky Family.

DALLAS ★ COWBOYS
Super Bowl XXVIII Champions

JOYCE & JOSEPH (JOE) BRODSKY
Assistant Coach
Running Backs

BIRTH DATES: *Joe* -- 6-9-34 (Miami, Fl.); *Joyce* -- (Brooklyn, N.Y.)

COLLEGES: *Joe* -- University of Florida (B.S. & M.S. in Administration and Supervision); *Joyce* -- University of Miami (B.A. -- Education)

GREATEST MOMENT AT SUPER BOWL XXVIII: The Entire Happening -- from the Pre- to the Post-

PLACES VISITED WHILE AT SUPER BOWL XXVIII: Wonderful Friends Visited Us

ENJOY MOST AS A DALLAS COWBOY: Camaraderie of the Coaches; and Quality of the Players as People

HONORS OR AWARDS: *Joe* -- Four-year Letterman in Football, Basketball, and Track at Florida; for 13 Seasons, One of South Florida's Most Successful High School Coaches; Won State Football Championship While Coaching High School; Had First Team in the State to Go 14-0; While Coaching Running Backs at University of Miami for 11 Seasons, Won Two National Championships; in 1992, Helped Guide His Prized Pupil (Third-Year Running Back Emmitt Smith) to His Second Straight NFL Rushing Title, Becoming the First NFL Player to Lead the League in Consecutive Years since 1983-'84; *Joyce* -- Graduated *Cum Laude* from University of Miami; and Valedictorian of Senior Class

HOBBIES & INTERESTS: *Joe* -- Golf, Fishing, and Family; *Joyce* -- Taking Care of Grandchildren (Amanda - 6 yrs.; and Joey - 3 yrs.); Reading, All Sports, Singing, and Traveling

FAVORITE AUTHOR: *Joyce* -- James Michener, and Leon Uris

FAVORITE TYPE OF MUSIC: *Joe* -- Country Western, and Classical; *Joyce* -- Pop, Country, and Classical

FAVORITE SPORTS HERO: *Joe* -- His High School Basketball Coach, Joe McNulty; *Joyce* -- Larry Brodsky

FAVORITE TV/MOVIE STAR: *Joe* -- John Wayne, and Three Stooges; *Joyce* -- Dustin Hoffman, and Paul Newman

FAVORITE FOOD: *Joe* -- Lobster, and Stone Crabs; *Joyce* -- Rack of Lamb, and Rice Pilaf

CHILDREN & AGES: Joe, Jr. - 36 yrs. (Wife: Robin; Two Grandchildren: Amanda and Joey); Larry - 33 yrs.; Jeffrey - 32 yrs. (Wife: Frances)

FITNESS & DIET TIP: Walk, at Least 50 Minutes, Three Times a Week - about Three Miles Each Time; and Eat No Red Meats or Fried Foods

LONG-RANGE CAREER GOALS: Three-Peat!

JOE BRODSKY'S WESTERN-STYLE GRITS

1 c. grits
4 c. water
1 t. salt
1/2 stick butter
1-1/2 c. *grated* Cheddar cheese
1/4 t. garlic powder
1/8 t. cayenne pepper
1 *small* can *cream-style* corn
1/2 can green chilies, *diced*
1 egg, *beaten*
milk or cream

Cook grits in water and salt (*according to package directions*). Stir in butter and cheese; *mix well*. Beat egg; add enough milk or cream to make 3/4 cup. Add liquid; *mix all well*. Pour into flat, *buttered* baking dish. Bake at 350 degrees for 45 to 50 minutes, *until bubbling and lightly-browned*.

JOYCE'S CHILI-CHEESE DIP

1 box Velveeta *Hot* Mexican Cheese
1 can Hormel Chili (*no beans*)
1 can Rotel Diced Tomatoes and Green Chilies (*10-oz. can*)

Place cheese in a casserole dish; *microwave* for 2 minutes. Add chili and tomatoes; *microwave* for 3 minutes, mixing *occasionally*. Microwave *until piping hot*. * GREAT *with tostitos chips*!

AMY & WILLIAM A. (BUCKY) BUCHANAN

Assistant Equipment Manager

BIRTH DATES: *Bucky* -- 6-9-61 (Alexandria, Virginia); *Amy* -- 4-3-65 (Little Rock, Arkansas)

YEARS IN PROFESSIONAL FOOTBALL: 4 months

PROFESSIONAL FOOTBALL EXPERIENCE: Enters First Year as the Assistant Equipment Manager, Joining the Cowboys This Spring; No Stranger to the Cowboys Equipment Department, Having Spent Many Weekends and Training Camps Helping His Father, William T. "Buck" Buchanan, Who Retired in the Spring after Serving 21 years as the Cowboy Equipment Manager

WIFE'S OCCUPATION: Administrative Assistant at EDS

HONOR OR AWARD RECEIVED: Having Buck Buchanan for a Father

HOBBIES & INTERESTS: *Bucky* -- Golf (Sports of All Kinds), and Family; *Amy* -- Water Skiing, Football, and Family

FAVORITE TYPE OF MUSIC: *Bucky* -- Rock 'n Roll; *Amy* -- All Kinds in General

FAVORITE FOOD: *Bucky* -- Steak and Potatoes

HOW YOU MET: Through Mutual Friends

CHILDREN & AGES: William (Thomas), II - 8 yrs.; and Jonathan (Brett) - 5 yrs.

DALLAS ★ COWBOYS
Super Bowl XXVIII Champions

Bucky and Amy Buchanan at family event in 1993.

Buchanan children: Thomas (8 years) and Brett (5 years).

BUCKY'S SANTA FE CHICKEN

1/4 lbs. BUTTERBALL Boneless, Skinless CHICKEN
 BREASTS
1 t. paprika
1 t. salt
1/4 t. pepper
1 T. cooking oil
1 *small* green pepper, *chopped*
1 *medium* onion, *chopped*
1 clove garlic, *chopped* (or 1 garlic powder equal to 1 clove)
1 can Rotel tomatoes
1-1/2 c. chicken broth
1-1/2 c. Minute Rice
3/4 c. *shredded* Cheddar or Monterey Jack cheese

Cut chicken into thin strips. Sprinkle with paprika, salt, and
pepper. Heat oil in 10" skillet over *medium-high* heat. Cook
chicken in oil for 2 minutes. Add onion, green pepper, and
garlic. Cook *until tender* (about 4 minutes), stirring
frequently. Add tomatoes and chicken broth. Bring *to a
boil*. Stir in the rice. Remove from heat. *Cover*; let stand
about 5 minutes, or *until all liquid is absorbed*. Sprinkle with
cheese and serve. Makes 4 servings.

AMY'S FUDGE PIE

1/2 lb. *melted* butter
1/2 c. cocoa
2 c. C & H GRANULATED SUGAR
1-1/2 c. PILLSBURY FLOUR
1/4 t. salt
4 eggs
1/2 t. vanilla

Mix all ingredients together. Pour into *greased* pie pan (2
cups per pan). Bake at 325 degrees for 20 to 30 minutes.
Let cool while making icing.

Icing: 1/3 c. butter   1-1/2 c. PILLSBURY
     2 T. milk   POWDERED SUGAR
     1 T. cocoa   1/8 t. vanilla

Mix ingredients together. Place on top of *cool* pie. * *This pie
is best when served warm*!

DALLAS ★ COWBOYS
Super Bowl XXVIII Champions

Kay and Dave Campo.

Campo kids -- Angie (20 years), Eric (18 years), Shelbie (14 years), and Michael (3 years).

KAY & DAVID (DAVE) CROSS CAMPO
Assistant Coach
Defensive Backs/Secondary

BIRTH DATES: *Dave* -- 7-18-47 (New London: Connecticut); *Kay* -- 7-22-56 (Ogden, Utah)

COLLEGES: *Dave* -- Central Connecticut State University (B.S. -- Physical Education); Albany State University (M.S. -- Education Communications); *Kay* -- Stevens Henager College (Assoc. Degree in Bus.)

GREATEST MOMENT AT SUPER BOWL XXVIII: When James Washington, One of My Players, Picked up the Ball and Ran It in for a Touchdown to Start the Second Half

PLACES VISITED WHILE AT SUPER BOWL XXVIII: *Kay* -- Coca-Cola Plant

FIRST PLAYED ORGANIZED FOOTBALL: As a Running Back and Defensive Back, for Robert E. Fitch, Sr., High School "Falcons"

ENJOY MOST AS A DALLAS COWBOY: Enjoy Being in an Organization with Great Tradition and a Commitment to Winning; Working in a Game I Love Twelve Months a Year at the Top Level of Competition

PROFESSIONAL COACHING EXPERIENCE: College Coaching -- 18 years; and Pro Coaching -- 6 years

HONORS OR AWARDS: Twice Earned All-East Honors at Shortstop at Central Connecticut State; in 1991, Received Alumni Distinguished Service Award from Central Connecticut State University; Man of the Year from the Southeastern Connecticut Amateur Athletic Association, in 1992; Last Season, Helped Direct Dallas Defense to a Top 10 Ranking in NFL in Total Defense; under Campo's Direction, the Dallas Secondary Has Grown into One of the Team's Deepest and Most Productive Units over the Past Five Years

HOBBIES & INTERESTS: *Dave* -- Music, Sports, and Golf; *Kay* -- Crafts, Reading, and My Children

FAVORITE AUTHOR: *Dave* -- Tom Clancy; *Kay* -- John Grisham

FAVORITE TYPE OF MUSIC: *Dave* -- 50's Rock and Roll, and Musical Sound Tracks; *Kay* -- Soul, and Country

FAVORITE SPORTS HERO: *Dave* -- Frank Gifford

FAVORITE FOOD: *Dave* -- Italian; *Kay* -- Chinese

CHILDREN & AGES: Angie - 20 yrs.; Eric - 18 yrs.; Becky - 17 yrs.; Tommy - 15 yrs.; Shelbie - 14 yrs.; and Michael - 3 yrs.

FITNESS & DIET TIP: Stay Active; Eat Low-Fat Diet; and Drink Lots of Water

DAVE CAMPO'S CHILI VERDE

2 T. shortening
3 lbs. *lean* pork chops, <u>trimmed of all fat</u>, *cut in 1/2" chunks*
1 clove garlic, *finely-minced*
2 cans *whole, mild* green chilies (*14-oz. cans*)
4 *chilies cans full* of water
2/3 c. shortening
2/3 c. PILLSBURY FLOUR (*approximately*)
salt, *to taste*

In a large heavy saucepan, melt the 2 T. shortening; add garlic and pork chunks. Cook over *medium* heat, stirring <u>occasionally</u>, *until the pork is cooked through and the moisture is absorbed*. Meanwhile, melt the 2/3 c. shortening in a fry pan. Add enough flour to make a <u>roux</u> the consistency of pancake batter. Stir with a wire whisk over *medium* heat *until the roux turns the color of peanut butter*. Set aside. Squeeze the green chilies through your hands, until they become *thin long shreds of chilies* (<u>wear gloves</u>). Add them to the *cooked* pork, along with water and salt. *Slowly bring to a boil.* Stir in enough of the browned roux to thicken the mixture; simmer *until the flavors blend*. Serve with homemade tortillas.

Homemade Tortillas:

Mix 4 c. PILLSBURY FLOUR, 1/2 T. salt, and 1 T. baking powder. Cut in 1/2 c. shortening. Add enough *hottest* tap water (1 to 1-1/2 cups) to make *a soft dough*. Kneed dough *until smooth*; let sit, *covered with a damp cloth*, for 15 to 30 minutes. Pinch off *golf-ball size* pieces of dough and flatten; roll out into circles <u>as thin as possible</u>. Bake on an *ungreased* griddle *heated to the highest temperature possible*, turning <u>once</u>. Place the cooked tortillas in a plastic bag *to soften*.

KAY'S CROCK POT HUEVOS RANCHEROS

1 c. dried pinto beans, *sorted and washed*
2 T. shortening, or bacon grease
1-2 t. salt
1/4 c. shortening, or bacon grease
1 lb. chorizo sausage, or 2 c. ham, *diced*
1/4 c. butter
12 eggs
1/2 c. milk
salt and pepper, *to taste*
1 jar ORTEGA GARDEN-STYLE SALSA (*approximately 16 ounces*)
2 c. *mild* Cheddar cheese, *grated*
2 c. *grated* Monterey Jack cheese

For serving: *chopped* green onions, sour cream, additional salsa, and homemade tortillas

In a large saucepan, place the beans and 2 T. shortening; *cover with water and bring to a boil*. Simmer *covered* about 3-1/2 hours, or *until almost tender*. Remove lid. Add salt and 1/4 c. shortening; bring to a <u>rolling boil</u>. Mash a few of the beans with a fork; continue boiling *until slightly thickened*. If using chorizo, fry *until cooked through*, breaking up the pieces. In another fry pan, melt the butter, and add the eggs and milk; scramble *until soft, but still slightly runny*, adding salt and pepper, *to taste*. In a large crock pot, place the beans; cover with sausage or ham, and top with the eggs. Cover the eggs with the salsa, and then, both cheeses. Turn the crock pot on *low*; cook until guests arrive (*about 1 hour -- but can up to 3 or 4 hours*). Serve with the onions, sour cream, additional salsa, and homemade tortillas.

JANET & DONALD RAY COCHREN
Athletic Trainer
Medical Records Coordinator

BIRTH DATES: *Don* -- 2-6-32 (Oakland City, Indiana); *Jan* -- 7-25-43 (Warrenton, Missouri)

COLLEGES: *Don* -- Purdue University (Physical Therapy); *Jan* -- Northeast Missouri State (Sociology and Psychology)

YEARS IN PROFESSIONAL FOOTBALL: 30 Years with Dallas Cowboys

ENJOY MOST AS A DALLAS COWBOY: Camaraderie with Players and Staff

HONORS OR AWARDS: *Don* -- Earned Physical Therapy Certificate at Pennsylvania; Joining Dallas Cowboys, in 1965, Became Medical Records Coordinator / Athletic Trainer, after Working 25 Seasons as Team's Trainer; One of 28 Trainers Selected from Colleges and Professional Sports Teams to Serve the United States Team at 1980 Winter Olympics in Lake Placid, New York; in 1984, Received 25-Yr. Honor Award from the National Athletic Trainers Association; in 1989, Chosen to Serve as a Member of the Professional Football Athletic Trainers/Gatorade Advisory Board; Honored by Purdue University by Presenting Him Their Distinguished Alumni Award, in 1992; *Jan* -- Nominee for Volunteer of the Year

HOBBIES & INTERESTS: *Don* -- Jogging, Spending Time with Family, and Going to Chris' Games; *Jan* -- Working with People, Traveling, Volunteer Work, and Being with Family and Friends

FAVORITE AUTHOR: *Don* -- Sidney Sheldon; *Jan* -- Danielle Steele

FAVORITE TYPE OF MUSIC: *Don* -- Good Jazz, and Country Western; *Jan* -- New Age

FAVORITE SPORTS HERO: *Don* -- Stan Musial; *Jan* -- Babe Ruth

FAVORITE FOOD: *Don* -- Spaghetti; *Jan* -- Tex-Mex

CHILDREN & AGES: Jeff - 29 yrs.; Wendy - 28 yrs.; Scott - 27 yrs.; and Chris - 17 yrs. (Wide Receiver and Defensive Back on Shepton High School Football Team, and Works with the Cowboys and the Dallas Mavericks)

FITNESS & DIET TIP: Keep Moving; and Stay Busy

DALLAS ⭐ COWBOYS
Super Bowl XXVIII Champions

Chris (17 years); Jeff (29 years) and new wife Tina; and Scott (27 years) - left to right.

Jan and Don Cochren; and Wendy (27 years) - left to right.

DON COCHREN'S SOUTHWEST BEEF FAJITAS

1 lb. BEEF BONELESS TOP ROUND STEAK, *about 1/2"
  thick*
1/4 c. lime juice
2 T. vegetable oil
2 t. ground red chilies
2 cloves garlic, *finely-chopped*
8 flour tortillas (*10" in diameter*), *warmed*

Cut beef steak <u>diagonally across grain</u> into thin slices, each
2" x 1/8". Mix remaining ingredients, *except tortillas*, in glass
or plastic bowl. Stir in beef *until well-coated*. *Cover*;
refrigerate 1 hour. Set oven control to *broil*. Place beef
slices on rack in broiler pan. Broil with tops 2"-3" from heat
until brown (about 5 minutes). Place 1/8 of the beef and
"Southwest Guacamole" on center of each tortilla. Fold one
end of tortilla up about 1" over beef mixture; fold right and
left sides over folded end, *overlapping*. Fold down remaining
end. Serve with guacamole. Makes 8 servings.

Southwest Guacamole:

     5 *ripe* avocados, *peeled and pitted*
     4 cloves garlic, *finely-chopped*
     1 *medium* tomato, *chopped* (about 1 cup)
     1/4 c. lime juice
     1/2 t. salt

Mash avocados in a medium bowl *until slightly lumpy*. Stir
in remaining ingredients. *Cover*; refrigerate 1 hour. Makes
3 cups guacamole.

JAN'S CHILE CON QUESO

1 c. *shredded* Cheddar or Monterey Jack cheese (*4 ounces*)
1 can *chopped* green chilies, *drained* (*4 ounces*)
1/4 c. half-and-half
2 T. *finely-chopped* onion
2 t. ground cumin
1/2 t. salt

Heat all ingredients over *low* heat, stirring <u>constantly</u>, *until
cheese is melted*. Serve warm with tortilla chips.
Makes 1-1/4 cups dip.

Tammy and Butch Davis at the Kentucky Derby - May, 1994.

Tammy, Drew, and Butch at training Camp - July '94.

TAMMY & PAUL (BUTCH) HILTON DAVIS
Assistant Coach
Defensive Coordinator

BIRTH DATES: *Butch* -- 11-17-51 (Talequah, Oklahoma); *Tammy* -- 2-3-61 (Wellington, Kansas)

COLLEGES: *Butch* -- University of Arkansas (B.S. -- Anatomy and Physiology); *Tammy* -- Florida Atlantic University (B.S. -- Business Administration); Currently, at Amber University

GREATEST MOMENT AT SUPER BOWL XXVIII: The Most Memorable Moment Was the Scene in the Locker Room after the Game, when the Players Were Able to Express the Sheer Love and Joy of What They Had Accomplished Together against All Odds

ENJOY MOST AS A DALLAS COWBOY: The Opportunity to Work with So Many Quality People, Both Players and Coaches

HONORS OR AWARDS: Defensive End at Arkansas; Coached Dallas' Defensive Line for Four Seasons; in 1992, Helped Cowboys Finish Season as the NFL's Top-Ranked Unit against the Rush; Promoted to Position of Defensive Coordinator in 1993 - Calling the Shots for a Super Bowl Champion Defense; the 1993 Defense Produced the Cowboys' First Pro Bowl Defensive Players since 1985 (Three Defenders Selected to Pro Bowl in 1993)

HOBBIES & INTERESTS: *Butch* -- Golf, Travel, Reading, Water Sports, and Family Activities; *Tammy* -- Golf, Tennis, Water Sports, and Reading

FAVORITE AUTHOR: *Butch* -- Tom Clancy, John Grisham, and Biographies; *Tammy* -- James Dobson (at This Time)

FAVORITE TYPE OF MUSIC: *Butch and Tammy* -- All Types of Music

FAVORITE FOOD: *Butch* -- Steak, Mexican, and Italian; *Tammy* -- Mexican, and Seafood

CHILDREN & AGES: Andrew Hilton "Drew" - Born 1-22-93

FITNESS & DIET TIP: Exercise; and Reduce Fat Content of Diet

BUTCH DAVIS' SOUR CREAM
AND CHICKEN ENCHILADAS

5 to 6 BUTTERBALL BONELESS, SKINLESS CHICKEN
  BREASTS
1 can of Rotel tomatoes
1 can of *diced* green chilies
onions, *sauteed* (*optional*)
flour tortillas
1 can cream of chicken soup
1 pt. of sour cream
Monterey and Cheddar cheeses, *combined together*

Boil 5 to 6 chicken breasts (at least 20 minutes). Cool; cut
into *small* pieces. Mix chicken, Rotel tomatoes (*strain a
little*), diced green chilies, and sauteed onions. Spray
casserole dish with *Pam*. Stuff flour tortillas; roll up. Mix
together cream of chicken soup and sour cream. Spread over
enchiladas. Spread Monterey and Cheddar cheeses over
casserole. Bake for 30 minutes at 350 degrees, *leaving cover
off for the last 15 minutes*.

TAMMY'S TEXAS SHEET CAKE

2 c. PILLSBURY ALL-PURPOSE FLOUR
2 c. C & H GRANULATED SUGAR
2 sticks margarine, *cut in chunks*
4 T. *unsweetened* cocoa powder
1 c. water
1/2 c. buttermilk   1 t. vanilla
2 eggs, *slightly-beaten*   1 t. baking soda

Sift flour and sugar into mixing bowl. Combine margarine,
cocoa, and water in pan; bring *to boil*. Pour over flour and
sugar; *mix well*. Mix in buttermilk, eggs, vanilla, and baking
soda. Pour into *greased* 15" x 11" sheet pan. Bake at 400
degrees for 20 minutes. * *Spread icing on cake while hot!*

Icing:

1 stick margarine
4 T. *unsweetened* cocoa powder
1/3 c. milk (*I use Pet Milk*)
1-lb. box C & H POWDERED SUGAR (*3-1/3 c. sifted*)
1 t. vanilla
1 c. nuts, *chopped fine*

While cake is baking, combine margarine, cocoa, and milk in
a saucepan; bring *to a boil*. Remove from heat. Beat in
sugar gradually; add vanilla. Stir in nuts. * *Spread on cake
while hot.*

JIM EDDY
Assistant Coach
Linebackers

BIRTH DATE: 5-2-39 (Checotah, Oklahoma)

COLLEGE: New Mexico State University (B.A. & M.A.)

FAVORITE ACADEMIC SUBJECT: Psychology

FIRST PLAYED ORGANIZED FOOTBALL: As a Freshman Running Back, for the Checotah High School "Wildcats"

HONORS OR AWARDS: For Ten Seasons - Including Three as Head Coach, Worked in the CFL, where His Teams Made Eight Post-Season Berths and Played in Four Grey Cup Championship Games; during Three Seasons with the Houston Oilers -- Team Earned Three Playoff Berths, Including the Franchise's First AFC Central Division Crown, in 1991 - Guided the Oilers' Defense, which Led the AFC - and Finished Third in the NFL in Total Defense, in 1992; in 1993, His First Year in Dallas, Added Defensive Knowledge and Experience to Help Land Three Cowboys Defenders in the Pro Bowl; in 1994, Moved from the Secondary to the Linebackers

HOBBIES & INTERESTS: Woodworking, Skiing, Hunting, and Fishing

FAVORITE AUTHOR: Stephen King

FAVORITE TYPE OF MUSIC: Popular

FAVORITE SPORTS HERO: Hank Aaron

FAVORITE TV/MOVIE STAR: Jody Foster

FAVORITE FOOD: Brownies

CHILDREN & AGES: Kelley Kathleen Tobin - 31 yrs.; and Connie Irene Eddy - 30 yrs.

FITNESS & DIET TIP: Jogging; and Watch Your Fat Intake

LONG-RANGE CAREER GOALS: Head Coach in NFL

261

Coach Jim Eddy.

JIM EDDY'S BAKED YAMS WITH
TOMATILLO SOUR CREAM

4 yams, *unpeeled and well-scrubbed*
2 t. vegetable oil
1/2 c. sour cream
1-2 T. commercial green tomatilla salsa
1 t. lime juice
salt and pepper, *to taste*
1 T. *fresh* cilantro

Preheat oven to 400 degrees. Rub yams with oil; place on an *ungreased* baking sheet. Bake for 30 minutes. *Prick skin in a few places with a fork*; bake 30 minutes more. In a bowl, combine sour cream, salsa, lime juice, and salt and pepper *to taste*. When potatoes are done, put on individual plates. Split potatoes *lengthwise*. Spoon a few tablespoons of sour cream mixture into each potato. Garnish with the cilantro. Serve <u>immediately</u>. Makes 4 servings.

EDDY'S CARAMEL NUT CRUNCH PIE

2 c. cream-filled chocolate sandwich cookies, *crumbled*
1/2 c. *unsalted, dry-roasted* peanuts, *chopped coarsely*
1/4 c. butter, *melted*
6 chocolate-coated, caramel-peanut nougat bars (*Snickers*) - (*2.07 ounces*)
1-1/2 qts. vanilla ice cream, *slightly-softened*
1 jar hot fudge sauce, *divided* (*11.75-oz. jar*)
1 jar hot caramel sauce, *divided* (*12-oz. jar*)

Combine first three ingredients; press into bottom and up the sides of 9"-deep dish pie plate. Bake at 350 degrees for 10 minutes. Set aside *to cool* <u>completely</u>. Chop candy bars into *small* pieces, and <u>reserve 2 tablespoons</u>. Spread *evenly* over crust. Drizzle with 2 T. fudge sauce and 2 T. caramel sauce. Sprinkle with reserved candy. Freeze *until firm*. Then, *cover*; return to freezer. Remove from freezer 20 minutes <u>before serving</u>. Serve with remaining fudge and caramel sauces.

Bobby, Janice, Coach Ford, and Jason enjoying the great outdoors.

Jason, Robert, and Bobby Ford.

JANICE & ROBERT L. FORD
Assistant Coach
Tight Ends

BIRTH DATES: *Robert* -- 6-21-51 (Belton, Texas); *Janice* -- 4-8-54 (Saginaw, Michigan)

COLLEGES: *Robert* -- University of Houston (B.S. -- Education); and Western Illinois University (M.A. -- Athletic Adm.); *Janice* -- Delta College

GREATEST MOMENT AT SUPER BOWL XVIII: Winning #2 and Being Able to Share It with Dave and Shirley (Janice's Parents), Laura and John (Family), and Our Good Friends (Cyndi, Tommy, Gene, and, of Course, Lulu!)

FIRST PLAYED ORGANIZED FOOTBALL: Twelve Years of Age, as a Running Back and Guard for the Smith Street "Bears"

HONORS OR AWARDS: Only Player in History of the NCAA to Catch Two 99-Yd. Touchdown Passes; Led Houston in Receiving, Punt Returns, and Kickoff Returns, in 1972, Earning Third-Team All-America Honors; College Hall of Fame Finalist; since First Season Coaching Tight Ends with the Cowboys, in 1991 -- No Other NFL Tight End Has Caught More Passes than Novacek's 127; in 1992, Novacek Hauled in More Passes than Any Other Tight End in Cowboys' History; in 1993, Coaching the Tight Ends -- Novacek Made His Third Consecutive Pro Bowl Appearance, and Named the 1993 NFL Alumni Tight End of the Year Award

HOBBIES & INTERESTS: *Robert* -- Golf, Reading, and Bowling; *Janice* -- Bowling, Football, and Reading

FAVORITE AUTHOR: *Robert* -- John Grisham, and Michael Creighton; *Janice* --John Grisham

FAVORITE TYPE OF MUSIC: *Robert* -- Soft Pop, and Rock; *Janice* -- Rhythm and Blues, and Jazz

FAVORITE SPORTS HERO: *Robert* -- Lenny Moore; *Janice* -- Jim Thorpe, and Jackie Robinson

FAVORITE FOOD: *Robert* -- Chicken Fried Steak, and Mashed Potatoes; *Janice* -- "My Own White Enchiladas"

CHILDREN & AGES: Bobby - 18 yrs. (Sophomore - Texas A & M University); and Jason - 16 yrs. (Junior - Coppell High)

FITNESS & DIET TIP: Walk 45 Minutes Every Day; Eat Bananas; Don't Overeat -- When You're Full, Stop; and Never Eat after 7 p.m.

LONG-RANGE CAREER GOALS: To Be a Head Coach

ROBERT FORD'S SOUTHWESTERN BAKED CHICKEN

4 to 5 BUTTERBALL Boneless, Skinless CHICKEN
 BREASTS
1 can cream of corn soup
1 *small* can *mild* green chilies, *chopped*
1/4 c. sour cream
1 shot of McILHENNY CO. TABASCO SAUCE
Mexican seasoning
salt and pepper, *to taste*
rice, or noodles

Heat oven to 350 degrees. Sprinkle chicken with salt,
pepper, and Mexican seasoning. Place in a 13" x 9" glass
baking pan. *Cover with foil.* Bake for 1 hour. In a small
bowl, combine soup, green chilies, sour cream, and Tabasco;
mix well. * *If sauce appears too thick, add some milk (2
tablespoons).* Spread sauce over chicken. Continue to bake
for 15 to 20 minutes, or *until golden brown.* *Serve with rice
or noodles.*

SHIRLEY'S NAVY BEANS

1 *large* bag *dried* navy beans, *sorted (to remove rocks),* and
 soak overnight
1/2 c. celery, *finely-chopped*
1 *small* onion, *finely-chopped*
1 carrot, *finely-chopped*
1/4 c. catsup
1 ham shank (or, *if you have any leftover ham,* 1 c. chopped
 ham)
salt and pepper, *to taste*
NUTMEG *(secret ingredient!)*

Throw away water that beans soaked in overnight. Using a
8-qt. pot, start with *fresh water,* filled to the top of pot (*over
the beans*). Add celery, onion, carrot, catsup, and ham.
Bring *to a boil.* Add salt and pepper, *to taste.* Lower heat to
simmer. Add a sprinkle or two of the *secret ingredient*
(NUTMEG)! Cook for 1-1/2 to 2 hours, or *until done.* * *Serve
with a slice of hot, buttered cornbread -- Robert's exclamation:
"Um-Um Good"!!!*

RAFFAELLA (RAFFY) & STEVE HOFFMAN
Assistant Coach
Kickers/Quality Control

BIRTH DATES: *Steve* -- 9-8-58 (Camden, New Jersey); *Raffy* -- 9-23-66 (Milan, Italy)

COLLEGES: *Steve* -- Dickinson College (B.A. -- Economics); St. Thomas University (M.A. -- Sports Administration); *Raffy* -- Oxford Institute of Languages (Monza, Italy)

GREATEST MOMENT AT SUPER BOWL XXVIII: Seeing the Proud Look on My Father's Face when I Shook His Hand after the Game

SPECIAL FOOD EATEN WHILE AT SUPER BOWL XXVIII: Italian Food at "LaGrotta" Restaurant

PROFESSIONAL COACHING EXPERIENCE: 6th Season with the Dallas Cowboys

ENJOY MOST AS A DALLAS COWBOY: Having the Chance Every Week to Be a Part of Something Most People Can Only Dream about

WIFE'S OCCUPATION: International Flight Attendant

HONORS OR AWARDS: All-Mid-Atlantic Conference Honors in Football, in 1978 and 1979; All-Mid-Atlantic Conference Honors in Baseball, in 1979 and 1980; Joining Cowboys in 1989 to Coach the Kickers, Received Added Duties of Quality Control, in 1990; Currently Coordinates the computer Scouting of All Cowboys' Future Opponents on Video Tape, while Providing Internal Analysis of the Cowboys' Own Tendencies and Productivity; Has Rapidly Developed a Reputation around the NFL for His Ability to Find and Develop Kicking Talents with Young Players; in 1993, Introduced Free Agent Punter John Jett to NFL - He Responded by Finishing Ranked Third in NFL in Net Punting Average (37.7)in '93

HOBBIES & INTERESTS: *Steve* -- Reading, Studying Italian, Listening to Music, and Watching Old Movies; *Raffy* -- Sewing, Decorating, Reading, Dancing, and Cooking

FAVORITE AUTHOR: *Steve* -- Leon Uris, Joseph Wambaugh, and James Clavell; *Raffy* -- Alberto Bevilacqua, Fracesco Alberoni, and John Grisham

FAVORITE TYPE OF MUSIC: *Steve* -- "Anything But Jazz"; *Raffy* -- Club Music . . . Also Soul and Good Country

FAVORITE SPORTS HERO: *Steve* -- Ed Podolak; *Raffy* -- Roberto Baggio

FAVORITE FOOD: *Steve* -- Pasta; *Raffy* -- Pasta; and Mexican

PETS: Two Dogs: Pongo and Boo Boo

FITNESS & DIET TIP: Vary Your Workouts So You Don't Get Bored; and Marry an Italian -- Eat Pasta for Every Meal

267

DALLAS ⭐ COWBOYS
Super Bowl XXVIII Champions

Raffy and Steve Hoffman, Raffy's dad and mom, and Steve's mom (from right to left).

STEVE HOFFMAN'S FIESTA ROLL-UPS

1 jar Picante Sauce (*for dipping*)
2 pkg. cream cheese (*8-oz. packages*)
4 oz. *chopped* black olives
4 oz. *chopped* green olives
1 oz. *chopped* jalapenos
1/2 pkg. taco seasoning mix
1 *small* onion, *chopped*
1 *big package* of *large* flour tortillas
5 to 6 drops McILHENNY CO. TABASCO SAUCE

Mix all ingredients with the cream cheese. Spread on
tortillas; roll up. Place on cookie sheet, *seam down. Cover*
with *plastic wrap or foil.* Refrigerate (*better if overnight!*).
To serve: Slice into 2-inch pieces; serve with Picante Sauce
for dipping.

* *Kissing is not recommended after eating a few of these
delicious rolls!!!*

RAFFY'S "ITALO-SOUTHWESTERN" PIZZA

1 jar ORTEGA GARDEN-STYLE SALSA
1 pkg. *shredded* Mozzarella cheese
1 c. *refried* beans
3 *medium* tomatoes, *diced*
1 c. *pitted* black olives
sliced jalapeno peppers
1/2 c. *minced* chives and cilantro mix
GROUND BEEF, *cooked and crumbled*

Make crust (*like you normally do for your traditional pizza*), or
buy your favorite kind. Spread a *thin* layer of refried beans;
cover with salsa. Add cheese, diced tomatoes, olives,
jalapeno peppers, and ground beef. Sprinkle the chives and
cilantro mix, and a little more cheese, on top. Bake for 20 to
30 minutes at 350 degrees.

Holly, Hudson, Elsie, and Scott Houck on vacation in Hawaii.

Holly and Scott celebrating Christmas.

DALLAS COWBOYS
Super Bowl XXVIII Champions

ELSIE & HUDSON HOUCK
Assistant Coach
Offensive Line

BIRTH DATES: *Hudson* -- 1-7-43 (Los Angeles, California); *Elsie* -- 12-22-47 (Rochester, Pennsylvania)

COLLEGES: *Hudson* -- U.S.C. (Education); *Elsie* -- University of Virginia (Bank Management)

GREATEST MOMENT AT SUPER BOWL XXVIII: Arriving Home, Stepping off the Plane, and Knowing that You Are World Champions

FIRST PLAYED ORGANIZED FOOTBALL: In 1957, Played Linebacker/Fullback for the Eagle Rock "Eagles"

PROFESSIONAL FOOTBALL OR COACHING EXPERIENCE: Los Angeles Rams - 9 yrs.; Seattle Seahawks - 1 yr.; and Dallas Cowboys - 1-1/2 yrs.

WIFE'S OCCUPATION: Regional Manager for Bank One

HONORS OR AWARDS: Played Three Seasons as a Center for U.S.C. - Including on the Trojans' 1962 National Championship Team; in 9 Years Coaching with the Los Angeles Rams, Developed One of the Most Dominate Lines in the NFL - No Team Sent More Offensive Lineman to the Pro Bowl than the Rams; in First Season in Dallas - 1993, Helped Guide Three Members of the Offensive Line to the Pro Bowl

HOBBIES & INTERESTS: *Hudson* -- Golf, Snow Skiing, and Fishing; *Elsie* -- Golf, Snow Skiing, Scuba Diving, and Travel

FAVORITE AUTHOR: *Hudson* -- John Grisham; *Elsie* -- Sidney Sheldon

FAVORITE TYPE OF MUSIC: *Hudson* -- Jazz, and Country Western; *Elsie* -- Oldies, and Country Western

FAVORITE SPORTS HERO: *Hudson* -- Vince Lombardi; *Elsie* -- Magic Johnson

FAVORITE TV/MOVIE STAR: *Hudson* -- Clint Eastwood; *Elsie* -- Michael Douglas

FAVORITE FOOD: *Hudson and Elsie* -- Mexican

CHILDREN & AGES: Troy - 30 yrs.; Scott - 25 yrs.; and Holly - 22 yrs.

FITNESS & DIET TIP: Walk Four Miles Every Day; Eliminate Fat from the Diet; and Drink Plenty of Water

271

DALLAS ⭐ COWBOYS
Super Bowl XXVIII Champions

HUDSON HOUCK'S CHILE RELLENOS
BREAKFAST CASSEROLE

2 *small* cans *diced* green chilies
1 c. Bisquick
6 eggs, *beaten*
1 c. cottage cheese
2 c. milk
2-1/2 c. *grated* Cheddar cheese
ORTEGA GARDEN-STYLE SALSA

Spray casserole dish with Pam. Sprinkle small cans diced green chilies and grated Cheddar cheese in dish. Mix Bisquick, eggs, cottage cheese, and milk together. Pour over chilies and cheese. Bake at 350 degrees for 45 minutes.
* *Serve with salsa.*

ELSIE'S SANTA FE CHICKEN

1 onion, *chopped*
1 green pepper, *chopped*
1 can Rotel tomatoes
1 clove garlic, *crushed*
1 c. Minute Rice
6 BUTTERBALL Boneless, Skinless CHICKEN BREASTS
Monterey Jack or Cheddar cheese
paprika
salt and pepper, *to taste*

Brown chicken breasts *until almost done* in a large skillet. Remove chicken; saute in same skillet (*add more oil, if needed*) onion, green, pepper, and garlic clove. *Drain juice from Rotel tomatoes into a one-cup measure*; add enough water to make *one cup of liquid*. Add Rotel tomatoes to onion and green pepper mixture. Add salt and pepper *to taste*, Minute Rice, 1 cup of *saved liquid*. Place chicken on top; sprinkle chicken with paprika. Cover with cheese. Let cook on *low* for 5 to 10 minutes. Serves 4 to 6.

272

ROSANNE & JIM MAURER

Assistant Trainer

BIRTH DATES: *Jim* -- 3-8-65 (Dallas, Texas); *Rosanne* -- 2-23-65 (Dallas, Texas)

COLLEGES: *Jim* -- Southern Methodist University (B.A. -- Physical Education); *Rosanne* -- Texas Tech

GREATEST MOMENT AT SUPER BOWL XXVIII: Seeing Bill Bates, after Major Knee Surgery, Playing in His First Super Bowl; and Being with My Wife and Parents after the Game

PLACES VISITED WHILE AT SUPER BOWL XVIII: The NFL Commissioner's Party, where We Danced in a Volcano

SPECIAL PEOPLE MET WHILE AT SUPER BOWL XVIII: *Jim* -- Kevin Costner

ENJOY MOST AS A DALLAS COWBOY: Helping Athletes in the Rehabilitative Process after an Injury; and Making Friends

HOBBIES & INTERESTS: *Jim* -- Golf, and Racquetball; *Rosanne* -- Reading (Fiction, and Non-Fiction)

FAVORITE TYPE OF MUSIC: *Jim* -- Bruce Springsteen; *Rosanne* -- Stevie Ray Vaughn

FAVORITE SPORTS HERO: *Jim* -- Walter Payton; *Rosanne* -- My Hero Is the Athlete Who Fights Hard through a Rehab after an Injury and Comes Back to Play the Game!

FAVORITE FOOD: *Jim* -- Barbecue Ribs

CHILDREN & AGES: Nick -- Born 1-12-89; Ben -- Born 6-9-92

FITNESS & DIET TIP: Consistent, Slow Progression when Using Weight Programs; and Look into a Lifestyle Change, Rather than a Quick-Fix Diet

LONG-RANGE CAREER GOALS: *Jim* -- To Be a Head Trainer in a Professional Athletic Setting; *Rosanne* -- To Teach Drama

Jim and Rosanne Maurer, with Ben and Nick.

DALLAS ★ COWBOYS
Super Bowl XXVIII Champions

JIM MAURER'S CHICKEN AND CHEESE ENCHILADAS

1/2 c. onion, *chopped*
1 garlic clove, *minced*
1 T. oil
2 c. *chopped, cooked* BUTTERBALL BONELESS, SKINLESS CHICKEN BREASTS
1 can *chopped* green chilies (*4-oz. can*)
1/4 c. chicken broth
2 t. chili powder
1 t. ground cumin
1 pkg. Philadelphia Cream Cheese, *cubed* (*4-oz. package*)
6 flour tortillas (*6-inch*)
1/4 lb. Velveeta Process Cheese Spread, *cubed*
2 T. milk
1/2 c. *chopped* tomato, *divided*

Microwave onion, garlic, and oil in 2-qt. microwave-safe casserole on *high* for 2 to 3 minutes, or *until tender*, stirring after 2 minutes. Stir in chicken, green chilies, broth, and seasonings. Spoon 1/3 c. chicken mixture into each tortilla; roll up. Place *seam-side down* in 8" square microwave-safe baking dish. *Microwave* process cheese spread, milk, and 1/4 cup tomato in medium microwave-safe bowl on *high* for 2 to 3 minutes, or *until Velveeta is melted*, stirring after each minute. Pour sauce over tortillas; top with remaining tomatoes. Microwave on *high* for 6 to 8 minutes, or *until thoroughly heated*, turning dish after 3 minutes. Makes 6 YUMMY servings!!!

ROSANNE'S CRAB QUESADILLAS

5 flour tortillas (*6-inch*)
3 green onions, *sliced*
1 tomato, *chopped*
1 T. *fresh* lime juice
1/2 t. ground cumin
1/4 t. ground red pepper
1 lb. *fresh* crab meat
1 c. *shredded* Monterey Jack cheese
1 c. *shredded* Cheddar cheese

Preheat oven to 450 degrees. Place tortillas on two cookie sheets. In a medium bowl, combine next 5 ingredients; add crab meat. In a small bowl, combine cheeses. Spoon 3/4 cup crab mixture over each tortilla; top with 1/3 cup cheese mixture. Bake for 7 to 9 minutes, or *until cheese melts*.
* Cut each tortilla into six wedges before serving.

Bruce and Kathy Mays at home in Coppell, Texas.

Laura, hugging sister Jennifer, at Jennifer's Pi Beta Phi initiation.

KATHRYN (KATHY) & BRUCE B. MAYS

Director of Football Operations

BIRTH DATES: *Bruce* -- 8-16-43 (Cleveland, Ohio); *Kathy* -- 1-6-48 (Detroit Michigan)

COLLEGES: *Bruce* -- Ohio Northern University (B.S. -- Education); University of Akron (M.S. -- Education); Oklahoma State University (Course Work Completed for Doctorate in Higher Education and Administration); *Kathy* -- Oklahoma State University (B.S. and M.S.)

GREATEST MOMENT AT SUPER BOWL XXVIII: Participating in Back-to-Back Super Bowls

ENJOY MOST AS A DALLAS COWBOY: The Ability of the Organization to Maintain an Even Keel during a Time of Great Pressure

WIFE'S OCCUPATION: Registered Dietitian at Cooper Clinic - Cooper Aerobic Center in Dallas

HOBBIES & INTERESTS: *Bruce* -- Reading, Golf, and Running; *Kathy* -- Reading, and Attending Musicals

FAVORITE AUTHOR: *Bruce* -- Ernest Hemingway; *Kathy* -- James Redfield

FAVORITE TYPE OF MUSIC: *Bruce and Kathy* -- Classical

FAVORITE SPORTS HERO: *Bruce* -- Ted Williams

FAVORITE FOOD: *Bruce and Kathy* -- Italian, and Chinese

CHILDREN & AGES: Kirsten - 25 yrs.; Jennifer - 19 yrs.; Laura - 17 yrs.; and Damien - 17 yrs.

FITNESS & DIET TIP: Exercise Consistently 3 to 5 Days per Week for 30 to 45 Minutes -- Include Three Days of Aerobics; Cut the Fat -- Increase the Carbohydrates; and Eat a Wide Variety of Foods

277

BRUCE MAY'S MEXICAN CHICKEN LASAGNA

1 *large* onion, *chopped*
2 T. canola oil
2 cloves garlic, *minced and mashed*
1 red bell pepper, *chopped*
2 cans condensed tomato soup (*10-3/4 oz. can*)
1 can enchilada sauce (*10-oz. can*)
1 pkg. Lasagna noodles, *cooked and drained*
1-1/2 t. salt
1/2 t. pepper
2 T. chili powder
1 t. cumin

Cheese Filling:

4 c. *cooked* BUTTERBALL Boneless, Skinless CHICKEN
   BREASTS, *cut in large pieces*
6 oz. *sliced* Cheddar cheese
6 oz. *sliced* Monterey Jack cheese

Heat oil, onion, garlic, bell pepper, and cook *until limp*. Add cans of soup, enchilada sauce, salt, pepper, chili powder, and cumin. Simmer sauce *uncovered* about 10 minutes, or *until thickened*. *Cover* shallow 4-qt. casserole with <u>half</u> of the *cooked* lasagna (*according to package directions*). Spread <u>half</u> of sauce mixture over noodles; then top with <u>half</u> of sliced cheese. Repeat. *Cover*; chill in refrigerator. Bake at 375 degrees for 50 minutes. * *If not chilled, then bake for 35 minutes*.

KATHY'S NEW MEXICO CORN BREAD

1 c. cornmeal
1/2 t. salt
1/2 t. baking soda
2 eggs
2 T. *melted* shortening

3/4 c. buttermilk
1 c. canned corn
1 *small* can *chopped* green
   chilies
1 c. *grated* Cheddar cheese

Combine cornmeal, salt, and baking soda. Stir in melted shortening. Add eggs; *mix well*. Stir in corn and buttermilk; *mix well*. Add 1/2 c. cheese and chilies; pour in *greased* 12" square pan. Sprinkle with 1/2 c. grated cheese on top. Bake at 400 degrees *until golden* (30 to 40 minutes).

DALLAS COWBOYS

Super Bowl XXVIII Champions

JAN & MIKE McCORD

Equipment Manager

BIRTH DATE: *Mike* -- 11-6-64 (Clovis, New Mexico); *Jan* -- 2-20-63 (Dimmitt, Texas)

COLLEGE: *Mike* -- University of Texas / Austin (Business Administration and Marketing); *Jan* -- West Texas State University (B.A. - Agri-Business)

GREATEST MOMENT AT SUPER BOWL XXVIII: The Confidence Expressed from the Team during Half-Time; and the Drive by the Dallas Offense in the Third Quarter when Emmitt Took over and Scored to Put the Game away

PLACES VISITED WHILE AT SUPER BOWL XXVIII: Atlanta Dome and Falcons' Complex

SPECIAL PEOPLE MET WHILE AT SUPER BOWL XXVIII: Rush Limbaugh

YEARS IN PROFESSIONAL FOOTBALL: 6th Year

ENJOY MOST AS A DALLAS COWBOY: The Relationships That Are Formed with the Guys Who Have the Same Commitment to Winning

HOBBIES & INTERESTS: *Mike* -- Golf, Basketball, Baseball, Tennis, Movies, and Country Dancing; *Jan* -- water skiing, dancing, and antiques

FAVORITE AUTHOR: *Mike* -- James Michener; *Jan* -- John Grisham

FAVORITE TYPE OF MUSIC: *Mike and Jan* -- Country

FAVORITE SPORTS HERO: *Mike* -- Mike Schmidt; *Jan* -- Troy Aikman

FAVORITE FOOD: *Mike* -- Italian; *Jan* -- Mexican

DOGS: Jasper and Sheeba

Mike and Jan McCord at wedding reception held at Bill Bates' Cowboy Ranch - May 21, 1994.

Mike and Jan McCord.

DALLAS ★ COWBOYS
Super Bowl XXVIII Champions

MIKE McCORD'S CHICKEN-RICE CASSEROLE

1-1/2 c. rice
1 can cream of mushroom soup
1 can cream of chicken soup
1 can cream of celery soup
1-1/2 *soup cans full* of water
1 can *sliced* mushrooms
1/2 c. *slivered* almonds
12 BUTTERBALL boneless, skinless CHICKEN BREASTS
salt and pepper, *to taste*
1/2 c. *melted* margarine

Place rice in a *buttered* pan; add the soups, water, mushrooms, and almonds. Sprinkle the chicken with salt and pepper; then, dip in margarine. Place on top of the rice mixture. *Cover.* Bake at 350 degrees for 1-1/2 hours.

JAN'S MEXICAN LASAGNA

1 lb. GROUND BEEF
4 flour tortillas (*7-inch*)
vegetable oil
1 can tomato sauce (*15-oz. can*)
1 pkg. taco seasoning mix (*1-1/4 oz. package*)
1 can *chopped* green chilies, *drained and divided* (*4-oz. can*)
1 can *frozen* avocado dip, *thawed* (*6-oz. can*)
1 c. *shredded* Monterey Jack cheese, *divided* (*4 ounces*)
1 jalapeno pepper, *sliced and seeded* (*optional*)
1 *hot* red pepper, *sliced and seeded* (*optional*)
fresh parsley sprigs (*optional*)

Cook ground beef in a skillet *until browned*, stirring to crumble. *Drain well*; set aside. Fry tortillas, <u>one at a time</u>, in 1/4" *hot* oil (375 degrees) about 5 seconds <u>on each side</u>, or just *until softened*. *Drain well* on paper towels; set aside. Combine tomato sauce and taco seasoning mix in a medium saucepan; bring *to a boil*. Reduce heat; simmer *uncovered* for 10 minutes. Remove from heat; <u>reserve 1/4 c. sauce mixture</u>. Add beef and <u>half</u> of green chilies to remaining sauce mixture. Place a tortilla and <u>half</u> of the meat mixture in a *greased* 8" or 9" cake pan. Layer with a tortilla, avocado dip, 1/2 c. cheese, and remaining green chilies. Top with a tortilla, remaining meat sauce, remaining tortilla, and 1/4 c. reserved sauce. Bake *uncovered* at 350 degrees for 40 minutes. Sprinkle with remaining 1/2 c. cheese; bake for 5 minutes, or *until cheese melts*. Garnish top with pepper slices and parsley, if desired. Makes 4 servings.

Anne and Kevin O'Neill.

McKenzie (age 9) and Kaitlyn (age 8) O'Neill.

DALLAS COWBOYS
Super Bowl XXVIII Champions

ANNE & KEVIN P. O'NEILL

Head Athletic Trainer

BIRTH DATE: *Kevin* -- 8-2-54 (Pittsburgh, Pennsylvania); *Anne* -- 12-26- (Los Angeles, California)

COLLEGE: *Kevin* -- University of Pittsburgh (B.S. -- Physical Education); and University of Arizona (M.S. -- Athletic Training); *Anne* -- Oregon State University (B.S. -- Home Economics)

SPECIAL PEOPLE MET WHILE AT SUPER BOWL XXVIII: Michael Jordan and His Wife, at the NFL Commissioner's Party

ENJOY MOST AS A DALLAS COWBOY: Camaraderie of Working with the Staff, Coaches, and Players

HOBBIES & INTERESTS: *Kevin* -- Jogging, Movies, and Spending Most of Free Time with Daughters

FAVORITE AUTHOR: *Kevin* -- John Grisham

FAVORITE FOOD: *Kevin* -- Italian; *Anne* -- Anything Chocolate

CHILDREN & AGES: McKenzie Jean - 9 yrs.; Kaitlyn Elizabeth - 8 yrs.

FITNESS & DIET TIP: Make Sure You Select a Proper Fitting Pair of Running/Workout Shoes; and Eat Five Servings of Fruit and Vegetables a Day for Better Health

SPECIAL COMMENTS: Being Involved with Football Has Given Us the Opportunity to Live in Many Different Places; Have Met the Most Wonderful People at Each Place; and Feel Very Fortunate to Have Had a Tremendous Amount of Success -- Including a National Championship and Two Super Bowl Titles

KEVIN O'NEILL'S ROASTED RED POTATOES

2 to 3 lbs. red potatoes, *quartered*
3 to 4 T. olive oil
Knorr's Aromat All-Purpose Seasoning
basil

Wash and quarter red potatoes. Put into bowl; add olive oil
and toss. Sprinkle <u>heavily</u> with Knorr's Aromat Seasoning
and sprinkle basil; toss again. Use roasting pan *with cover.*
Coat with Pam. Put potatoes into roasting pan. Sprinkle top
of potatoes *lightly* again with seasoning and basil. Bake in
oven at 400 degrees for 45 minutes to 1 hour, or *until
potatoes are tender and browned lightly.*

ANNE'S TEXAS HOT CHICKEN "WINGS"

3 lbs. chicken wings
6 T. *Louisiana-style* hot sauce
1/2 c. butter, *melted*
Bleu cheese dressing

Split wings at each joint. *Discard tips.* Put wing sections in
baking dish. Bake at 325 degrees for 35 minutes. Place in
bowl. Combine hot sauce and butter; pour over chicken
wings. *Cover*; refrigerate for *at least* 3 hours. Before
serving, place wings in baking pan and bake at 425 degrees
for 10 minutes. *Serve with Bleu cheese dressing (for dipping)!*

284

MIKE WOICIK
Assistant Coach
Strength and Conditioning

BIRTH DATE: 9-26-56 (Baltimore, Maryland)

COLLEGE: Boston College (B.A. -- History); Springfield College (M.A. -- Physical Education)

GREATEST MOMENT AT SUPER BOWL XXVIII: The Locker Room after the Win, and Having My Parents There to See the Game

ENJOY MOST AS A DALLAS COWBOY: The Players with Whom I Work

HONORS OR AWARDS: Outstanding Discus Thrower at Boston College, Setting a School Record of 180' 5"; Earned All-East Honors and Qualified for the NCAA Championships; Came to Dallas after Serving Ten Years as the Strength and Conditioning Coach at Syracuse University; Named NFL Strength Coach of the Year, in 1992, (as Voted by Peers); Developed the Dallas Cowboys into One of the Healthiest and Best-Conditioned Teams in the NFL; since Coming to Dallas in 1990, Has an Overall Record of 50-22, with 7 Play-Off Victories, and 2 Super Bowl Titles

HOBBIES & INTERESTS: Bowling, Fishing, Reading, and Music

FAVORITE AUTHOR: Robert Ludlum

FAVORITE SPORTS HERO: Willie Mays

FAVORITE FOOD: Prime Rib

FITNESS & DIET TIP: Do Something Every Day

DALLAS ★ COWBOYS
Super Bowl XXVIII Champions

Coach Mike Woicik.

MIKE WOICIK'S SOUTHWESTERN PECAN PIE

3 eggs
2/3 c. C & H GRANULATED SUGAR
dash of salt
1 c. *dark* corn syrup
1/2 c. *melted* butter or margarine
1 c. pecan halves
1 *unbaked* pastry shell (*9-inch*)

Beat eggs <u>thoroughly</u> with sugar, salt, corn syrup, and melted butter. Add pecans. Pour into *unbaked* pastry shell. Bake in *moderate* oven (350 degrees) for 50 minutes, or *until knife inserted halfway between outside and center of filling comes out clean*. Cool before serving.

MIKE'S DYNAMITE BEEF BITES

1-1/2 lbs. BEEF FLANK STEAK
1/2 c. ORTEGA GARDEN-STYLE SALSA
12 *whole* jalapeno peppers, *halved lengthwise and seeded*
1/4 c. *herbed* cream cheese
toothpicks

Thinly slice steak in 1/4" thick strips, 4" long. Cut <u>across grain</u>, *holding knife at an angle*. In glass dish, or sealable plastic bag, marinate beef strips in salsa for one hour. Fill each jalapeno <u>half</u> with 1/2 t. cream cheese. Wrap filled jalapenos with one steak strip, covering cream cheese as you wrap. Fasten steak ends with toothpick. Grill, or broil.
4 inches from heat for 4 minutes, *turning after 2 minutes*. <u>Do not overcook!</u>

Zampese children: Laurie, Jon, Ken, and Kristin at Ken's wedding rehearsal dinner in Pacific Palasides, California - 1992.

Zampese grandchildren: Jullian Rae, Boone Jennings, Chelsey Marie, Jesse Jon, and Jenna Leigh - Easter '93 in Blossom Valley.

JOYCE & ERNIE ZAMPESE
Assistant Coach
Offensive Coordinator/Quarterbacks

BIRTH DATES: *Ernie* -- 3-12-36 (Santa Barbara, California); *Joyce* -- 11-23-35 (Chicago Illinois)

COLLEGES: *Ernie* -- University of Southern California / Cal Poly / San Luis Obispo (B.A. and M.A. - Education); *Joyce* -- Marymount College, Westwood / U.C.S.B. / Cal Poly / San Luis Obispo (B.A. and M.A. - Education)

FAVORITE ACADEMIC SUBJECT: *Ernie* -- Biology; *Joyce* -- Merchandizing and Psychology

GREATEST MOMENT IN SPORTS: San Diego Charger Victory over Miami in the 1981 Playoffs

FIRST PLAYED ORGANIZED FOOTBALL: As Tailback for Santa Barbara Dons, in 1951

PROFESSIONAL COACHING EXPERIENCE: San Diego Chargers (1976 and 1979-1986); Scouting for Jets (1977-1978); Los Angeles Rams (1987-1993); Came to Dallas Cowboys (1994)

HONORS & AWARDS: *Ernie* -- High School Football Player of year in Southern California (1953); Has Been Leader of Some of the Most Powerful Offensive Teams in the League over the Past Several Years - in Eleven Years as Offensive Coordinator, His Teams Have Ranked in the Top Five in Total Offense Six Times; Almost Every Team Record on Offense Was Established during Zampese's Time with both the San Diego Chargers and the Los Angeles Rams; *Joyce* -- Santa Barbara High School Homecoming Queen, Marymount College Freshman Class Queen, and Loyola University Homecoming Queen

HOBBIES & INTERESTS: *Ernie* -- Reading, Baby Sitting Grandchildren, Family Gatherings, and Barbecuing; *Joyce* -- Sewing, Crafts, Reading, Grandchildren, and Children

FAVORITE AUTHOR: *Ernie* -- Louis L'Amour; *Joyce* -- Taylor Caldwell

FAVORITE SPORTS HERO: *Ernie* -- Joe DiMaggio; *Joyce* -- My Husband

FAVORITE TV/MOVIE STAR: *Ernie* -- John Wayne

FAVORITE FOOD: *Ernie* -- Steak; *Joyce* -- Buttered Popcorn

CHILDREN & AGES: Kristin - 32 yrs.; Laurie - 30 yrs.; Ken - 27 yrs.; Joe - 19 yrs.

GRANDCHILDREN & AGES: Jillean - 9 yrs.; Boone - 7 yrs.; Chelsey - 5 yrs.; Jesse - 3 yrs.; and Jenna - 3 yrs.

FITNESS & DIET TIP: Walking; and Don't Over-Indulge

ERNIE ZAMPESE'S BEANS

1/2 onion, *chopped*
1/2 stick margarine
1 t. oil
1 t. parsley
1/2 can tomato paste (*6-oz. can*)
1 can tomato sauce (*16-oz. can*)
2 lbs. dried pinto beans
2 ham hocks

Chop onion; saute in margarine. Add oil and parsley. Mix tomato paste and tomato sauce together. Add to onion mix; simmer for 10 minutes. Put in a large pot with pinto beans. Add water to 3/4 level. Put in ham hocks. Cook slowly for 4 hours, *stirring occasionally*. Take out ham hocks; remove meat. Return meat to pot.

DARLENE KOFLER'S SOMBRERO SPREAD

1 lb. GROUND BEEF
1/2 c. *chopped* onion
1/2 c. catsup
1 t. chili powder
1 t. salt
1 can kidney beans, *mashed - with liquid* (*16 or 32 oz. can*)
grated Cheddar cheese
1/2 c. *chopped* onions
1/2 c. *chopped* black olives
king-size Fritos

Brown ground beef; add onion. Stir in catsup, chili powder, and salt. Add mashed beans and liquid. Heat at 325 degrees for 30 minutes. Garnish with Cheddar cheese, chopped onions, and black olives. *Serve with king-size Fritos.*

VIKKI & MIKE ZIMMER
Assistant Coach
Defensive Assistant

BIRTH DATES: *Mike* -- 6-5-56 (Peoria, Illinois); *Vikki* -- 6-9-59

COLLEGES: *Mike* -- Illinois State University (B.A. - Physical Education); *Vikki* -- Weber State / University of Utah (Dance Degree)

FAVORITE ACADEMIC SUBJECT: *Mike* -- Foreign Language (Spanish); *Vikki* -- History

GREATEST MOMENT IN SPORTS: Playing for My Dad; and Coaching One of the Best Defenses in the Country - Building Them to That Point

FIRST PLAYED ORGANIZED FOOTBALL: In Sixth Grade, for the Kelvin Grove Hornets

PROFESSIONAL COACHING EXPERIENCE: Coached Best Defense in School History at Washington State (1992-1993); Best Record in School History at Weber State College (1987) and at Washington State (1992); Coached Blue-Grey All-Star Game, in 1993

HONORS & AWARDS: *Mike* -- Two-Time All-Conference Quarterback at Lockport, Illinois, High School; Quarterback and Linebacker at Illinois State University; *Vikki* -- Miss Weber State College; Dance Instructor for 21 Years; Member of Ballet West Co.; Weber State Cheerleader for 3 Years; and U.S.A. Cheerleader

HOBBIES & INTERESTS: *Mike* -- Hunting, Fishing, and Racquetball; *Vikki* -- Dance, Judging Pageants and Competitions and Cheerleaders, Cooking, Crafts, Homemaking, and Love People

FAVORITE AUTHOR: *Vikki* -- Helen Steiner Rice

FAVORITE TYPE OF MUSIC: *Mike* -- Country; *Vikki* -- All Types

FAVORITE SPORTS HERO: *Mike* -- Joe Namath; *Vikki* -- Mike, and His Dad, Bill

FAVORITE TV/MOVIE STAR: *Mike* -- Arnold Swartzenegger; *Vikki* -- Bob Hope, and Mary Tyler Moore

FAVORITE FOOD: *Mike* -- Mexican; *Vikki* -- Shrimp

CHILDREN: Adam William - 10-1/2 yrs.; Marti Nichole - 7-1/2 yrs.; and Corri Dawn - 4-1/2 yrs.

FITNESS & DIET TIP: Get in a Routine and Vary Exercises to Keep Interesting; Cut out the Fat; and Work Out

291

DALLAS ★ COWBOYS
Super Bowl XXVIII Champions

Zimmer Family in Lockport, Illinois - 1993.

1993 Christmas card in Pullman, Washington, after Copper Bowl in Arizona.

MIKE ZIMMER'S SOUTHWESTERN SUCCESS

1 bag of Success Rice
3/4 lb. *extra lean* GROUND BEEF
1/2 c. *chopped* onion
1/2 c. water
1-1/2 c. *thinly-sliced* zucchini
1 pkg. taco seasoning mix (*1-1/2 oz. package*)
1/2 c. *frozen, whole-kernel* corn
1 can stewed tomatoes (*14-1/2 oz. can*)
1 c. *shredded, reduced-fat* Cheddar cheese

Prepare rice (*according to package directions*). In large skillet, brown ground beef; *drain*. Stir in remaining ingredients, *except rice and cheese*. Remove from heat. Add *cooked* rice; sprinkle with cheese.

VIKKI'S GRANDMA HARTMAN'S
SOUTHERN FRIED CHICKEN

6 BUTTERBALL Boneless, Skinless CHICKEN BREASTS
3/4 c. fried bread crumbs
3 T. PILLSBURY FLOUR
salt and pepper, *to taste*
1/2 t. basil leaves
1 t. dry parsley
1/2 t. paprika
3-4 T. *melted* butter

Mix bread crumbs with flour; add seasonings. Remove skin from chicken pieces. Dip chicken in water; then, roll in bread crumbs. Drizzle butter <u>evenly</u> in *foil-lined* baking pan. Lay chicken in pan. Bake at **400** degrees for 20 minutes. Then, turn chicken. Bake for **20** minutes more. * *Bread crumbs can be replaced with saltine crackers (crushed).*

Super Bowl XXVIII.

RECIPE INDEX

DALLAS ★ COWBOYS
Super Bowl XXVIII Champions

DALLAS COWBOYS
Super Bowl XXVIII Champions

RECIPE INDEX

Page

297

DALLAS ★ COWBOYS
Super Bowl XXVIII Champions

Page

(Sandwiches and Fixings)

CASSEROLES

(Cheese, Meat, Pasta, Rice, and Vegetable)

COOKIES & BARS

MEAT DISHES

(Beef Dishes)

Page

(Pork Dishes)

(Seafood Dishes)

PASTA DISHES

PIES, TARTS, & COBBLERS

SALADS, SOUPS, CHILI, & STEWS

SAUCES, SPREADS, DIPS, AND MEAT RUB

DALLAS COWBOYS
Super Bowl XXVIII Champions

DALLAS ★ COWBOYS
Super Bowl XXVIII Champions

Super Bowl XXVIII.

SPONSORS

DALLAS ★ COWBOYS
Super Bowl XXVIII Champions

SPONSORS

for the

**1994
DALLAS COWBOYS WIVES'
FAMILY COOKBOOK and PHOTO ALBUM
(SOUTHWESTERN EDITION)**

*Our Grateful Appreciation
for Being the Sponsors in 1994
to Help the Boys and Girls
Who Live, Work, and Study at
HAPPY HILL FARM ACADEMY/HOME*

— — — — — — — — —

THE TROY AIKMAN FOUNDATION

BOB AND MARY BREUNIG

BUTTERBALL FRESH CHICKEN

DR. PEPPER

FRIENDLY CHEVROLET - DALLAS

INTERSTATE BATTERIES

INCREDIBLE UNIVERSE

KROGER

PILLSBURY

TEXAS BEEF COUNCIL

WALLS INDUSTRIES

A.1 Steak Sauce

Bush's Baked Beans

C & H Granulated Sugar

Lea & Perrins Worcestershire Sauce

McIlhenny Co. Tabasco Sauce

Ortega Garden-Style Salsa

Planters Honey Roasted Peanuts

BOY, WHAT WE CAN LEARN

Look into their big, bright eyes and you'll see nothing but curiosity and innocence. Their ability to learn is infinite; their capacity to love, larger than life itself. They're excited by a bird, a butterfly, the moon, a piece of paper blowing in the wind or water dripping from a leaky faucet.

They're so happy with just a hug and kiss. When they meet someone, they see no color. They don't question the person's religion, financial status, sexual preference or political views. They give so much and ask nothing.

Maybe if we could see things through their eyes for just a couple of minutes we'd try to make this world a better place for them to grow up in. Sometimes it's hard to believe we all started out as children.

Boy, what we can learn from them...

Kathy Ramarui

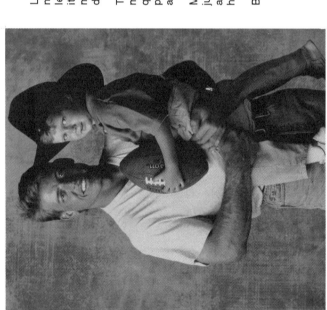

"One Dream At A Time
THE
Troy Aikman
FOUNDATION

P.O. Box 201326
Arlington, TX 76011
Metro 817/469-8160

Dr Pepper...
The Only True Texan!

Cooking With
The Dr

DR PEPPER BOTTLING COMPANY OF TEXAS

Dr Pepper.

DALLAS • FT. WORTH • HOUSTON • WACO

All of us at

Interstate Batteries

are pleased to continue our support of

Happy Hill Farm

and the Dallas Cowboys Wives Cookbook.

We're proud to be associated with
an organization that provides a warm
and caring, Christian atmosphere for
children who need it most.

Official sponsor of the NFL

NEED NEW IDEAS FOR DINNER?

CALL
1-800-284-BEEF

We're happy to help with your recipe for success.

Happy Hill Farm Recipe

- Take one child
- Add patience and understanding
- Mix in kindness
- Blend in a strong family unit
- Add a healthy helping of Christian values
- Sprinkle with discipline
- Top off with a solid education
- Season with plenty of love

Note: This recipe has served hundreds of children, but with additional support could serve many other boys and girls who still need help.

DALLAS COWBOYS
Super Bowl XXVIII Champions

To order additional copies of the DALLAS COWBOYS WIVES' FAMILY COOKBOOK and PHOTO ALBUM (SOUTHWESTERN EDITION), simply fill out the convenient order form, clip, and mail to:

COOKBOOK (SOUTHWESTERN ED.)
HAPPY HILL FARM ACADEMY/HOME
STAR ROUTE, BOX 56
GRANBURY, TEXAS 76048

***** Please Make Your Check or Money Order Payable to: *****
HAPPY HILL FARM

Please send _____ Cookbook(s) (SOUTHWESTERN ED.) to:

Name _____

Address _____

City, State, Zip _____

Enclosed is a check or money order for **$12.95 for each** Cookbook, plus **$4.00 each for postage and handling**.

$ _____ **Total Amount Enclosed**

Please send _____ Cookbook(s) (SOUTHWESTERN ED.) to:

Name _____

Address _____

City, State, Zip _____

Enclosed is a check or money order for **$12.95 for each** Cookbook, plus **$4.00 each for postage and handling**.

$ _____ **Total Amount Enclosed**

DALLAS COWBOYS
Super Bowl XXVIII Champions

To order additional copies of the DALLAS COWBOYS WIVES' FAMILY COOKBOOK and PHOTO ALBUM (SOUTHWESTERN EDITION), simply fill out the convenient order form, clip, and mail to:

COOKBOOK (SOUTHWESTERN ED.)
HAPPY HILL FARM ACADEMY/HOME
STAR ROUTE, BOX 56
GRANBURY, TEXAS 76048

***** Please Make Your Check or Money Order Payable to: *****
HAPPY HILL FARM

Please send _____ Cookbook(s) (SOUTHWESTERN ED.) to:

Name _____

Address _____

City, State, Zip _____

Enclosed is a check or money order for **$12.95 for each Cookbook, plus $4.00 each for postage and handling**.

$ _____ **Total Amount Enclosed**

Please send _____ Cookbook(s) (SOUTHWESTERN ED.) to:

Name _____

Address _____

City, State, Zip _____

Enclosed is a check or money order for **$12.95 for each Cookbook, plus $4.00 each for postage and handling**.

$ _____ **Total Amount Enclosed**